FIVE STAR CUISINE

Dr. B.K. Chakravarti

M.Sc. DN (Cal.) Dip in HM & Tourism (Raj.)
Ph.D. (Cal.) AHCIMA (London) FIIBM
Visiting Faculty
Department of Hotel Management & Catering Technology
Birla Institute of Technology (Deemed University) Mesra, Ranchi
Former Principal & Senior Faculty IHM, Patna and IHM, Kolkata

A P H PUBLISHING CORPORATION
5 ANSARI ROAD, DARYA GANJ
NEW DELHI-110 002

Published by
S.B. Nangia
A P H Publishing Corporation
5 Ansari Road, Darya Ganj
New Delhi-110002
☎ 23274050

ISBN 81-7648-918-2

Typesetting at
Paragon Computers
B-36, Chanakya Place
New Delhi-110 059
☎ 25509417

Printed in India at
Efficient Offset Printers
New Delhi-110 035

The book is dedicated to Vincent Gomes (Nivaran) who is no more. Vincent belonged to a family of great Chefs - his Grand father was with Maharaja of Patiala and father was the Kitchen master of Late Pandit Jawaharlal Nehru. Vincent started modestly, but rose to the level of celebrated chefs of the country. He headed Food Production Dept. in Oberois and many other leading hotels. He had the opportunity to instruct at IHM, Kolkata to transfer his skills to many of his brilliant students who are working all over the World. Five of his sons, took up family profession and all of them are well known for their skills and art in the Culinary faternity.

I had about four decades of personal association with him and was greatly impressed and attracted towards his professional skills and dedication in cookery. Unfortunately, he could not translate his experiences and knowledge in any print media for the generation to follow, except the fortunate few who received direct coaching from him. My wife Subhra was lucky to receive his direct instruction and inspiration for the culinary Art. In fact, Vincent was the driving force for me to write this book in particular.

Dr. B.K. Chakrvarti

PREFACE

In recent time there has been a growing tendency among the people to eat outside. This tendency has developed to a great extent almost in every part of the world. Secondly, due to spread of urbanization and various economic factors people started eating out atleast one or two meals almost every day particularly those who have to go to work leaving their homes early.

It has also become a fashion to eat out in star hotels and in good quality restaurants once a while along with the family members, friends, professionals and acquaintance, etc.

From the survey of the public food service since early 1800 A.D. it could be seen that there has been a considerable change in the style, menu, service, price and consumer's behaviour in the public eating houses throughout the world. In India also, we have seen sea of changes in public eating houses and the eating pattern. There has been a growth of star hotels and good quality restaurants, serving not only Indian cuisine but also cuisine of the various parts of the world.

In the above background, the author thought that it would be appropriate to produce a volume highlighting some of the important features about the cuisine of the public eating places and the inner stories of food preparation in star category eating establishments. It may be mentioned here that there is wide difference between home cooking and cooking of outside eateries. The major differences are they cook items on the basis of popularity, market acceptability and internal managements to prepare those dishes for quick service to the customers as and when foods are ordered in the restaurants. The restaurant items which are to be sold are displayed in various manner and styles and with price of the dishes. Universally, the display of food items with price for customers through print media is called menu.

In order to serve the menu item's, the eating places have to organize themselves suitably, so that food items can be served to the customers as per the reputation of the eating establishments, not only for one or two days but, sometime for years for uninterrupted reputation in the market, regarding the quality, service and items to be served.

With this end in view, the author has arranged the text in such a manner that even the beginners and other interested groups in quality cuisine, shall find the book useful for the purpose of preparing food items which are particularly and popularly sold in various star category hotels and restaurants of repute all over the world.

Dr. B.K. CHAKRAVARTI

ACKNOWLEDGEMENTS

The author is grateful to all those people who have assisted in the production of this book by way of lending professional services.

The author is thankful to M/S CBS Publishers, New Delhi and M/S Pitman Publishing, London in particular for providing permission and help for references used in the text.

Thanks are due to Late U. Mallick , GM Hotel Chanakya , Patna, Mr. R. D'Costa, MD, Hotel Boulevard, Jamshedpur, Mr. C.M. Kapoor, Hotel Chinar, Ranchi, Mr. K.K. Chopra, Hotel Yuvaraj, Palace, Ranchi, Mrs. Subhra Chakravarti, President, Institute of Culinary Management & Research, Kolkata, Mr. J.M. Choudhary, the then Corporate Chef Hotel Ashoka, New Delhi, Ms. Inga Nam, Chef Hors d'Oeuvers, Culinary writer, USA, Mr. Dennis Powell, Deptt. of F & B Operation, Culinary Institute of America, Mrs. Jyotsna Bhosle & Mrs. Merci Mathew, Teachers, Catering College, Mumbai for their help, ideas, and encouragement.

Author is also thankful for the support from Prof. A.M. Agarwal, Deptt. of Hotel Management & Catering Technology, B.I.T. Mesra. Author is deeply indebted to Prof. S.K. Mukherjee VC, BIT, Mesra , Ranchi for his generous help and providing all facilities to pursue academic development and research in the field of Hospitality and culinary Arts in particular.

The author also acknowledges the services of Mr. Manish Pandey formerly with IHM, Patna and Shri Kashi Nath Dutta of ICMR, Kolkata for script typing and of numerous other friends and colleagues in various Hotel Management Institutes and Hotels in India and abroad.

The author extends thanks to Shri S.B. Nangia of M/S APH Publishing Corporation, New Delhi, for his keen interest in publishing the Book with expert care.

Dr. B.K. Chakravarti

CONTENTS

REPRINTS OF MENUS OF SOME SELECTED EATERIES

FASE '79

Food Accommodation Service Education
FRIDAY 20 APRIL 1979
LUNCHEON

• • •

Egg Mayonnaise
Half Fresh Grapefruit
Chilled Fruit Juices
Cream of Onion Soup
Consomme Brunoise

• • •

Deep Fried Fillets of Haddock Only
Roast Leg of Lamb, Mint Sauce
Madras Curry Chicken, Patna Rice

• • •

Creamed Swedes Garden Peas
Boulangere and Parmentiere Potatoes

• • •

COLD BUFFET
Ox Tongue, Cheese, Roast Ham, Grosvenor Pie,
Salmon Mayonnaise, Roast Beef,
Fresh Salads in Season

• • •

Blackcurrant Cream Cheese Cake
Baked Rice Pudding
Gooseberry Pie and Custard Sauce
Assorted Ice Creams
Cheese and Biscuits

• • •

Coffee

Biftorifche Gaftftatten

Albrecht Durer Strabe 3
90403 Nurnberg (Germany)
Tel : 0911/20 38 26 *Fax :* 0911/24 18 117

Medieval banquet
in the historical convent cellar, year of our Lord 1592,
at the feet of the "Noiserburg"
feel to have stepped back into the time of
robber-barron "Eppelein von Gaillingen".
Thou lay down stress and enjoy the time of the 16th
century and following Nurnberg traditions
henceforth thou are called
"WEFS" and "WERAS"
(Women and Men)
Do not sit down at the table
before thou have washed thy hands properly &
take the knife in thy hand, this shall be thy only cutlery
but thy hands
Where once the nunns feasted,
the robber-barons maids and servants welcome thou & serve the meal
Do not forget to break the bread because this thou will need
to push the food into thy mouth. And this will be served
Meal served in a bullocks horn

• • •

flat cake with lord and delicate flavoured herbs from Grandmas garden

• • •

home-made jellied meat

• • •

Rich beef-tea with small dumplings

• • •

filled quail wrapped in bacon fresh from the oven

• • •

Grilled spareribs with cabbage salad and lambs lettuce

• • •

Apple pancakes Grandmas style

• • •

Cheese and fruits

• • •

What thou will left over will
under the old tradition be distributed among the poor and the old
Shallst thou not follow every rule
correctly and if thou not say "to thy health" before
drinking, thou will be punished with the Iron Maiden.
Did thou enjoy the meal;
tell it to other people;
Did thou miss something;
tell it to the servants and mainden.

MENU

Ashok Hotel
New Delhi

CONTINENTAL MENU

NON-VEGETARIAN	**VEGETARIAN**
• • •	• • •
CREAM OF ASPARAGUS SOUP	CREAM OF ASPARAGUS SOUP
• • •	• • •
MEUNIERED FILLET OF SOLE SERVED WITH ALMOND & PISTA MAYONNAISE	FRIED PARCELS OF GARDEN VEGETABLE SERVED WITH ALMOND AND PISTA MAYONNAISE
• • •	• • •
ESCALOPE OF CHICKEN STUFFED SERVED WITH CHIMAY SAUCE	COTTAGE CHEESE STEAKS STUFFED SERVED WITH CHIMAY SAUCE
• • •	• • •
PARSLEY POTATOES SPINACH MOUSSE GLAZED CARROTS	PARSLEY POTATOES SPINACH MOUSSE GLAZED CARROTS
• • •	• • •
MALAKOFF PUDDING WITH SABAYAN SAUCE	MALAKOFF PUDDING WITH SABAYAN SAUCE
• • •	• • •
COFFEE	COFFEE

CONTINENTAL MENU Norbreck Castle Hotel (UK)

THE CHEF WILL BE PLEASED TO DISCUSS ANY PARTICULAR ALTERNATIVE YOU MAY REQUIRE

THESE ARE ONLY SUGGESTED ITEMS

Appetisers

Florida Cocktail	50p	Seafood Pancake au Gratin (Max 100)	80p
Grapefruit Cocktail	40p	Morecambe Potted Shrimps	£1.25
Tomato Mainaisseque (with Tuna Padagarnish)	60p	Avocado pear & Prawns	£1.40
Egg Mayonnaise	50p	Melon & Parma Ham	£1.35
Melon & Pineapple Cocktail	60p	Cornets of Smoked Salmon with Prawns	£1.60
Egg à la Russe	50p		
Melon Gondola	65p		
Flaked Salmon Mayonnaise	£1.10		
Prawn Cocktail	£1.00		
Hors d'Oeuvre Norbreck Castle	£1.00		

Soups

Cream of Tomato	45p	French Onion Soup	50p
Cream of Asparagus	45p	Hot Vichyssoise	50p
Chicken Noodle	45p	Minestrone with parmesan	50p
Cream Ambassadeur	45p	Royal Game Soup Laced with Port	65p
Cream Portugaise	45p	Lobster Bisque	65p
Consommé Royale	45p		
Consommé Julienne	45p		
Cream of Celery	45p		
Cream of Leek	45p		
Scotch Broth	45p		

Fish Courses

Poached Fillet of Whiting Bonne Femme	45p	Grilled Rainbow Trout Meunière or Almondine	50p
Seafood vol au Vent (Max 200)	45p	Grilled Halibut Maître d' Hotel	50p
Poached Fillet of Haddock provencale	45p	Deep Fried Jumbo Scampi with Tartare Sauce (Max 200)	50p
Paupiettes of Sole in Shrimp Sauce	45p	Scampi Thermidor	65p
Grilled Fillet of Plaice Belle Meunière	45p		65p
Poached Fillet of Sole Dugère	45p		
Deep Fried Goujons of Plaice with Tartare Sauce (Max 200)	45p		
Poached Fillet of Sole Veronique	45p		
Poached Scallops Parisienne	45p		
Poached Sole on Courgette with White Wine & Cucumber	45p		

Main Courses
Inclusive of Potatoes and one Vegetable

Half a roast wide Chicken with Seasoning	£2.40	Roast Stuffed Saddle of Lamb Mint Sauce	£2.75
Cold Roast Chicken & Ham Salad	£2.40	Norfolk Tu Chipolata & Seasoning	£2.75
Roast Fylde Chicken Forestiere	£2.40	Roast Leg of Pork Apple Sauce Seasoning	£2.80
Sugar Gammon with Madeira Sauce & Cherries	£2.40	Contrefillet of Beef au Hanguraine	£2.75
Roast Leg & Lamb with Mint Sauce	£2.40	Entrecote Steak Bordelaise	£3.00
Roast Rib of Beef Yorkshire Pudding	£2.75	Hole Roast with Bacon and Seasoning	£3.25
		Tender Fillets of Beef Chaisseur	£3.25
		Grilled Fillet Steak Royale	£3.80

Sweets

Cheese and Biscuits	40p	Fresh Cream Sherry Trifle	55p
Pear Condé	55p	Fresh Fruit Salad and Cream	55p
Fresh Pineapple with Kirsch	65p	Fresh Cream Gateau	55p
Charlotte Russe	55p	Gateau St Honore	45p
Black Forest or Chocolate Mint or Strawberry Gateau	55p		80p
			65p

A SELECTION OF SPECIALITY ICE-CREAM DISHES CAN BE PRESENTED AS FOLLOWS

Champagne Bucket	75p
Barrel Open Book or Slipper	55p
Beer Stein	50p
Gateau	45p

*EXTRA VEGETABLE 40p *COFFEE 30p *COFFEE WITH CREAM 35p *SORBET OF YOUR CHOICE 35p

ALL PRICES INCLUSIVE OF VAT AT 8%

MENU

HOTEL SAMARAT INTERNATIONAL PATNA

CONTINENTAL
LUNCH & DINNER

(12 Noon To 3 P.M. & 7.30 P.M. To 11 P.M.)

Appetizers Hors d'Oeuvre

Russian Salad	32.00

(Vegetables and fruits served on the bed of Mayonnaise garnished with boiled Eggs)

Fisherman's Salad	39.00

(Diced fish in cocktail sauce garnished with boiled prawns)

Soup-Les-Potage

Cream' of Tomato/Vegetable Soup	15.00
Ministronne Soup	18.00
French Onion Soup	19.00
Cream of Chicken Soup	18.00
Cream of Mushroom Soup (Veg.)	18.00
Cream of Mushroom Soup (N. Veg.)	20.00
Cream of Asparagus (Veg.)	20.00
Cream of Asparagus (N. Veg.)	21.00

Vegetables Legumes

Vegetable-Au-Gratin	32.00

(Garden fresh vegetable & mushrooms baked with cheese)

Potato Shalimar	31.00

(Green Peas, Dhaniya patta, Green Chilli, Coconut, Mushroom Mashed Potato stuffed fried and serve with vegetable, Chips and Cold Cut Salad)

Vegetable Cake-Roll	31.00

(Vegetables, Onion Mushroom with pan cake stuffed bread Crumb fried and serve with vegetables & Cold Cut Salad).

Vegetable Mis-Mar	31.00

(Macroni, Green peas, concasse sauce and topped with grated cheese and baked)

Vegetable Cannalonie	31.00

(Mixed vegetables, pancake and concasse sauce topped with grated cheese and baked)

Vegetable Ala Kiev	35.00

(Minced vegetables stuffed with chopped gherkin & mushrooms rolled in bread crumb, deep Fried & served on mashed Potatoes)

Cabbage-Farci	35.00

(Cabbage stuffed with chopped vegetables, tomato cancasse & baked with cheese)

Vegetable Shashlick	35.00

(Cottage cheese fresh vegetable cooked on skewers in oven served on bed of rice)

FISH-POISSON

Fish Mayonnaise	46.00

(Boiled fillet of fish dressed on Potato salad, covered with Mayonnaise sauce, garnished with boiled eggs)

Fish Bonne-Famine	45.00

(Poached fillet of Beckti with mushrooms in white sauce)

Fish Ala Portugese   45.00

(Fillet of fish simmered in Tomato sauce with capsicum & garlic served with french fries & boiled vegetables)

Fish Florentine   45.00

(Poached fillet dressed on spinach, Puree enriched with cream & glazed with grated cheese)

Steak De Beckti Mai-Mai   46.00

(Fresh Beckti Meuniere topped with ham, Pineapple & poached egg served with boiled vegetable)

Fish Fried with Tartre Sauce   39.00

(Fillet of fish marinated in spices deep fat fried. Served with boiled vegetable & french fries, Accompanied with tartre sauce)

Grilled Fish   45.00

(Fillet of fish grilled with Tomato sauce)

Fish Molina   45.00

(Fish in Cream Curry masala on bed of Rice grains with Jullienne of garlic Ginger and green chilli)

Fish Rice   45.00

(Capsicum Tomato, Green peas Mushroom, Egg and Cream Curry sauce)

Fish Ala Samrat Special   50.00

(Our Chefs special recipe)

CHICKEN-POULET

Poulet Vallee D' Auge   55.00

(Stewed chicken with white wine mushrooms and cream served with boiled rice)

Chicken Cordon Bleu   55.00

(Tender escalopes of chicken stuffed with slice of ham & cheese & shallow fried)

Chicken Paprika   55.00

(Boneless fillet of white chicken simmered in paprika sauce served with capsicum, sweet potatoes, boiled vegetables and rice)

Roast Chicken   50.00

(Pot roasted chicken simmered in brown sauce served with boiled vegetables & french fries)

Chicken Chesseur   62.00

(Boneless chicken cooked in Espagnole sauce with cream capsicum, mushroom, Pickle onion and Tomato finished with Tomato sauce)

Chicken Ala Kiev   50.00

(Chicken, Butter Bread Crumb fried, Mushroom, served with Mashed potato & garden vegetables)

Chicken Ala King   51.00

(Chicken Peeled Tomato, Capsicum, Rice mushroom, Egg, White Cream sauce)

Chicken a-la Samrat Special garden chicken   62.00

(Our chefs special recipe)

Chicken pepper Steak Chef's Singapore   62.00

(Boneless chicken seasoned with Pepper & cooked in brown sauce topped with pineapple and grilled Tomato served with boiled Rice)

Murgh Shashlick   55.00

(Boneless chicken onion capsicum, Tomato cooked on skewers in oven served on bed of Rice)

Chicken Mercury   62.00

(Breast of chicken panfried in butter placed on noodles and white Mushrooms covered with white sauce baked with cheese)

Chicken Imperial	55.00
Chicken Japanese	65.00

PORK

Pork Winner Escalope	45.00

(Lemon, Parsley, Dhania patta Potato, vegetables with Concasse sauce)

Pork Escalope Millannaise	45.00

(Spagheti, Tomato, Fried pork eggs and concasse sauce)

OUR SIZZLING PLATTER

Chicken steak sizzler Singapore	60.00
Mutton steak sizzler Singapore	50.00
Vegetable steak sizzler Singapore	39.00

ASSORTED GARDEN FRESH SALADS

Green Salad (L)	15.00
Green Salad (S)	9.00
Chicken Salad	46.00
Oriental Salad	31.00
Fish Salad	34.00

INDIAN

LUNCH & DINNER

(12 Noon To 3 P.M. & 7.30 P.M. To 11 P.M.)

From Our Fisher Man's Net

Fish Punjabi   45.00

(Pieces of fish flavoured with spices)

Fish Butter Masala   47.00

(Fish cooked in butter Masala gravy)

Fish Curry   40.00

(Fish cooked in curry sauce)

Fish Masala   48.00

(Fish prepared in rich spices)

Fish Do Piaza   45.00

(Fish prepared in mildly spiced onion sauce)

Prawn Samrat Special   84.00

Prawn Mughlai   72.00

Prawn Do Piaza   65.00

Prawn Butter Masala   72.00

Prawn Curry   58.00

From Our Game-Keepers Cage

Chicken Samrat Special   71.00

(Chicken chap delicately prepared in rich sauce)

Chicken Leg Kabab Butter Masala 62.00

(Chicken legs roasted in tandoor, prepared in butter masala gravy)

Murg Mussallam (Full)   97.00

Murg Mussallam (Half)   52.00

(Chicken cooked in special gravy)

Chicken Tikka Butter Masala   62.00

(Chicken Tikka in butter masala gravy)

Chicken Mughlai   65.00

(Tender chicken delicately

prepared in mughlai sauce)

Chicken Jahangir   59.00

(Chicken cooked in cream sauce)

Chicken Shahi Korma   59.00

(Boneless Chicken cooked in rich cream sauce)

Chicken Bharta   59.00

(Boneless Chicken cooked in thick sauce)

Chicken Butter Masala   60.00

(Chicken prepared in butter masala gravy)

Chicken Badam pasanda   62.00

(Chicken prepared in special thick gravy enriched with almonds)

Chicken Masala   59.00

(Chicken prepared in thick gravy with eggs)

Chicken Palak   52.00

(Chicken cooked with spinach)

Chicken Do Piaza   52.00

(Chicken prepared in mildly spiced onion sauce)

Chicken Curry   43.00

(Chicken prepared in curry sauce)

Chicken Patiala   62.00

(Minced Chicken with Egg round shaped fried cooked in mughlai sauce garnished with fried Egg)

Chicken Chakori   100.00

(Chicken Palak Mushroom Keema & cooked with Chef's special Gravy)

Chicken Apsana 117.00

(Chicken liver Keema Mushroom Egg Tomato & Paneer & cooked with Chefs special gravy)

Chicken Ambala 125.00

(Chicken liver Keema Mushroom Tomato & cooked with rice creamy gravy)

From Our Butcher's Shop

Mutton Rogan Josh 40.00

(Mutton legs cooked in thick gravy)

Mutton Shahi Korma Rampuri 44.00

(Boneless mutton pieces cooked in creamy gravy)

Mutton Do Piaza 43.00

(Mutton prepared in mildly spiced onion sauce)

Mutton Shahjehani Curry 44.00

(Our chefs special recipe)

Mutton Masala 44.00

(Mutton prepared in rich masala gravy)

Mutton Dolma 44.00

(Minced mutton and eggs delicately spiced in sauce)

Mutton Korma 40.00

(Tender mutton pieces prepared in korma sauce with Indian herbs)

Keema Mutter 38.00

(Minced meat with green peas)

Mutton Kofta Begum-Bahar 45.00

(Minced meat balls stuffed with nuts and cooked in rich gravy)

Keema Egg Curry 40.00

(Minced meat cooked with eggs)

Mutton Sagwala 43.00

(Mutton cooked with spinach)

From Our Vegetable Garden

Aloo Mumtaz 25.00

(Potatoes stuffed with sultanas and khoya simmered in gravy sauce)

Aloo Do Piaza 24.00

(Potato cooked in mildly spiced onion sauce)

Stuffed Tomato 25.00

(Tomatoes stuffed with Vegetables)

Stuffed Capsicum 26.00

(Capsicum stuffed with Vegetables)

Paneer Shahi Korma 28.00

(Cottage cheese cooked in Korma sauce)

Paneer Kofta Dilkhush 30.00

(Minced cottage cheese balls stuffed with sultanas cooked in gravy)

Paneer Butter Masala 32.00

(Cottage cheese cooked in butter masala gravy)

Malai Kofta 28.00

(Minced cheese Rolls with fresh cream cooked in rich sauce)

Mutter paneer 25.00

(Cottage cheese with green peas)

Vegetable Jhal Ferzi 23.00

(Fresh seasonal vegetables, cheese sauted with onion capsicum and Tomato)

Vegetable Navrattan Korma 30.00

(Fresh seasonal vegetables cooked in Korma garnished with fruits)

Vegetable Kofta 23.00

(Minced vegetables in rich gravy)

Aloo Dum Banarasi 23.00

(Potatoes cooked in rich gravy topped up with cream)

Sag Paneer 28.00

(Cottage cheese cooked with spinach)

Shabnam Curry 33.00

(Fresh mushrooms & green peas cooked in rich gravy)

Green Peas Fry 15.00

(Green peas fried with onion and spices)

Green Peas Butter Masala 21.00

(Green peas prepared in butter masala gravy)

Vegetable Samrat Special 38.00

(Our chef's special recipe)

Mixed Vegetable 22.00

(Fresh seasonal vegetables cooked in Indian style)

Rani Palak 39.00

Shahi Kofta 33.00

Paneer Pasanda 34.00

From Our Egg Basket

Egg do Piaza 21.00

Egg Curry 20.00

From Our Chef's Special Hundi

Chicken Masala Briyani 59.00

(Chicken fried rice cooked in mughlai style)

Mutton masala Briyani 48.00

(Mutton fried rice cooked in mughlai style)

Green Peas/Phool Pulao 24.00

(Fried rice with cauliflower/Green peas)

Navrattan Pulao 30.00

(Fried rice with carrot beans dry fruits and cottage cheese)

Kashmir! Pulao 30.00

(Fried rice cooked in kashmiri style mixed with (fried onion - optional) garnished with pineapple and cherries)

Shahi Pullao 30.00

Hyderabadi Briyani 71.00

Moti Mahal Briyani 65.00

Noor Mahal Briyani 71.00

Dal Makhani 19.00

(Dal fried in butter)

Dal Fried 17.00

Rice 15.00

Choice of Raita 18.00

(Tomato Khira Onion mixed or pineapple)

TANDOOR

Tandoori Chicken (Full) 72.00

Tandoori Chicken (Half) 39.00

Kalmi Kabab 55.00

Chicken Seekh Kabab 55.00

Chicken Reshmi Kabab 55.00

Chicken Boti Kabab 56.00

Chicken Tikka 49.00

Chicken Chap 55.00

Chicken Ginger Kabab 78.00

Chicken Shahjehani Kabab 123.00

Samrat Special Tandoori Chicken 78.00

Fish Tandoori 45.00

Fish Tikka 45.00

Fish Reshmi Kabab 45.00

Fish Ginger Kabab 78.00

Paneer Seekh Kabab 28.00

Keema Naan/Paratha/Kulcha (126, 138, 147) 18.00

Chicken Stuffed Keema Naan 23.00

Tandoori Roti 4.00

Tandoori Paratha 6.00

Nan/Kulcha (254, 147) 8.00

Stuffed Naan/Paratha/Kulcha (139, 140, 146) 13.00

Special Naan 15.00

Kashmiri Stuffed Naan 15.00

Papad Dry 4.00

Masala Papad 5.00

CHINESE

LUNCH & DINNER

(12 Noon To 3 P.M. & 7.30 P.M. To 11 P.M.)

Soup (For Non-Vegetarian)

Chicken Noodle	20.00
Chicken Sweet Corn	18.00
Egg Sweet Corn	16.00
Tomato Egg Drop	16.00
Chicken Asparagus	22.00
Chicken Wanton	25.00
Chicken Mushroom	22.00
Chicken Hot 'N' Sour	22.00
Talumein Soup	25.00

Sea Food

Fish Mendarin	42.00
Fish Sweet 'N' Sour	45.00
Sliced Fish Garlic Sauce	42.00
Sliced Fish/Vegetable	42.00
Fish Chilli	42.00
Prawn Chilli	65.00
Garlic Prawn	65.00
Sweet 'N' Sour Prawn	65.00
Sijuan Prawn	65.00

Chicken

Ginger Chicken	52.00
Chilli Chicken	52.00
Chilli Chicken (Boneless)'	57.00
Garlic Chicken (Boneless)	58.00
Lemon Chicken (Boneless)	57.00
Sijuan Chicken (Boneless)	57.00
Chicken Manchoorian (Boneless)	57.00
Sweet 'N' Sour Chicken	52.00
Shredded Chicken with Mushroom & Bambooshoot	60.00
Chicken with Pineapple (Boneless)	57.00
Chicken with Vegetables (Boneless)	57.00
Spring Chicken	52.00
Kashmiri Chicken	59.00
Chicken with Cashewnut	59.00

Pork

Fried Chilli Pork	35.00
Sweet 'N' Sour Pork with P/A	34.00
Sliced Pork with mushroom and Bambooshoot	36.00
Sliced Pork with Shredded capsicum	34.00

Chowmein

Chicken Chowmein	41.00
Pork Chowmein	33.00
Fish Chowmein	38.00
Egg Chowmein	29.00
Mix Chowmein	45.00
Singapore Noodles	39.00
Singapore Chicken Sing-Chow	45.00

(Rice and Noodles mixed with diced chicken and vegetables prepared in Chinese sauce)

Prawn Chowmein	52.00

Chopsuey

American Chopsuey	49.00
Chinese Chopsuey	49.00
Chicken Chopsuey	43.00
Vegetable Chopsuey	43.00

Chinese Rice

Chicken Fried Rice	41.00
Pork Fried Rice	33.00
Fish Fried Rice	38.00
Egg Fried Rice	29.00
Mix Fried Rice	45.00
Samrat Special Fried Rice	46.00
Vegetable Fried Rice	29.00
Prawn Fried Rice	52.00

For The Vegetarians

Vegetable S/C Soup	15.00
Vegetable Noodle Soup	16.00
Vegetable Asparagus Soup	18.00
Vegetable Hot 'N' Sour Soup	18.00
Vegetable Mushroom Soup	18.00
Vegetable Wanton Soup	18.00
Vegetable Chowmein	28.00
Vegetable Sweet N Sour	20.00
Vegetable Manchoorian	20.00
Vegetable Balls in Garlic Sauce	20.00
Diced Vegetable in Garlic Sauce	20.00
Paneer Chilli	32.00
Potato Chilli	21.00

Spring Rolls

Chicken Spring Roll	52.00
Egg Spring Roll	38.00
Pork Spring Roll	35.00
Vegetable Spring Roll	29.00

Desserts

Fruit Salad with Cream	20.00
Fruit Salad with Ice Cream	26.00
Caramel Custored	20.00
Rasmalai/Channa Payes	16.00

Choice of Ice Cream

Chocolate Ice Cream	18.00
Vanilla/Strawberry	17.00
Pista Ice Cream	21.00
Tutti/Fruti Ice Cream (S)	22.00
Tutti/Fruti Ice Cream (L)	36.00
Double Sunday Ice Cream	39.00
Cold Coffee	15.00
Cold Coffee with Ice cream	23.00
Fruit Basket	40.00
Tea	7.00
Coffee	7.50
Esp Coffee	8.50

TAXES   AS   PER   APPLICABLE

CHINESE MENU

APPETIZERS

Pot Stickers (6)	$3.60
Fried Wonton (8)	2.25
Egg Rolls (one)	1.15
Barbecued Spare Ribs (4)	3.75
Fried Shrimps	4.50
Shrimp Toast (4)	3.95
Assorted Appetizers Plates	6.00

SOUPS

(Person)	1	2	3
Sizzling Rice	$1.75	3.25	
Sweet Corn Chicken	1.75	3.25	4.75
Egg Drop	.95	1.75	2.50
Hot and Sour	1.75	3.25	4.75
Vegetarian	1.75	3.25	4.75
Wonton	1.75	3.25	4.75
San Shan	2.25	4.25	6.25

FRIED RICE

Chicken	$4.25
Beef	4.25
Pork	4.25
Shrimp	5.25
Mandarin	5.25

CHOW MEIN

Chicken	$5.25
Beef	5.25
Pork	5.25
Shrimp	6.25
Mandarin	6.25
Mandarin Lo Mein	6.25

SEA FOOD

Shrimp with Garlic Sauce	$7.95
Shrimp with Chinese Vegetables	7.95
Sauteed "Happy Family"	9.95
Sweet and Sour Shrimp	7.95
Shrimp with Green Peas	7.95
Shrimp Sizzling Rice	8.95
Princess Prawns	9.95
Snow Peas with Shrimp	7.95
Sweet and Sour Fish Fillet	7.95
Lobster with Chinese Vegetable	12.95
King Crab Mandarin Style	8.95
Shrimp with Lobster Sauce	7.95
Lake Tungting Shrimp	7.95
Chow San Shan	9.95
Braised Fish	11.50
Hot Braised Fish	11.50
Sweet and Sour Fish (whole)	11.50
Crab Tien Tsin	8.25
Assorted Seafood and Vegetable with Sizzling Rice	11.95

BEEF

Mongolian Beef	$6.95
Ginger Beef	6.25
Ming's Beef	6.25
Oyster Sauced Beef	6.25
Onion Beef	6.25
Pepper Steak	6.25
Beef with Garlic Sauce	6.25
Beef with Chinese Vegetable	6.25
Beef with Broccoli	6.25
Snow Peas with Beef	6.95

PORK

Sweet and Sour Pork	$5.95
Mushroom Pork	6.95
Moo Shi Pork	6.95
Pork with Garlic Sauce	6.95
Twice Cooked Pork	5.95
Pork with Chinese Vegetable	5.95
Pork with Pea Pods	5.95
Bean Curd Szechwan Style	6.95

FOWL

Snow White Chicken	$6.95
Princess Chicken	5.95
Curry Chicken	5.95
Black Mushrooms Chicken	6.95
Garlic Chicken	5.95
Almond Chicken	5.95
Chicken with Plum Sauce	5.95
Sweet and Sour Chicken	8.25
Peking Duck (one day advance notice is required)	22.00
Deep Fried Crispy Duck	9.50
Chicken with Chinese Vegetable	$6.95
Cashew Chicken	6.25
Lemon Chicken	6.25

VEGETABLES

Sauteed Snow Peas	$5.95
Northern Style Vegetable Deluxe	5.25
Snow Peas with Black Mushrooms	5.95
Oyster Suace with Broccoli	5.95
Braised Bean Curd	5.95

Delicious Decisions

For all your Meals

For reservation & Parties
Call 343-5700
Thein TSIN Restaurant
Route 104 East Oswego New-YORK
13126 (315)- 343-5700

IMPERIAL DINNERS		FAMILY DINNERS	
A. FOR TWO	$20.00	**A. FOR TWO**	$15.00
Sizzling Rice Soup		Egg Drop Soup	
Egg Rolls & Fried Won Ton		Egg Rolls	
Monogolian Beef		Almond Chicken	
Sweet & Sour Shrimp		Sweet & Sour Pork	
B. FOR THREE	30.00	**B. FOR THREE**	22.00
Sizzling Rice Soup		Egg Drop Soup	
Egg Rolls & Fried Won Ton		Egg Rolls	
Monogolian Beef		Almond Chicken	
Moo Shi Pork		Sweet & Sour Pork	
Sweek & Sour Shrimp		Pepper Steak	
C. FOR FOUR	40.00	**C. FOR FOUR**	30.00
Sizzling Rice Soup		Egg Drop Soup	
Egg Rolls & Fried Won Ton		Egg Rolls	
Monogolian Beef		Almond Chicken	
Sweet & Sour Shrimp		Sweet & Sour Pork	
Chow San Shan		Pepper Steak	
Moo Shi Pork		Assorted Vegetables Deluxe	
D. FOR FIVE	50.00	**D. FOR FIVE**	37.00
Sizzling Rice Soup		Egg Drop Soup	
Egg Rolls & Fried Won Ton		Egg Rolls	
Monogolian Beef		Almoud Chicken	
Sweet & Sour Shrimp		Sweet & Sour Pork	
Moo Shi Pork		Pepper & Steak	
Chow San Shan		Pork with Chinese, Vegetable	
Sweet & Sour Fish		Assorted Vegetables Deluxe	
E. FOR SIX	60.00	**E. FOR SIX**	45.00
Sizzling Rice Soup		Egg Drop Soup	
Egg Rolls & Fried Won Ton		Egg Rolls	
Monogolian Beef		Almond Chicken	
Sweet & Sour Shrimp		Sweet & Sour Pork	
Garlic chicken		Pepper Steak	
Chow San Shan		Pork with Chinese Vegetable	
Moo Shi Pork		Assorted Vegetables Deluxe	
Sweet & Sour Fish		Shrimp with Green Peas	

ORDER COMES WITH STEAMED RICE AND TEA

MENU

BRITISH AIRWAYS

LONDON — DELHI
('79)

Continental	कान्टीनेन्टल
Breakfast	सुबह का नाश्ता
Orange Juice	संतरे का रस
• • •	• • •
Fresh Melon and Citrus Fruit	ताजे और रसीले फल
• • •	• • •
Wholegrain roll and blueberry muffin Butter and marmalade	पाव रोटी और ब्लू बेरी मफिन मक्खन और मुरब्बा
• • •	• • •
Coffee or Tea	काफी या चाय

Dinner	रात का भोजन
Our Well Being in the Air menu offers you an alternative dining style. Light easily digested dishes made from the freshest ingredients	हमारी हवाई उड़ान का मीनू आपको तरह तरह के भोजन प्रस्तुत करता है। ताजे समान से बनाया गया हल्का-फुल्का पाचक भोजन।
• • •	• • •
Katchumber Salad	कचुम्बर का सलाद
• • •	• • •
Escalope of turkey with provencal sauce stir-fried vegetables and new potatoes or Vegetarian speciality peas and mushroom masala dal makhani and vegetable biriyani	बोटी टर्की जायकेदार चटनी के साथ भुनी सब्जी और तले आलू या विशेष शाकाहारी भोजन मटर मशरूम मसाला दाल मक्खनी और सब्जी बिरयानी
• • •	• • •
Strawberry and rhubarb mousse	स्ट्राब्री और रूबार्ब मीठी क्रीम में
• • •	• • •
Cheese and crackers with butter	पनीर और क्रेकर मक्खन के साथ
• • •	• • •
Coffee, decaffeinated coffee or Tea	काफी, डिकैफिनेटैड काफी या चाय

MENU

AMERICAN PLAN MENU CARTE

APPETISSERS

Petits Hors d' Oeuvres
Prawns Cocktail
English Plate
Fruits Cocktail

Or

SOUP

Asparagus
Mulligatawny
Minestrone

Tomatoes Egg Soup

• • •

FISHES

Fried with Tartare Sauce
Bonne Femme
Duglere
Louisianne
Sweet and Sour Fish
Chinese Roast Fish

ENTREES

Grill Chicken Chicken Shaslick
Chicken Curry
Tandoori Chicken
Grill Pork Chop
Ham Steak Singapore
Mutton Curry, Mutton Liver & Kidneys
Brochette Chicken Livers Madeira Sauce

• • •

VEGETABLES

Fried Potatoes
Sauted Potatoes
Mashed Potatoes
Green Peas in Butter
French Beans
Mixed Vegetables
Vegetables Gratin
Salads

DESSERTS

Cold Chocolate Souffle
Apple Pie A La Mode,
Cup Belle Helene
Cup Jamaique
Fruits Salad + Ice Cream
Assorted Ice Cream
Fresh Fruit
Tea/Coffee

ASHOKA HOTEL
New Delhi

MENU

ASHOK HOTEL

New Delhi

NON-VEGETARIAN

CHOOSE ANY THREE

SALAD-E-SURAT
(Dices of carrots, beans, turnip and apple served in cream)

SABZ-E-KHET
(Fresh from the farm-tomatoes onion, radish and cucumber served with lemon)

SIMLA CHAT
(Potatoes and apple served with chatpata masala)

ACHARI SALAD
(Home made seasonal vegetables)

KACHUMBER
(Dices of onions, cucumber, tomatoes, capsicum and cabbage in lemon dressing)

CHOOSE ANY ONE

TOMATO SHORBA
(Extract of red tomatoes tempered with home made masala)

BOULA BOULA
(Garden-fresh green pea soup served with croutons)

PYAO-E-KHUMB
(Extract of fresh mushroom with swirl of cream)

HOT & SOUR SOUP
(Brunoise of vegetales and tofu cooked in vinegar and chillies)

MULLIGATAWNY SOUP
(Curry flavoured lentil soup served with rice finished with lemon)

CHOOSE ANY TWO

MACCHI RERIWALI
(Derne of fish marinated in chatpata masala and deep fried)

WHOLE GRILLED SALMON
(Whole salmon marinated and grilled, served with wafers)

KERALAMIN
(Fish stuffed with chutney, finished in Kerala style)

MURGI MASALEDAR
(Pieces of chicken cooked with capsicum, onion and tomatoes)

SAAG MURG
(Chicken pieces marinated in Indian spices cooked with spinach)

RARRA CHICKEN
(Succulent pieces of chicken cooked with tomatoes and capsicum and finished with Indian spices)

ACHARI GOSHT
(Tender pieces of lamb marinated in Achar Masala)

DAL MEAT
(Delicious combination of mutton and chana dal cooked in Punjabi style)

CHOOSE ANY ONE

PANEER DURBAR
(Paneer cooked in butter and tomatoes served with cream)

KADAIPANEER
(Cottage cheese cooked with capsicum and onion served on Hot Tava)

PANEER PEPPER STEAK
(Cottage cheese steak finished with pepper)

MUSHROOM TAVAWALA
(Fresh khumb from Chaat prepared in conventional renwala style)

CHOOSE ANY THREE

MATAR-DO-PIAZA
(Cooked green peas and onion tempered with Garam Masala)

HARIALI KOFTA
(Paneer palak kofta simmered in delicious palak gravy)

GOBHI MASALEDAR
(Tandoori gobhi cooked in Bombay masala)

SUBZ DILKUSH
(Colourful assortment of fresh vegetables cooked in home made masala)

SPAGHETTI FLORENTINE
(Delicately cooked spaghetti served on a bed of green spinach)

EGG PLANT IN GARLIC SAUCE
(Hote brinjals cooked in chilli-garlic sauce)

CHOOSE ANY ONE

DAL KAMADRA
(Creamy urad dal cooked in traditional Kashmiri style)

CHANA-PESHWARI
(Mildly spiced white chana cooked in Peshwari style)

DAL PANCHMAHAL
(Assortment of five lentils cooked in Rajasthani style)

CHOOSE ANY ONE

SABZI RAITA
(A variable combination of fresh

vegetables mixed with Dahi)

ASSAEME RAITA
(Diced pineapple mixed with sweet curd)

PAKORI RAITA
(Small pakori in dahi served with sonth)

CHOOSE ANY ONE

KASHMIRI PULAO
(Rich pulao with cherries, fruits and nuts)

JEERA PULAO
(Delicately jeera tempered rice)

SUMDRA PULAO
(Lemon flavoured)

CHOOSE ANY TWO

KULCHA/PARATHA/POORI/MISSI ROTI
Achar Papad Chutney

CHOOSE ANY TWO

NARAM GARAM
(Honey flavoured Gulabjamun served piping hot)

LUCKNAWI RASMALAI
(Milk soaked rasmalai made in Lucknavi Nawabi style)

CHOICE OF SOUFFLE
(A wide range of souffles)

BARFLI BAHAFI
(Choicest ice-cream served at Hill temperature)

JASHN-E-KASHMIR
(Freshly cut apples, bananas and cherries served soaked in sugar syrup)

VEGETARIAN (SPECIAL)
TOMATO SHORBA
(Extract of Red Tomatoes Tempered with Home-made Masala)

INDIAN BAR-BE-CUE

PANEER TIKKA

ALOO MATTAR CHAAT ON TAVA

MUSHROOM TAVA WALA

ROOMALI ROTI

• • •

CHINESE FOOD COUNTER

VEG. SPRING ROLLS

VEG. MANCHURIAN

VEG. ALMONDS

CHILLI PANEER

VEG. HAKKA NOODLES

SOUTH INDIAN

MASALA DOSA (BABY)

UTTAPAM (BABY)

VADA

SAMBAR/CHUTNEY

SOUTH INDIAN PARATHA

HANDI

MATAR PANEER

VEG. JALFREZI

ALOO GOBHI

PINDI CHANNA

SALAD COUNTER

RAW GREEN SALAD

RUSSIAN SALAD (without eggs)

CHEESE & PINEAPPLE SALAD

CHANNA DAL SALAD

TOSSED SALAD

DESSERT COUNTER

GARAM JALEBI

GAJAR HALWA

RASMALAI

BLACK FOREST CAKE

ICE-CREAM

JEERA PULAO

NAAN PARATHA

RICE PAPAD

AMRITSARI PAPAD

DAHI BHALLA

NON-VEGETARIAN SPECIAL

SELECT ANY ONE (SOUP)
CREAM OF ALMOND
CREAM OF MUSHROOM
HOT & SOUR SOUP
CONSOMME XAVIER
CREAM OF ASPARAGUS

SELECT ANY ONE
MURG MAKHNI
MURG SHAJEHANI
MURG MASALA
MURG MUSSALAM

SELECT ANY ONE
BOONDI RAITA
CUCUMBER RAITA
MIXED RAITA
LAUKI RAITA
DAHI BHALLA

SELECT ANY ONE
SHAHI PANEER
MATTAR PANEER
PALAK PANEER
MUSHROOM PEAS CURRY

SELECT ANY ONE
DAL MAKHNI
CHANNA MASALA

KHATTE RAJMAH
SUKHI DAL
PICKLE/CHUTNEY/PAPAD

SELECT ANY ONE

COLD BUFFET
ROAST MUTTON
SPICED HAM
HAM & ASPARAGUS ROLLS
CHICKEN GALATINE
PATE MAISON
CHEESE & PINEAPPLE SALAD
RUSSIAN SALAD
COLE SLAW MEXICAN
GREEN SALAD

SELECT ANY ONE
FRIED FISH
FISH AMRITSARI GOAN
FISH CURRY
FISH MUSSALAM

SELECT ANY ONE
MUTTON ROGAN JOSH
GOSHT PALAK
GOSHT KORMA
TAKATIN

SELECT ANY THREE
PEAS & MAKHANA CURRY
NAVRATTAN KORMA
VEGETABLE JALFREZI
MALAI KOFTA CURRY
VEGETABLE AU GRATIN
VEGETABLE A LA KIEV
SWEET & SOUR VEGETABLE ALOO
DUM
OR
ANY SEASONAL VEGETABLE

SELECT ANY TWO
PEACH GATEAU
MERINGUE SUCHARD
ALMOND/PISTA SOUFFLE
FRUIT JELLY
CARAMEL CUSTARD
FRUIT TRIFFLE
FRESH FRUIT SALAD
ICE CREAM/FRESH FRUIT
SALAD
TEA/COFFEE

SELECT ANY ONE
TANDOORI CHICKEN
CHICKEN IRANI
RESHMI KABAB
CHICKEN TIKKA
BOTI KABAB

SEEKH KABAB
SHAMI KABAB
FISH TIKKA

SELECT ANY ONE
VEGETABLE KABAB
VEGETABLE SHASLIK
PANEER TIKKA
TANDOORI TIKKA
TANDOORI SALAD
TANDOORI GOBI

SELECT ANY TWO
NAAN/PARATHA/ROTI KULCHA/POORI

SELECT ANY ONE
NAVRATTAN PULAO
PEAS PULAO
JEERA PULAO
VEGETABLE PULAO
VEGETABLE FRIED RICE

SELECT ANY ONE
RASGULLA
RASMALAI
GULAB JAMUN
SHAHI TUKRANAWABI
COLA/LIMCA/ORANGE/LEMON - Rs. 15/
- PER BOTTLE

BOTTLE, CANNED JUICE - Rs. 10/- PER
GLASS (SMALL)

VEGETARIAN

CHOOSE ANY THREE

SALAD-E-SURAT
(Dices of carrots, beans, turnip and apple
served in cream)

SABZ-E-KHET
(Fresh from the farm-tomatoes, onion,
radish and cucumber served with lemon)

SIMLA CHAAT
(Potatoes and apple served with chatpata
masala)

ACHARI SALAD
(Home made seasonal vegetables)

KACHUMBER
(Dices of onions, cucumber, tomatoes,
capsicum and cabbage in lemon dressing)

CHOOSE ANY ONE

TOMATO SHORBA
(Extracts of red tomatoes tempered with
home made masala)

BOULA BOULA
(Garden fresh green peas soup served
with croutons)

PYAO-E-KHUMB
(Extract of fresh mushroom with swirl of
cream)

HOT & SOUR SOUP
(Brunoise of vegetables and tofu cooked
in vinegar and chillies)

MULLIGATAWNY SOUP
(Curry flavoured lentil soup served with
rice finished with lemon)

CHOOSE ANY ONE

PANEER DURBAR
(Paneer cooked in butter and tomatoes served with cream)

KADAIPANEER
(Cottage cheese cooked with capsicum and onion served on Hot Tava)

MUSHROOM TAVEWALA
(Fresh khumb from chail prepared in conventional reriwala style)

CHOOSE ANY THREE

MATAR-DO-PIAZA
(Cooked green peas and onion tempered with Garam Masala)

HARIALI KOFTA
(Paneer palak kofta simmered in delicious palak gravy)

GOBHI MASALEDAR
(Tandoori gobhi cooked in Bombay masala)

SUBZ DILKUSH
(Colourful assortment of fresh vegetables cooked in home made masala)

SPAGHETTI FLORENTINE
(Delicately cooked spaghetti served on a bed of green spinach)

EGG PLANT IN GARLIC SAUCE
(Hot brinjals cooked in chilli garlic sauce)

CHOOSE ANY ONE

DALKAMADRA
(Creamy urad dal cooked in traditional Kashmiri style)

CHANA PESHWARI
(Mildly spiced white chana cooked in Peshwari style)

DAL PANCHMAHAL
(Assortment of five lentils cooked in Rajasthani style)

CHOOSE ANY ONE

SABZI RAITA
(Variable combination of fresh vegetables mixed with Dahi)

ASSAEME RAITA
(Diced pineapple mixed with sweet curd)

PAKORI RAITA
(Small pakori in dahi served with sonth)

CHOOSE ANY ONE

KASHMIRI PULAO
(Rich pulao with cherries, fruits and nuts)

JEERA PULAO
(Delicately jeera tempered rice)

SUMDRA PULAO
(Lemon flavoured pulao)

CHOOSE ANY TWO

KULCHA/PARATHA/POORI/MISSI ROTI
Achar-Papad-Chutney

CHOOSE ANY TWO

NARAM GARAM
(Honey flavoured Gulabjamun served piping hot)

LUCKNAVI RASMALAI
(Milk soaked rasmalai made in Lucknavi Nawabi style)

CHOICE OF SOUFFLE
(A wide range of souffles)

BARFILI BAHAR
(Choicest Ice-cream served at hill temperature)

JASHN-E-KASHMIR
(Freshly cut apples, bananas and cherries served soaked in sugar syrup)

MENU

HOTEL PRESIDENT (PATNA)

CONFERENCE MENU

TWO NON-VEGETARIAN

SOUP (ANY ONE)
TOMATO SOUP VEGETABLE SOUP S/
CORN SOUP GR. PEAS SOUP

FISH (ANY ONE)
FISH CURRY FISH FRIED

MUTTON (ANY ONE)
MUTTON CURRY
MUTTON DOPYAJA
MUTTON ROGAN JOSH
MUTTON MASALA
MUTTON KORMA

CHICKEN (ANY ONE)
CHICKEN BUTTER
MASALA CHICKEN
DOPYAJA CHICKEN
CURRY CHICKEN MASALA

PANEER (ANY ONE)
PANEER BUTTER MASALA
MATTAR PANEER
PALAK PANEER
PANEER TOMATO
PANEER SAHI KORMA

VEGETABLE (ANY ONE)
MALAI KOFTA
VEGETABLE KOFTA
NAVRATAN KORMA
VEGETABLE JAIPURI

VEGETABLE (ANY ONE)
Mixed VEGETABLE
VEGETABLE JHALFREZI
ALOO DUM
VEGETABLE MANCHURIAN
ALOO GOBHI

DAL (ANY ONE)
DAL MAKHANI
DAL GHANA
MIXED DAL

PULAO (ANY ONE)
VEGETABLE PULAO
PEAS PULAO
PLAIN PULAO
ZEERA PULAO
NAVRATTAN PULAO

BREAD & NAAN (ANY TWO)
ROTI
NAAN
KULCHA
STUFFED KULCHA
TANDOORI PARATHA
PURI/HING KACHORI
STUFFED NAAN

SALAD (ANY ONE)
POTATO SALAD
GREEN SALAD
ONION SALAD

PAPAD

RAITA (ANY ONE)
MIXED RAITA
PINEAPPLE RAITA
BUNDI RAITA
POTATO RAITA
DAHI WADA

DESSERT (ANY ONE)
VANILA ICE CREAM
S.B. ICE CREAM
FRUIT SALAD WITH CREAM

MENU

HOTEL GOMOTI LUCKNOW

कुछ ठंडा कुछ गरम

फलों का रस आपकी पसंद (डिब्बा बंद)
(अनन्नास/संतरा/आम)
(अनन्नास, संतरा, आम) छोटा
(अनन्नास, संतरा, आम) बड़ा
सेब का रस
लस्सी
(मीठी/नमकीन/मसाला)
कोल्ड कॉफी आइसक्रीम के साथ
मिल्क शेक
(वनीला/स्ट्रावेरी/चाकॅलेट)
सॉफ्ट ड्रिंक
फ्रेश लाइम सोडा
सोडा
मिनरल वाटर
चाय/कॉफी
वार्नवीटा/हॉट चॉकलेट

सुप तुरीन

क्रीम सूप आपकी पसंद का
टमाटर/मशरूम/वेजिटेबल/चिकन
स्वीट कार्न सूप
(वेज/नॉन वेज)

अंगारों से (तंदूरी विशिष्टतायें)

तंदूरी मुर्ग (आधा)
मुर्ग टिक्का
मालाई सीक कबाब
पनीर टिक्का

कढ़ाई से

मुर्ग मखानी
मुर्ग टिक्का लबाबदार
मुर्ग मसाला
गोश्त शाही कोरमा
गोश्त सुमई
भुना गोश्त

TWO-IN-ONE ICE CREAM

KUCHHA THANDA KUCHHA GARAM
(NOT 'N' COLD BEVERAGES)

PHALON KA RAS AAP KI PASAND KA
(Canned juice)
(Pine Apple/Orange/Mango)

(Pine Apple/Orange/Mango) Small	15.00
(Pine Apple/Orange/Mango) Large	20.00
Apple Juice	25.00
Lassi	15.00
(Sweet/Salted/Masala)	
Cold Coffee With Ice Cream	25.00
Milk Shake	20.00
(Vanila/Strawberry/Chocolate)	
Soft Drink	12.00
Fresh Lime Soda	12.00
Soda-Water	10.00
Mineral-Water	25.00
Tea/Coffee	10.00
Bournvita/Hot Chocolate	15.00

SOUP TUREEN

(12.30 P.M. To 3.00 P.M. / 7.30 P.M. to 11.00 P.M.)
Cream Soup Aap Ki Pasand Ka
(Cream Soup of your choice)

Tomato/Mushroom/Vegetable/Chicken	20.00
Sweet-Corn Soup	20.00
(Veg./Non-Veg.)	

Angaron Se (From Tandoor)

Tandoori Murg (Half)	55.00
Murg Tikka	60.00
Malai Seekh Kabab	35.00
Paneer Tikka	35.00

KADHAI SE

Murg Makhani	60.00
Murg Tikka Lababdar	70.00
Kadhai Murg	45.00
Murg Masala	45.00
Gosht Shahi Korma	40.00
Gosht Surmi	40.00
Bhuna Gosht	40.00

शाकाहारी

पनीर मखानी
कढ़ाई पनीर
शाही पनीर
मलाई कोफ्ता
काजू मटर खुम्ब करी
भरवां आलू दम
भरवां टमाटर
सब्ज सदाबहार (सूखी मौसमी सब्जी)
दाल मखानी
रायता
(कचुम्बर/आलू/बूंदी/अनन्नास)

डेग से

सफेद चावल
मटर पुलाव/जीरा पुलाव
यखनी पुलाव
कश्मीरी पुलाव

सांझा चूल्हा

तंदूरी रोटी
नान
पराठा
मिस्सी रोटी
कुलचा

शेफ के खजाने से

रोस्ट चिकन
अमेरिकन फ्राइड चिकन
चिकन शासलिक
पनीर शासलिक
मटन स्टू
बेजिटेबिल औगेतिन

शब्बा खैर

आइसक्रीम
बनीला/चॉकलेट/स्ट्रोबेरी/केसरपिस्ता
बनाना बोनन्जा
टूटी–फ्रूटी

VEGETARIAN

Paneer Makhani	35.00
Kadhai Paneer	35.00
Shahi Paneer	30.00
Malai Kofta	30.00
Kaju Matar Khumb Curry	35.00
Bharwan Aloo Bum	25.00
Bharwan Tamatar	25.00
Sabz Sadabahar (Dry seas veg.)	25.00
Dal Arhar	20.00
Dal Makhani	20.00
Raita	18.00
(Kachumber, Potato, Boondi, pineapple)	
Green Salad	12.00

Deg se

Safed Chawal	15.00
Pea Pulao/Jeera Pulao	20.00
Murgh Biryani	40.00
Yakhni Pulao	35.00
Kashmiri Pulao	25.00

Sanjha Choolha

Tandoori Roti	04.00
Naan	06.00
Paratha	06.00
Missi Roti	08.00
Kulcha	08.00

CHEF KE KHAZANE SE
(continental offerings)

Roast Chicken	70.00
American Fried Chicken	70.00
Chicken Shashlik	70.00
Mutton Stew	40.00
Paneer Shashlik	40.00
Vegetable Augratin	30.00

Shabbah Khair

Ice Cream	20.00
(vanilla/chocolate/strawberry/ mango/kesar pista)	
Banana Bonanza	30.00
Tuti-Fruity	30.00

स्नेक्स

10.30 से 12.00 दोपहर
एवं 3.00 बजे से 8.00 बजे रात्री
ताजा फल का रस
जलजीरा
टमाटर सूप
क्रीम सूप (चिकेन/मशरूम)
फीश-एन-चीप्स
फीस फिंगर
फ्राईड चिकेन
चिकेन पिपर स्टेक
फ्रेन्च फ्राइस

बिटबिन-द-टू
टो स्टेड से डबीच (चार पीस)
(चीज या चिकेन)
ग्रील्ड चीज टोस्ट
चीज या चिकेन से डबीज (चार पीस)
टमाटर या खीरा से डबीज (चार पीस)
चिकेन पकौड़ा
काजू
पीनटस
चीज वा अनानास स्टीक

आईसक्रीम
दर्पण डिलाइट
च्वाईस आफ आईसक्रीम
(वेनिया, स्ट्राबेरी)
फ्रूट सलाद
फ्रूट सलाद आईसक्रीम सहित

दिन एवं रात्री भोजन
12.30 बजे से 2.45 से अपराह
एवं 8.00 से 10.45 तक

स्टाटर
जलजीरा
इवाईयन चीक

Snack Timers

Served From 10.30 a.m. to 12.00 noon &
3.00 p.m. to 8.00 p.m.

Freshly Squeezed Juice	35.00
(Seasonal Fresh Fruit Juice)	
Jeera Pani	10.00
Tomato Soup	25.00
Cream Soup	
(mushroom or vegetable)	25.00
Fish 'N' Chips	65.00
Fish Finger	65.00
Fried Chicken	80.00
Chicken Pepper Steak	90.00
French Fries	20.00

Between The Two

Toasted Sandwiches (4 PC.)	35.00
(Cheese or Chicken)	
Grilled Cheese Toast	35.00
Cheese or Chicken	
Sandwich (4 PC.)	30.00
Tomato or Cucumber	
Sandwich (4 PC.)	25.00
Vegetable Pakora	20.00
Paneer Pakora	30.00
Chicken Pakora	65.00
Cashewnuts	60.00
Peanuts	20.00
Cheese & Pineapple Stick	36.00

For The Sweet Tooth

Darpan Delight	40.00
Choice of Ice Cream	25.00
(Vanilla, Strawberry)	
Fruit Salad	25.00
Fruit Salad With Ice Cream	40.00

Lunch & Dinner

Service From 12.30 p.m. to 2.45 p.m. &
8.00 p.m. to 10.00 p.m.

Starters	
Jeera Pani	10.00
(Spicy Aperitif Flavoured With	
Cumin & Mint)	
Hawaian Chic	45.00
(Chicken & Pineapple Dressed in	
Mayonnaises)	

हॉट पॉट
क्रीम ऑफ टोमेटो
क्रीम ऑफ वेजिटेविल
क्रीम ऑफ चिकेन

कोन्टीनेन्ट
भारतीय विशिष्ट व्यज्जन
दावत–ए–हिन्द
फीस एन्ड चिप्स
फ्राइड चिकेन
वेजिटेबुल आंगान

तन्दूरी
फीस टिक्का
(मसालेदार दही में भिगोया हुआ मछली)
मुर्ग तन्दूरी आधा
(मसालेदार दही में भिगोया हुआ तन्दूरी मुर्गा)
चूजा मलाई टिक्का
(क्रीम एवं बादाम में बनाया हुआ मुर्गा)
टिक्के–ए–मुर्ग
(चकेन के टुकड़े दही के साथ बनाया हुआ)

ऐ गुलिस्तां हमारा
फीश करी
(मसालेदार हड्डी रहित मछली के टुकड़े)
मुर्ग मक्खन यादगार
(तन्दूरी मुर्गा, टमाटर एवं मक्खन के साथ)

From The Hot Pot

Cream of Tomato	25.00
Cream of Vegetable	25.00
Cream of Chicken	25.00

From The Continent
Indian Specialities

Daawat-E-Hind

Fish & Chips	65.00

(Crumbed Fried Fillet of Fish
Served with French Fries)

Chicken Pepper Steak	90.00

(Grilled Breast of Chicken Cooked
in Tongue Tingling Pepper-Sauce)

Fried Chicken	80.00

(Deep Fried Crumbed Chicken
Served with Golden French Fries)

Vegetable Augratin	50.00

(Boiled Vegetable Cooked in
White Sauce with Cream &
Gratinated with Cheese)

Tandoor-Se

Fish Tikka	70.00

(Morsel of Fish Marinated in
Spiced Yoghurt & Cooked in
Earthen Oven)

Murgh Tandoori Half	70.00

(Spring Chicken Marinated in
Spiced Yoghurt & Cooked in
Earthen Oven)

Chooza Malai Tikka	85.00

(Boneless Chicken Marinated in
Cream Nuts & cooked in
Earthen Oven)

Tikka-E-Murgh	80.00

(Boneless Chicken, marinated
in Spiced Yoghurt & cooked
in Earthen Oven)

Yeh Gulistan Hamara

Fish Curry	65.00

(Boneless pieces of Fish in
Spicy Gravy)

Murgh Makhani Yadgar	80.00

(Tandoori Chicken simmered in
rich Tomato & Butter Gravy)

MENU

TAKSHILA

(HOTEL CHANAKYA PATNA)

NORTH

FRONTIER

SPECIALITY

12 Noon to 3.30 P.M. 7.30 P.M. to 10.30 P.M.

SHORBA

TAMATAR KA SHORBA	30.00
MURGH YAKHNI	35.00
"GORI" KA SHORBA	40.00

SHAKAHARI

SUEZ TANDOORI	150.00
PANEER SAUFIA TIKKA	85.00
BHARWAN ALOO	50.00
TANDOORI PHOOL	50.00
TANDOORI MIRCH	50.00
PANEER KESARI PASANDA	90.00
PANEER BUTTER MASALA	80.00
BHARWAN TAMATAR	50.00
DIWANI HANOI	75.00
ALOO ANARWALI	65.00
KOFTA SABZ BAHAR	100.00
TRI COLOUR KOFTA	85.00
DAL TAKSHILA	40.00

MANSAHARI

MURGH MALAI KEBAB	130.00
(Tender pieces of chicken, marinated with cream and soft cheese)	
MURG RESHMI KEBAB	120.00
(Chicken mince cooked on a skewer)	
TANGRI BHARWAN	120.00
PESHAWARI TANDOORI MURGH	150.00
MURGH MIRCH KEBAB	130.00
RANN-E-TAKSHILA	250.00

(Whole baby mutton leg, marinated in special spices cooked in the tandoor)

MUTTON PASANDA KEBAB	80.00
KHAAS SEEKH KEBAB	80.00
KARAH KEBAB	80.00
FISH TIKKA	100.00
FISH NOORANI	100.00
MURGH MAKHNI (FULL)	140.00
CHOOZA MUSALLAM	150.00
BALTI MURGH	150.00

ROTI

PESHAWARI NAAN	18.00
TAKSHILA NAAN	25.00
BUTTER NAAN	15.00
SADA NAAN	12.00
BHARWAN KULCHA	16.00
ROTI	10.00
KHASTA ROTI	15.00
ROOMALI ROTI	12.00
MESI ROTI	15.00
PAKHTOONI NAAN	25.00
KABULI BIRYANI	105.00

DESSERTS

SHAKOORI PHIRNI	30.00
PISTA KULFI	30.00
GULAB JAMUN	20.00
RASMALAI	20.00

MENU

BANQUET

TWO NON-VEGETARIAN

SOUP (ANY **ONE**)
TOMATO SOUP
VEGETABLE SOUP
MINISTRONE SOUP
S/CORN SOUP
GR. PEAS SOUP
ALMOND SOUP

FISH (ANY **ONE**)
FISH CURRY
FISH FRIED
TOMATO BAKED FISH
FISH MAYONNAISE
FISH AMRITSARI

MUTTON (ANY **ONE**)
MUTTON CURRY
MUTTON DOPIYAJA
MUTTON BHUNA
MUTTON ROGAN JOSH
MUTTON MASALA
MUTTON KORMA

CHICKEN (ANY **ONE**)
CHICKEN BUTTER MASALA
CHICKEN DOPYAJA
CHICKEN HARA MASALA
CHICKEN CURRY
CHICKEN METHI
CHICKEN MASALA

PANEER (ANY ONE)
PANEER BUTTER MASALA
MATTAR PANEER
PALAK PANEER
PANEER TOMATO
PANEER SAHI KORMA
PANEER PASANDA

VEGETABLE (ANY **ONE**)
SHABNAM CURRY
MALAI KOFTA
VIGETABLE KOFTA
BAKED VEGETABLE
NAVRATTAN KORMA
VEGETABLE JAIPURI

VEGETABLE (ANY **ONE**)
MIXED VEGETABLE
VEGETABLE JHALFREJI

ALOO DUM
VEGETABLE MANCHURIAN
ALOO GOBI
ALOO JEERA

DAL (ANY **ONE**)
DAL MAKHANI
DAL GHANA
PINDI GHANA

PULAO (ANY **ONE**)
VEGETABLE PULAO
PEAS PULAO
PLAIN PULAO
ZEERA PULAO
NAVRATTAN PULAO

BREAD & NAAN (ANY **TWO**)
ROTI
NAAN
KULCHA
STUFFED KULCHA
TANDOORI PARATHA
PURI
STUFFED NAAN

SALAD (ANY **ONE**)
POTATO SALAD
GR. SALAD
RUSSIAN SALAD
SPROUTED SALAD

PAPAD

RAITA (ANY **ONE**)
MIXED RAITA
PINEAPPLE RAITA
BUNDI RAITA
POTATO RAITA
DAHI WADA
DAHI PAKORI

DESSERT (ANY **ONE**)
VANILLA ICE CREAM
S.B. ICE CREAM FRUIT SALAD
TWO-IN-ONE ICE CREAM
FRUIT TRIFFLE

VEGETARIAN

SOUP (ANY ONE)

TOMATO SOUP
VEGETABLE SOUP
MINISTRONE SOUP
S/CORN SOUP
GR. PEAS SOUP
ALMOND SOUP

PANEER (ANY ONE)

PANEER BUTTER MASALA
MATAR PANEER
PALAK PANEER
PANEER TOMATO
PANEER SAHI KORMA
PANEER PASANDA

VEGETABLES (ANY ONE)

SHABNAM CURRY
MALAI KOFTA
VEGETABLE KOFTA
BAKED VEGETABLE
NAVRATTAN KORMA
VEGETABLE JAIPURI

VEGETABLE (ANY ONE)

MIXED VEGETABLE
VEGETABLE JHAL FREJI
ALOO DUM
VEGETABLE MANCHURIAN
ALOO GOBI
ALOO JEERA

DAL (ANY ONE)

DAL MAKHANI
DAL GHANA
PINDI GHANA

PULAO (ANY ONE)

VEGETABLE PULAO
PEAS PULAO
PLAIN PULAO
ZEERA PULAO
NAVRATTAN PULAO

BREAD & NAAN (ANY TWO)

ROTI
NAAN
KULCHA
STUFFED KULCHA
TANDOORI PARATHA
PURI
STUFFED NAAN

SALAD (ANY ONE)

GR. SALAD
POTATO SALAD
RUSSIAN SALAD
SPROUTED SALAD

PAPAD

RAITA (ANY ONE)

MIXED RAITA
PINEAPPLE RAITA
BUNDI RAITA
POTATO RAITA
DAHI WADA
DAHI PAKORI

DESSERT (ANY ONE)

VANILLA ICE CREAM
S. B. ICE CREAM
FRUIT SALAD
TWO-IN-ONE ICE CREAM
FRUIT TRIFFLE

Courtesy : **Hotel Chankya, Patna INDIA**

MENU

```
┌─────────────┐
│    MOTEL    │
└─────────────┘
```

AJ's RESTAURANT U.K.

MAIN COURSES

STARTERS & SOUPS

GARLIC BREAD	90P
ORANGE JUICE	90P
HONEYDEW MELON	95p

(Slice of Fresh Melon with Ground Ginger)

BOWL OF PIPING HOT SOUP £1.40

Cream of Tomato	Minestrone
Hearty Oxtail	Rich Mulligataway
Celery	Cream of Chicken

Serve with Roll and Butter Your server will advise you of today's choices

PRAWN COCKTAIL £2.25
Served complete with Brown Bread

DIPPERS DELIGHT (Serves 2) £3.95
Chicken Nuggets, Garlic Mushrooms, Scampi and Battered Onion Rings with a Choice of Dip.

DEEP FRIED MUSHROOMS £2.05
Garlic Mushrooms, deep fried with a choice of Dip.

SEAFOOD DIP £2.25
Scampi pieces with Tartare Dip

BAKES & GRILLS

SERVED WITH EITHER, SALAD, RICE, CHIPPED, NEW OR JACKET POTATO

ROAST CHICKEN £5.50
Half an oven Roasted Chicken served with Garden Peas and Sweetcorm with a Rich Gravy

GAMMON STEAK £5.30
Griddled Prime Gammon served with a Pineapple Ring and Garden Peas

SIRLOIN STEAK £6.95
Tender Sirloin Steak served with Mushrooms, Onion Rings and Garden Peas

BEEF STEW & DUMPLINGS £4.95
A traditional tasty alternative

FARMHOUSE GRILL £4.60
Griddled Egg, Bacon, Tomatoes, Sausage, Hamburger served with Garden Peas and Mushrooms

PORK SCHNITZEL £4.95
Tender Crumbed Pork served with Tomatoes, Garden Peas and Button Mushrooms

BURGERS

Lean Beef served with Coleslaw and Relishes and Choice of Salad or Chipped Potatoes

BACONBURGER £4.15
Topped with Bacon and Grated Cheese

PINEBURGER £3.45
Open Burger with Pineapple and Coleslaw

EGG BURGER £3.35
Crowned with a Griddled Egg

CHILLI BURGER £3.45
Hot & Spicy Vegetable chilli

AJ's "MAJORBURGER" £4.50
On Lean Beef and served with any two of the following
a Cottage Cheese
b Griddled Egg
c Cheddar Cheese
d Tomato
e Griddled Bacon
f Vegetable Chilli
g Mushrooms
h Pineapple

CHICKEN BURGER £3.35
Tender Chicken in Batter

FISH

Served with either Salad, Rice, Chipped, New Or Jacket Potato

FILLET OF PLAICE £4.55
Breaded and deep-fried, served with Garden Peas, Lemon and Tartare, Sauce

LIVER AND BACON £4.45
Griddled Liver and Bacon served
with Onion Rings, Tomatoes,
Garden Peas and Gravy

LASAGNE £4.75
Traditional Italian Pasta served with
Garden Peas

FILLET OF HADDOCK £4.55
Crispy battered and deep : fried,
served with Garden Peas and Lemon

SCAMPI PLATTER £5.75
Golden Crumbed Scampi pieces
served with Garden Peas, Lemon and
Tartare Sauce

MENU

PUB RESTAURANT U.K.

AJ's RESTAURANT U.K.

MAIN COURSES

STARTERS

GARLIC BREAD	£1.25
CHEESY TOPED	£1.75
PRAWN COCKTAIL with Granary Bread	£2.95
HOMEMADE SOUP with French Bread	£1.95
KING PRAWNS in Filo **PASTRY** with Dip and Salad Garnish	£2.95
HOMEMADE PATE and Toast	£2.50
GARLIC MUSHROOMS & French Bread	£2.50

SANDWICHES (LUNCH TIME ONLY)

Choice of Granary or White Bread

HOMECOOKED HAM	£2.25
ROAST BEEF	£2.50
TASTY CHEDDAR	£1.75
PRAWNS IN SAUCE	£2.95
PRAWNS & CHEESE	**£3.50**

PLOUGHMAN'S LUNCHES

(Lunch time Only)

Homecooked Ham	£4.00
Stilton	£4.00
Cumberland Sausage	£4.00
Tasty Cheddar	£3.50

FILLED JACKET POTATO

(Lunch time Only) All served with
crispy salad and a choice of two
fillings £3.95

Ham, Cheese, Onion, Tomato,
Coleslaw, Pineapple & Baked Beans
(Prawn & Cheese is Extra) £1.00

MEAT DISHES

PRIME RUMP STEAK	£7.95
MEGAMDIED GRILL	£8.75
PRIME FILLET STEAK	£8.95
GAMMON STEAK & PINEAPPLE	£6.50

Our Chef will be delighted to serve
either Chasseur or Diane Sauce to
compliment your Grill. All the above
served with a choice of potato, fried
onions, mushrooms, grilled tomatoes
and crispy salad.

CUMBERLAND SAUSAGE
Served with French Fries and Baked
Beans £3.75

CHICKEN FILLETS
served with French Fried & Salad £5.95

HOMEMADE STEAK & KIDNEY
Pie with a selection of fresh
Vegetables £4.95

HOMEMADE MEAT LASAGNE
Served with French Fries & Salad £4.75

CHILDREN'S MENU

CHICKEN NUGGETS & CHIPS	£2.50
SAUSAGE, BEANS & CHIPS	£2.50
SCAMPI & CHIPS	£2.50

LIAN SOON

CHINESE RESTAURANT

Mumbai, INDIA

Time : 11.30 a.m to 3.00 p.m.
7.00 p.m. to 12.00 p.m.

FREE HOME DELIVERY

CALL US AT :
6366484 / 6300697

We also undertake party orders before 24 hours.

LIAN SOON SPECIAL

1.	Lian Soon Special Soup	40.00
2.	Chicken Sweet Corn Soup	35.00
3.	Egg Sweet Corn Soup	35.00
4.	Talu Mein Soup	35.00
5.	Lung Fung Soup	35.00
6.	Manchow Soup	35.00
7.	Hot & Sour Soup	35.00
8.	Wanton Noodles Soup	40.00
9.	Wanton Soup	35.00
10.	Chicken Noodles Soup	35.00
11.	Prawns Noodles Soup	35.00
12.	Chopsouy Soup	35.00
13.	Chicken Clear Soup	35.00
14.	Egg Cream Veg. Soup	35.00

VEG. SOUP

15.	Veg. Sweet Corn Soup	30.00
16.	Plain Sweet Corn Soup	28.00
17.	Veg. Clear Soup	28.00
18.	Veg. Noodles Soup	30.00
19.	Veg. Hot & Sour Soup	30.00
20.	Veg. Manchow Soup	30.00
21.	Veg. Me Fung Soup	35.00
22.	Tomato Soup	30.00
23.	Veg. Wanton Noodles Soup	35.00
24.	Veg. Wanton Soup	30.00

VEG.

25.	Veg. American Chopsouy	45.00
26.	Veg. Chinese Chopsouy	45.00
27.	Triple Schezwan Rice and Noodles	55.00
28.	Veg. Fried Rice	40.00
29.	Veg. Schezwan Fried Rice	45.00
30.	Veg. Singapore Fried Rice	45.00
31.	Veg. Chow Noodles with Gravy	45.00
32.	Veg. Haka Noodles	40.00
33.	Veg. Schezwan Noodles	45.00
34.	Veg. Singapore Haka Noodles	45.00
35.	Veg. Spring Roll	38.00
36.	Veg. Ball Schezwan Sauce	38.00
37.	Veg. Ball Hongkong	38.00
38.	Veg. Ball Manchurian	38.00
39.	Sweet & Sour Veg	38.00
40.	Garlic Veg. Sauce	38.00

PLEASE NOTE : NO BEEF NO PORK

41. Veg. Chow - Chow	38.00
42. Veg. Mushroom Chow-Chow	45.00
43. Veg. Fried Fingers Schezwan	40.00
44. Veg. Fried Wanton	40.00
45. Veg. Steam Rice	50.00
46. Paneer Chilly	45.00
47. Mushroom Chilly	45.00

CHOPSOUY

48. Schezwan Chinese Chopsouy	60.00
49. Mix Chinese Chopsouy	60.00
50. Chicken Chinese Chopsouy	50.00
51. Mix American Chopsouy	60.00
52. Chicken American Chopsouy	50.00
53. Plain Crisp Noodles	30.00

RICE

54. Chicken St. Wanton	50.00
55. Triple Schezwan Rice & Noodles	60.00
56. Chicken Steam Rice	60.00
57. Chicken Fried Rice	45.00
58. Mixed Fried Rice	48.00
59. Prawns Fried Rice	45.00
60. Egg Fried Rice	45.00
61. Mix Singapore Fried Rice	50.00
62. Chicken Singapore Fried Rice	48.00
63. Prawns Singapore Fried Rice	48.00
64. Egg Singapore Fried Rice	48.00
65. Mix Schezwan Fried Rice	50.00
66. Chicken Schezwan Fried Rice	48.00
67. Prawns Schezwan Fried Rice	48.00
68. Egg Schezwan Fried Rice	48.00
69. Plain Steam Rice	25.00

NOODLES

70. Chicken Chow Mein with Gravy	50.00
71. Mix Haka Noodles	48.00
72. Chicken Haka Noodles	45.00
73. Prawns Haka Noodles	45.00
74. Egg Haka Noodles	45.00
75. Mix Schezwan Haka Noodles	50.00
76. Chicken Schezwan Haka Noodles	48.00
77. Prawns Schezwan Haka Noodles	48.00
78. Egg Schezwan Haka Noodles	48.00
79. Mix Singapore Haka Noodles	50.00
80. Chicken Singapore Haka Noodles	48.00

PLEASE NOTE : NO BEEF NO PORK

81. Prawns Singapore Haka Noodles	48.00
82. Egg Singapore Haka Noodles	48.00

SPRING ROLL

83. Mix Spring Roll	45.00
84. Chicken Spring Roll	40.00
85. Prawns Spring Roll	40.00
86. Egg Spring Roll	40.00
87. Fried Wanton	45.00
88. Lolly Pop Chicken	55.00
89. Chicken Fingers	55.00

CHICKEN PRAWNS, FISH. LAMB

90. Chicken Hot Garlic	45.00
91. Chilly Chicken Boneless	45.00
92. Manchurian Chicken Boneless	45.00
93. Garlic Chicken Boneless (Sweet)	45.00
94. Ginger Chicken Boneless	45.00
95. Roast Chicken Chilly	60.00
96. Chicken Green Sauce	45.00
97. Diced Chicken Chilly White Sauce	45.00
98. Spring Chicken	55.00
99. Chicken Meat Ball Garlic (Sweet Sauce)	55.00
100. Hunan Chicken	60.00
101. Chicken Veg. Cashewnut	60.00
102. Chilly Prawns	50.00
103. Manchurian Prawns	50.00
104. Garlic Prawns (Sweet)	50.00
105. Ginger Prawns	50.00
106. Fried Prawns	50.00
107. Fish Manchurian.	55.00
108. Fish Chilly	55.00
109. Fish Garlic Sauce (Sweet)	55.00
110. Fish Ginger Sauce	55.00
111. Fish Fried	55.00
112. Mandarin Fish	56.00
113. Lamb Meat Ball Chilly	60.00
114. Lamb Meat Ball Schezwan	60.00
115. Lamb Meat Ball Hongkong	60.00

SWEET AND SOUR

116. Sweet & Sour Chicken Boneless	45.00
117. Sweet & Sour Fish	55.00
118. Sweet & Sour Prawns	50.00

SCHEZWAN SPECIAL

119. Schezwan Chicken Boneless	45.00
120. Schezwan Prawns	50.00

PLEASE NOTE : NO BEEF NO PORK

121. Schezwan Fish	55.00
122. Hongkong Chicken Boneless	45.00
123. Hongkong Prawns	50.00
124. Hongkong Fish	55.00

MUSHROOM CHOW-CHOW

125. Chicken Mushroom Veg. Chow-Chow	55.00
126. Prawns Mushroom Veg. Chow-Chow	60.00
127. Fish Mushroom Veg. Chow-Chow	65.00
128. Chicken Capsicum with Mushroom	60.00
129. Prawns Capsicum with Veg. Chow-Chow	65.00
130. Fish Capsicum with Mushroom	65.00

CHOW- CHOW

131. Chicken Veg. Chow-Chow	45.00
132. Prawns Veg. Chow-Chow	50.00
133. Fish Veg. Chow-Chow	55.00

COLD DRINKS

134. Thumps - up	15.00
135. Pepsi	15.00
136. Fanta	15.00
137. Coca - Cola	15.00
138. Mineral Water	15.00

OUR SPECIAL ORDER
BEFORE 24 HRS.

139. Sui Mai (Per Dozen)	200.00
140. Momo (Per Dozen)	120.00
141. Steam Chicken in Garlic	220.00
142. Steam Fish (Full) Medien	200.00
143. Fried Chicken in Soya (Full)	220.00
144. King Prawns in any Style	220.00
145. Fried Crispy Chicken (Full)	220.00

Note : For All Extra Sauce Gravy Etc. Rs. 12/- Will Be Charged.

PLEASE NOTE : NO BEEF NO PORK

CROISSANTS

Plain Croissants	10.00
Mushroom & Corn Croissants	20.00
Garlic N Cheese Croissants	20.00
Spicy Veg.	20.00
Veg. Kolhapuri	20.00
Paneer Bhurji	20.00
Chicken 'N' Cheese	22.00
Barbeque Chicken	22.00
Chicken Manchurian	22.00
Ham 'N' Cheese	22.00
Chocolate Croissants	25.00

PUFFS AND STRUDDLES

Veg Curry Puff	18.00
Cheese & Garlic Puff	18.00
Mushroom Onion Puff	18.00
Dingri Mutter Struddle	20.00
Ham 'N' Cheese Struddle	25.00
Chicken Puff	22.00
Mutton Keema Puff	22.00
Chicken Schezwan Struddle	25.00
Apple Struddle	20.00

CALIZZA [FOLDED PIZZA]

Farm House [All Veg]	30.00
Barbeque Chicken	32.00
Peppery Paneer	30.00
Caliza Special Non Veg	32.00

ROLLS AND QUICHES

Reshmi Kebab Roll	22.00
Chicken Kathi Roll	45.00
Chicken Whopper	45.00
Veg Quiche	20.00
Chicken Quiche	25.00

SALADS

Veg. Salad (From the Salad Bar}	45.00
With 1 Scoop Chicken Jungli	70.00
Pre-packed Veg Salad (Small)	30.00
Pre-Packed Non Veg Salad	50.00
Chicken Salad [Small]	40.00
Chicken Salad [Large]	60.00

SANDWICHES

Chef's Special	20.00
Tomato "N" Cheese	20.00
Chicken Jungli	25.00

Tuna Jungli	25.00
Extra Cheese	05.00

DOUBLE DECKERS AND PREMIUM SANDWICHES

Chicken Exotic/Chicken Tikka	
Sandwich	45.00
Chicken Jungli	45.00
Chef's Special	35.00
Veg. Double Decker	35.00
Veg. Jungli	35.00

CROISSANDWICHES AND SUBMARINES

Veg. Croissandwich	30.00
Chicken Croissandwich	35.00
Veg. "N" Cheese Submarine	35.00
Chicken Indiana Jones	45.00
"with extra cheese"	05.00

GRILLED SANDWICHES AND MELTS

Grilled Chicken Sandwich	45.00
Tomato Cheese "N" Potato	35.00
Chicken Melt	45.00
"with extra cheese"	05.00

BURGERS

Veg Burger	35.00
Chicken Burger	45.00
with extra cheese	05.00

MINI MEALS
(Available only in select outlets)

Veggie Lasagne	50.00
Chicken Lasagne	65.00
Spaghetti Nepolitiane {Veg.}	50.00
Spagheett	65.00
Chicken Biryani	50.00
Veg. Biryani	40.00
Tomato "N" Cheese Pizza	35.00
Barbeque Chicken Pizza	45.00
Extra Cheese	05.00

MOUSSE/TARTS/DESSERTS

Chocolate Mousse	30.00
Mango Mousse (Seasonal)	30.00
Strawberry Mousse (Seasonal)	30.00
Black Forest Pudding	15.00
Truffle Tart	20.00
Lemon Tart	20.00
Rum Bail	15.00

TEA TIME BAR CAKES

Mawa Cake	80.00
Madiera Cake	80.00
Fruit Cake	90.00
Plum Bar	140.00
Orange Bar	80.00
Date & Walnut Cake	90.00
Choco Chip Cake	90.00

CAKES AND PASTRIES

	Pastry	Small	Large	Special order	Fancy Chocolate
Chocolate Truffle	35.00	175.00	350.00	350.00	380.00
Dutch Truffle	35.00	175.00	350.00	350.00	380.00
Black Forest Ananas	35.00	175.00	350.00	350.00	380.00
Krokani	35.00	175.00	340.00	340.00	380.00
Strawberry	35.00	170.00	340.00	340.00	380.00

PREMIUM PASTRIES

	Pastry	Small	Large	Special order
Dutch Noughat	40.00	175.00	350.00	350.00
Festive Chocolate Gateau	40.00	175.00	350.00	350.00
Black magic Gateau	40.00	175.00	350.00	350.00
Peach "N" Apricot	40.00	175.00	350.00	350.00
Fig "N" Honey	40.00	175.00	350.00	350.00
Black Currant	40.00	17500	350.00	350.00
Chocolate Ribbon	40.00	175.00	350.00	350.00
Chocolate Chip	40.00	175.00	350.00	350.00

EGGLESS CAKES AND PASTRIES

	Pastry	Small	Large	Special order	Fancy Chocolate
Dutch Truffle Chocolate	35.00	175.00	350.00	350.00	380.00
Truffle	35.00	175.00	350.00	350.00	380.00
Black Forest Pineapple	35.00	175.00	350.00	350.00	380.00
Fresh Cream Strawberry	35.00	170.00	340.00	350.00	360.00
Crush	35.00	170.00	340.00	350.00	360.00

BUTTER CREAM CAKES

	Pastry	Small	Large	Special order	Fancy Chocolate
Chocolate Butter Cream	30.00	150.00	300.00	300.00	330.00
Strawberry Butter Cream	25.00	140.00	280.00	280.00	300.00
Pineapple Butter Cream	25.00	140.00	280.00	280.00	300.00
Noughat Vanilla Butter Cream	30.00	157.00	350.00	280.00	
Stripped Delite Butter Cream	25.30	170.00	340.00		
Butter Scotch Butter Cream	30.00	170.00	340.00	280.00	

CAKES FOR SPECIAL OCCASIONS AND OTHERS

Tier Cakes with Royal Icing	440.00
Tier Cakes with Fondant Icing	440.00
Tier Cakes with Marzipan Royal Icing	450.00
[Available in chocolate truffle or in plum cake]	
Holy Communion Cakes	
Christening Cakes	
Barbie Doll	440.00

NOTE : Please refer to the fancy cake album before placing the order. Our cakes other than the Butter Cream Cakes are made with fresh cream and has to be consumed within six hours of purchase even if refrigerated.

CHEF COOKS IN FRONT OF U

BADNAAM

the tava 'n' tandoor place

KOLIWADA FRY

Machli	80/-
Jheenga	90/-

TAVA LUCKHNAWI

Mutton

Bheja hatela	60/-
Dhoke baaz kaleji	60/-
Tikka boti	60/-
Kheema	60/-
Gurda	60/-
Kapoora	60/-
Chapein	60/-

Chicken

Tapori tikka	60/-
Chaalbaaz tange	60/-
Sheekh kabab	60/-
Tandoori chicken tawa masala	75/-
Tandoori tikka tawa masala	75/-

Samandar ke

Awara jhinge	
Matawali machli (rawas)	70/-
Machalti machli (pomfret)	100/-

Tandoori badmashiyan

Poora murga	100/-
Aadha murga	55/-
Murg tikka	60/-
Roti	5/-
Naan	10/-
Butter naan	15/-
Lehsuni naan	15/-
Lachcha paratha	15/-

BEIMAAN BIRYANI

Chicken	50/-
Mineral water	5/-
Aerated drinks	8/-

FREE DELIVERY

DROP IN OR DINE AT HOME
6341275, 6348041. R.N.A. - LOKHANDWALA - ANDHERI (W), MUMBAI
INDIA

Image

Delux Family
Restaurant & Bar

FREE HOME
DELIVERY
M E N U

10% DISCOUNT

Opp. Kamats Klub, S. V. Road,
Goregaon (W),
Mumbai - 400 062.

Tel. : 876 7225 / 874 1251 / 876 7869

IBTIDA
Light Bites

cheese cocktail	80.00
cheese pakoda	80.00
paneer pakoda	80.00
chicken pakoda	60.00
harabhara kabab/chole palak kabab	65.00
mix vegetable pakoda	60.00
alu chat	50.00
potato chips	50.00
papad roll	60.00
vegetable kabab platter	175.00

US PAAR SE
from the continent

club sandwich (chicken or mutton)	60.00
club sandwich (veg.)	50.00
mutton sandwich	50.00
cheese sandwich	50.00
vegetable sandwich	40.00
grill sandwich (veg.)	55.00
grill sandwich (non-veg.)	60.00

HINDUSTANI MIRCH MASALA
shuruaat

an overture to the meal	
apple juice (gold coin)	40.00
fresh lime soda	25.00
fresh lime water	25.00
soft drinks	30.00
fresh fruit juice	45.00

SHORBA SOUPS

chicken shorba	50.00
mutton shorba	50.00
tomato shorba	50.00
vegetable shorba	50.00
green peas shorba	50.00
cheese onion shorba	50.00
dal shorba	50.00
palak shorba	50.00

AATISH - E - TANDOOR
clay oven specials

tandoori daawat	325.00
murg tandoori	150.00
tandoori pomfret	as per size
rawas tandoori	as per size
reshmi kabab	105.00
karela kabab	110.00
murg tikka	105.00
tangdi kabab	110.00
sheekh kabab	100.00
shole kabab	110.00
jumbo prawns(tandoori)	200.00
fish tikka	110.00
paneer tikka/tandoori gobi	100.00
hariyali kabab/shikari kabab	100.000
hazzari kabab/multani kabab	110.00
achari kabab	110.00
tangdi mumtaz	110.00
kathi rolls (veg.)	95.00
kathi rolls (chicken/mutton)	100.00

MURG KHASIYAT
the spring chicken

murg malai methi	100.00
murg jalfreizy	100.00
murg chop masala	100.00
murg saagwala	100.00
murg resham bahar	100.00
murg kadai	110.00
tandoori murg makhani	110.00
murg shahi khorma/chicken	
mughlai	100.00
murg tikka masala	110.00
murg raada	100.00
murg capsicum	100.00
murg phudhina	110.00
murg pathani/reshmi kabab makhani	120.00
tawa chicken	120.00
dhaba chicken	120.00

GOSHT - E - BAHARAIN
from the chef's pan

degchi gosht	105.00
gosht makhani	105.00
kadai gosht	110.00

gosht jalfreizy	100,00
gosht roganjosh	105.00
gosht seekh kabab makhani	105.00
gosht resham bahar	105.00
gosht chop masala	105.00
gosht saagwala	100.00
gosht kheema mutter	105.00
gosht pudhina	105.00
dal gosht	100.00
dhaba gosht/tawa gosht	120.00
gosht meat ball masala	110.00

SAMUDRA ZEWAR
jewel of the deep sea

lobster masala	as per size
special crab masala/crab dry fry	as per size
tiger prawns fry/masala	as per size
jumbo prawns fry/masala	160.00
prawns masala	110.00
prawns fry	110.00
fish pudhina masala	100.00
fish masala	110.00
fish fry koliwada	110.00
fish fry with chips	11000
fish fingers	110.00
full rawas fry/masala	220.00

TAJE FASAL
for our vegetarian guests

methi malai mutter	35.00
vegetable chop masala	65.00
vegetable tikka masala	35.00
cheese tomato masala/stuffed capsicum	30.00
vegetable harabhara masala	55.00
mushroom babycorn masala	105.00
kaju khorma masala/paneer shahi khorma	105.00
navratan khorma/veg. anarkali	90.00
malai kofta/veg begam bahar	90.00
vegetable kadai/veg. milli jhulli	90.00
vegetable kheema masala	90.00
dal maharani	75.00
dal tadka	55.00
paneerpalak/paneerpasanda	35.00

paneer methi masala/paneer hyderabadi	65.00
bhendi/gobi masala	65.00
baked vegetable cheese	100.00
vegetable kofta makhnwala	100.00
dum aloo kashmiri/punjabi	90.00

ROTIYON KI BAHAR
Indian Bread

kheema naan	35.00
vegetable stuffed paratha/naan/ kulcha	25.00
methi/muli/pudinaparatha	2500
tawa reshmi paratha	20.00
paratha/kulcha/naan	15.00
methi/muli/pudina parath.a	15.00
roomali/missi roti	15.00
roti	10.00
roti ki tokri	130.00
kashmiri naan/cheese naan	25.00

LAZZAT - E - BASMATI
pearl of the kitchen

hydrabadi biryani	110.00
vegetable dum biryani	50.00
chicken dum biryani	105.00
mutton dum biryani	105.00
prawns dum biryani	105.00
vegetable pulao	50.00
special kashmiri pulao	50.00
nawabi rice	45.00
khichdi/dahi bhat/palak bhat	90.00
jeera rice	60.00
paneer dum biryani	95.00

SAATH - SAATH
the accompaniments

russian salad	50.00
green salad	35.00
boondi raitha	40.00
mix raitha	40.00
pineapple raitha	45.00
lassi (sweet or salt)	35.00
curd	35.00

OVER THE WALL
thong soups (non-veg.)

soups (non-veg)	55.00
hot and sour wanton soup	55.00
lung fung soup	55.00
manchow soup	55.00
hot and sour soup	55.00
sweet corn chicken soup	55.00
tomato egg cream soup	55.00
chicken mushroom soup	55.00
chicken clear soup	55.00
talumein soup	55.00

THONG
Soups (veg.)

sweet corn vegetable soup	50.00
vegetable wanton soup	50.00
vegetable hot and sour soup	50.00
vegetable manchow soup	50.00
talumein soup	50.00
vegetable noodles soup	50.00
vegetable lung fung soup	50.00

THAVPOON
Spring rolls (starters)

chicken spring roll	85.00
prawns spring roll	85.00
vegetable spring roll	75.00
mix spring roll	75.00

KAI
Chicken

chicken lollypop/cripsy chicken	100.00
chicken roasted (half)	110.00
chicken mangolian garlic sauce	100.00
chicken bambino	110.00
chicken in oyster sauce	100.00
chicken in thai sauce	100.00
fried chicken chilly/chicken hot chilly	100.00
fried ginger chicken	100.00
fried spring chicken	11000
chicken manchurian	100.00
chicken garlic sauce	100.00
chicken chow chow	100.00
chicken almonds	110.00

chicken cashewnut	110.00
chicken sweet & sour	110.00
chicken schezwan style	100.00
chicken pepper salt	100.00

HOISEEN
Sea food

lobster schezwan style	as per size
fish schezwan style	110.00
fish manchurian	110.00
fried fish chilly	110.00
fish chow chow	110.00
fried fish ginger	110.00
fish garlic sauce	110.00
fish sweet & sour	110.00
prawns garlic sauce	110.00
prawns hot garlic sauce	110.00
prawns manchurian	110.00
fried prawns ginger	110.00
prawns honkong style	110.00
prawns sweet & sour	110.00
prawns chow chow	110.00
prawns schezwan style	110.00
jumbo prawns	180.00
(in sauce of your choice)	
prawns pepper salt	110.00
cripsy prawns	as per size
crabs in lemon butter sauce	as per size

CHOY
Vegetable

vegetable hot chilly/crispy vegetable	80.00
crispy spinach balls	60.00
vegetable fried garlic sauce	80.00
vegetable balls in garlic sauce	80.00
vegetable almonds	30.00
vegetable chow chow	80.00
vegetable sweet & sour	80.00
vegetable cashewnut	80.00
vegetable shezwan style	90.00
vegetable hong kong	90.00
vegetable manchurian	60.00
paneer manchurian	110.00
egg plant singapuri	110.00
cauliflower manchurian	100.00
fried paneer chilly	100.00

paneer schezwan style	100.00
baby corn mushroom	100.00
(in sauce of your choice) vegetable pepper salt	60.00
vegetable fingers in schezwan sauce	60.00

FAAN
Rice

chicken fried rice (schezwan style)	65.00
prawns fried rice (schezwan style)	65.00
mixed fried rice (schezwan style)	65.00
chicken fried rice	85.00
prawns fried rice	65.00
mix fried rice	65.00
vegetable fried rice	75.00
mushroom fried rice	65.00
egg fried rice	75.00
seven jewel rice (veg)	100.00
seven jewel rice (non-veg.)	105.00
mix stewed rice	90.00
chicken stewed rice	90.00
prawns stewed rice	90.00
vegetable stewed rice	60.00
non-veg. triple schezwan	120.00
veg. triple schezwan	110.00

MEIN NOODLES

manchow noodles (non-veg)	90.00
santumin noodles (non-veg)	105.00
mix hakka noodles	90.00
chicken hakka noodles	90.00
prawns hakka noodles	90.00
vegetable hakka noodles	60.00
mix chow mein	90.00
chicken chow mein	90.00
prawns chow mein	90.00
american chopsuey (non-veg.)	90.00
american chopsuey (veg.)	60.00
chinese chopsuey(veg.)	60.00
chinese chopsuey (non-veg.)	90.00
fu young (chicken/prawns/crab)	75.00

JAL PAN
Beverages

cold coffee with ice cream	65.00
cold coffee	60.00

milk shake with ice cream	65.00
milk shake	60.00
vanilla hot chocolate sauce	65.00
tea	25.00
coffee	25.00

MEETHE SAPNE
Sweet sensations

cassata	55.00
kesar pista/butter scotch	55.00
choconut	55.00
vanilla	50.00
strawberry	50.00
chocolate	50.00
fruit salad	50.00
fruit salad jelly	50.00
fruit salad ice-cream	55.00
matka kulfi	55.00
ras malai	50.00
black magic/golden fantasy	65.00

 Do Visit Us

Yin and Yang - (Taj)

(Harmony in the Right Proportion)

Intertwined with the love of good food is also the ancient basic philosophy of China, the belief in harmony, of the balance of nature, of the duality of existence, of the blending of contrasts. Yin and Yang, the two elements, are as significant in the Chinese kitchen as they are in the temple. Yin is soft, yielding, dark, feminine. Yang is hard, bright, masculine, vigorous. In the wok, the hotpot or the steamer, Yin and Yang combine and complement each other. Sweet contrasts with sour. The two basics of stir-frying - ginger and spring onions - arc Yang and Yin. Crunchy sea salt goes with Sichuan peppercorns.

Steamed chicken goes with stir fried fresh greens, the Yang of fiery chillies goes with the gentle Yin of sugar. The contrast of taste and texture, colours and cooking methods, which results in any balanced Chinese meal, is a triumph of the philoso-phical theory of Yin and Yang. A Chinese meal, ordered correctly, should be orchestrated like a Mozart symphony : hot and cold, sweet and sour, plain and spicy, meat and pickle, fish and greens, Yin and Yang.

STEAMED SPECIALITIES

Steamed Mandrin Style Chicken		225.00
Steamed Whole Pomfret Mandrin Style		395.00
Steamed King Prawns Mandrin Style		275.00
Steamed Chicken in Chefs Prized Recipe		225.00
Whole Pomfret in Chef's Prized Recipe		395.00
King Prawns in Chef's Prized Recipe		275.00
Steamed Chicken with Celery		225.00
Steamed King Prawns in Black Bean Sauce		275.00
Steamed Tofu with Bell Peppers ex Broccoli		175.00
Stuffed Bean Curd (Choice of Sauce)	Veg	60.00
	Non Veg	225.00
Steamed Wanton	(Veg)	120.00
	(Non-Veg)	145.00
Summai or Dumplings	(Veg)	160.00
	(Non Veg)	195.00
Steamed Chinese Bread (2 pcs)		60.00
Steamed Crabs or Lobster (Choice of Sauce)		As per Size

SOUPS

Mongolian Steam Boat (6 Persons)		295.00
Yin & Yang Soup		85.00
Spicy Crab Meat Soup		85.00
Sea Food Clear Soup		85.00
Sea Food Chowder		85.00
Talomein Soup	(Veg)	75.00
	(Non Veg)	95.00
Pork Meat Ball Soup with Bean Curd		85.00
Sweet Corn	(Veg)	55.00
(Choice of Meat)		65.00
Tom Yum	(Veg)	60.00
	(Chicken)	70.00
	(Prawns)	75.00
Hot & Sour	(Veg)	55.00
	(Non Veg)	70.00
Manchow	(Veg)	55.00
	(Non Veg)	70.00
Veg Jade Soup with Bean Curd	65.00	
Wanton Soup	(Veg)	65.00
	(Non Veg)	75.00
Clear Chicken Soup with Vegetables	75.00	
Thai Soup	(Veg)	60.00
	(Non Veg)	75.00
For 1 × 2 Extra Charge	20.00	

SEA FOOD

Pomfret Chilli Wine	(L)	395.00
	(S)	275.00
Pomfret with Spring Onion Sauce	(L)	395.00
	(S)	275.00
Ginger Fish	(L)	395.00
	(S)	275.00
Pomfret as you like	(L)	395.00
	(S)	275.00
Jumbo Prawns Choice of Sauce		495.00
King Prawns Zen Pepper		275.00
King Prawns in Thai Sauce		275.00
Kung Pao King Prawns		275.00
King Prawns Hunnan Style		275.00
Singapore Chilli Prawns		275.00
King Prawns as you like		275.00

Prawn Ball Manchurian		225.00
Crab/Lobster as you like		As per size

APPETIZERS

Li Kou Fu Style Roast Chicken	(Full)	325
(Classical Chinese Roast braised		
with Rice Wine & Herbs)	(Half)	175
Roast Chicken Schezwan Style	(Full)	325
	(Half)	175
Satay King Prawns		275
Golden Fried King Prawns		275
Pepper Prawns Cupsi		225
Tsing Hai Cupsi Prawns		225
Pepper Salt Cupsi prawns		225
Soft Hearted Shrimp Balls		225
Crispy Fish Fingers		225
Hakka Pomfret		225
Tofu Roll with Shrimp Mousse		175
Prawns Sesame Toast		145
Gin Ball Chicken		195
Satay Chicken		175
Tsing Hai Chicken		160
Pepper Salt Chicken		160
Hakka Chicken		160
Pepper Chicken		160
Chicken Wings Oriental		150
Pork Spare Ribs		165
Satay Paneer		165
Chilly Paneer"		165
Tofu Rolls with Mushrooms		155
Hakka Vegetables		145
Golden Fried Babycorn		95
Cauliflower Manchurian		95
Onion Pan Cake		95
Vegetable Sesame Toast		95
Crispy Fried Onion Rings		90
Straw Potatoes Schezwan Style		90
Fried Wantons (Veg)		90
Fried Wantons (Non Veg)		95
(Choice of Chicken, Prawn or Pork)		
Spring Rolls (Non Veg)		95
(Choice of Chicken, Prawn Or Pork)		
Spring Rolls (Veg)		85

SPECIAL MEAL COMBOS

Jade Surprise   110.00
  (A Combination of Spinach Button Mushrooms Bean
  Curd in Tomato base on Fluffy Rice)
Lo Hans Steam Rice   135.00
  (Assortment of Chinese Mushrooms Braised in Oyster
  Sauce and topped with Crispy Bean Curd.
  Truly A Mushroom Freak's Delight!)
Prawn Jadiette Rice   195.00
  (The very best of Shrimps along with Crab Meat
  Sauce cooked with Shiaoxing Rice Wine)
King Prawn at their best   275.00
  (Fresh King Prawns with choicest Chinese Vegetables in Oyster
  Sauce)
Sea World's Gift   275.00
  (Bite Size Fillets of Pomfret Stir
  Fried with Chinese Greens and
  Soya)
Mofu Tofu   175.00
  (Pork and Bean Curd Mince gently simmered with Tomatoes and
  Button Mushrooms)
Epicures Delight   185.00
(Sliced Pork Braised in our Chef
  Spl. Sauce with Mushrooms and
  White Radish. A tribute to Chinese Home Style Cooking)
Chicken and Bean Rice   185.00
(Minced Chicken simmered with
  Black Bean Paste)

POULTRY

Roast Chilli Chicken (Full with Bones)	300
(Half with Bones)	175
Chicken &. C'Mushroom in Plum	
Sauce	185
Fung Chhang Chicken	185
Thai Chicken in Red Or Green Sauce	175
Sliced Chicken Spring in Oyster	
Sauce	175
Diced Chicken Red Pepper in Wine Sauce	175
Chicken Tepan Yaki	175
Crispy Lemon Chicken	175
Diced Chicken Almond Cashewnut	175
Soho Chicken	175
Garlic Chicken (Hot/Sweet)	175

Ginger Chicken	175
Kung Pao Chicken	175
Chicken Chilli Garlic	175
Chicken with Hot Bean Sauce	175
Chicken as you like	195

PORK AND TENDERLOIN

Stir Fried Minced Pork with Mofutofu	155
Roast Pork Cantonese Style	155
Chilli Fried Roast Pork	155
Sweet and Sour Pork	155
Tenderloin with Mushroom, Red Green Pepper	155
Stir Fried Tenderloin with Oyster Sauce	155
Tenderloin with Spring Onion and Chilli	155
Pork as you like	175

VEGETABLES

Royal Imperial Vegetables	155
Medley of Mushrooms with Babycorn on Chinese Cabbage	145
Diced Vegetables with Almonds and Cashew	145
Cottage Cheese in choice of Sauce	145
Buddha's Delight	145
Three Treasure Vegetables in choice of Sauce	145
Crackling Spinach with Potatoes	145
Stuffed Egg Plant in choice of Sauce	105
Stuffed Capsicum in Chef's special Sauce	105
Stir Fried Chinese Greens	105
Crispy Vegetables in choice of Sauce	105
Lady's Finger Pepper Salt	105
Sauted Potatoes choice of Sauce	105

RICE AND NOODLES

Chef's Special Fried Rice	(Veg)	95
(Choice of meat)		115
Chef's Spl. Yam Mein Noodles (Veg)	95	
	(Non Veg)	115
Fried Rice	(Veg)	85
(Choice of meat or egg)		95

Steam Rice Home Style	(Veg)	105
(Choice of meat)		135
American Chopsuey	(Veg)	95
(Choice of meat)		125
Chinese Chopsuey	(Veg)	95
(Choice of meat)		125
Tepan Shoba	(Veg)	105
(Choice of meat)		135
Hakka Noodles	(Veg)	95
(Choice of meat)		125
Singapore Mefun	(Veg)	105
(Choice of meat)		135
Cantonese Fried Noodles	(Veg)	105
(Choice of meat)		135
Plain Steamed Rice	(Large)	75
	(Small)	55
Choice of two meats or more i.e. (mix) extra		30

STEAKS AND SIZZLERS
(all served with fries & vegetables and garlic bread or rice)

Veg surprise	190
Paneer Shashlik	210
Chicken Steak Pepper	215
Chicken Shashlik	235
Hamburger Steak	215
Pork Chops	215
Beef Steak	215
Mixed Grill	245
Singapore Special Chicken Steak	245
Seafood Sizzler	315

DESSERTS

Caramel Custard	75.00
Baba Au Rum	95.00
Souffle Surprise	75.00
Honey Tossed Flat Noodles	95.00
Honey Tossed Flat Noodles with Ice Cream	125.00
Choice of Toffee	95.00
Choice of Toffee with Ice Cream	125.00
Choice of Ice Cream	75.00
Day's Special	135.00
Candid Fresh Fruit with Ice Cream	135.00

Food Prices are inclusive of all taxes

KEBAB KING

VEGETARIAN

CLASSIC VEGGIE*
  (Shahi Paneer, Tandoori Aloo)   119
VEG. DELUX
  (Veg Kofta, Paneer Tikka*)   119
CREATE YOUR OWN COMBO
  (Choice of any 3+Baby Naans OR Roomali Roti, Onion Laccha.
  Green Chutney)   129
  Choose between Shahi Paneer, Veg Kofta, Dal Kebab King,
  Tandoori Aloo, Gobhi Kebab, Hara Kebab, Kandh Kebab,
  Paneer Tikka and Veg Seekh Kebab, Dal Kebab King.

NON VEGETARIAN

JOSH-E-PATHAR
  (Gosht-E-Josh, Pathar Kebab   149
CHICKEN DELUX
  (Murg Makhni Andaaz, Kebab-
  E-Bannu   154
TANDOORI KURRY
  (Shahi Paneer, Tandoori Chicken   154
  Dal Kabab King, Baby Naans or Roomali Roti Onions Laccha Green Chutney
CREATE YOUR OWN KURRY COMBO
  (Choice of any 3+Baby Naans OR Roomali Roti, Onion Laccha, Green Chutney
  Choose between Pathar Kebab, Garhi Kebab, Seekh Kebab. Kebab-E-Hazaarvi,
  Kebab-E-Bannu, Hasina Murg Kebab, Murg Tandoori, Tandoori Aloo, Gobhi
  Kebab, Hara Kebab, Kandh Kebab, Paneer Tikka and Veg Seekh Kebab)   169

BARBEQUE PLATTERS *New*

VEGETARIAN

GARDEN FRESH
  (Tandoori Aloo, Gobhi Kebab, Hara Kebab*   99
VEG GOURMET
  (Paneer Tikka. Kandh Kebab, Hara Kebab)*   109

NON VEGETARIAN

CLASSIC TANDOORI
(Tandoori Chicken, Seekh Kebab*)   119
BARBEQUE DELUX
Hasina Murg Kebab, Seekh Kebab*   119
KEBAB-E-KHAAS
(Garhi Kebab, Kebab-E-Bannu*)   129
TANDOORI SPECIAL
Pathar Kebab, Kebab-E-Hazarvi*   139
CHICKEN GOURMET
(Tandoori Chicken. Kebab-E-Hazaarvi*)   139
CHICKEN SUPREME
(Kebab-E-Bannu, Hasina Murg Kebab*)   139

KEBAB KING

CREATE YOUR OWN COMBO
(Choice of any 2 Kebabs + Dal
Kebab King, Boby Naans or Roo-
mali Roll, Onion Laccha, Green Chutney)
Choose between Pathar Kebab, Garhi Kebuti, Seekh Kebab Kebab E.-Hazaarvi
Dal Ki Kebab King Baby Naans or Roomali Roti Onion Laccha Chutney

EXQUISITE KEBABS

NON VEGETARIAN
RAAN AALISHAAN
   Tender leg of Lamb delicately marinated in rum and rare spices, roasted
   in the tandoor)   259
PATHAR KEBAB
   (Slices of Mountain Lamb gently rubbed with spices and cooked on
   a hot stone)   159
GARHI KEBAB
   (Delicious chops of mutton, marinated with herbs and cooked in the tandoor) 159
SEEKH KEBAB
   (Tender Rolls of finely minced mutton cooked on charcoal fire)   119
KEBAB-E-HAZAARVI
   (Boneless pieces of chicken marinated in cheese, cream, lime juice and
   chillies, roasted in the tandoor),   159
KEBAB-E-BANNU
   (Succulent pieces of tender chicken marinated in egg, vinegar
   and pepper, roasted in the tandoor)   159
HASINA MURG KEBAB
   (Tender Rolls of minced chicken cooked on charcoal fire)   159
MURG TANDOORI (FULL)   169
                  (HALF)   99
AJWAINI FISH TIKKA (SEASONAL)
   (Chunks of river sole, marinated
   with rare herbs and finished in the tandoor)   169

VEGETARIAN
TANDOORI ALOO
   (Potatoes stuffed with vegetables
   and herbs, finished in the tandoor)   89
GOBHI KEBAB
   (Golden Brown fried coins of grated cauliflower with spices)   99
HARA KEBAB
   (A blend of green peas with aromatic herbs, cooked to perfection)   99
KANDH KEBAB
   (Chefs own creation of zimikandh and sesame seeds   99
PANEER TIKKA
   (Kebabs of fresh home made cheese)   104
VEG SEEKH KEBAB
   (Minced Rolls' of garden fresh vegetables, skewered and cooked in the tandoor) 109

KEBAB KING

DELICACIES FROM THE HANDI

NON VEGETARIAN

MURG MAKHNI ANDAAZ
  (Tandoori Chicken cooked with Tomatoes finished in butter and topped
  with cream)   (FULL)   239
                                                           (HALF)   144
BONELESS
                                                           (FULL)   254
                                                           (HALF)   149
MURG-E-JOSH
  (Chicken Roganjosh, Chefs own creation)   139
RARA MURG
  (Pan roasted Chicken, mixed with juliene of Ginger. Slit Green Chillies,
  tempered with whole Red Chilli in a thick Indian Masala spiced extravagantly) 139
GOSHT-E-JOSH
  (Mutton roganjosh, an all time favourite)   149
RARA GOSHT
  (Pan roasted Mutton, mixed with juliene of Ginger, Slit Green Chillies,
  tempered with whole Red Chilli in a thick Indian Masala spiced extravagant)   149
KOFTA FRONTIER (CHICKEN/ MUTTON)
  (Minced balls of chicken or mutton, cooked to perfection in chef's own style) 149

VEGETARIAN

SHAHI PANEER
  (Home made cottage cheese, cooked with tomatoes, finished in butler
  and topped with cream)   119
VEG KOFTA FRONTIER
  (Minced balls of mixed vegetables, cooked to perfection in chef's own style) 114
DAL KEBAB KING
  (A harmonious combination of lentils)   79

BREADS FROM TANDOOR

BUTTER NAAN   24
PLAIN NAAN   19
LACCHA PARANTHA   24
PUDINA PARANTHA   24
ULTE TAWA KA PARANTHA   19
BHARWA KULCHA (Stuffed with a choice of cottage cheese, potatoes or onion) 29
TANDOORI ROTI   9
ROOMALI ROTI   9

DESSERTS

BROWNIE   4
PHIRNI   29
GULABJAMUN   29

KEBAB KING

KURRY PIZZAS New

VEGETARIAN

	Regular Serves	Medium Serves
PANEER MAKHNI	139	209
CREAMY MUSHROOM	129	194
VEGGIE KOFTA	119	174

NON VEGETARIAN

BUTTER CHICKEN	159	239
MUTTON CURRY	149	229
CHICKEN CURRY	149	229

TANDOORI PIZZAS

VEGETARIAN

TANDOORI MARGHERITA (An all time favourite . . . Just baked differently)	79	119
TANDOORI VEGGIE (Mushroom, Capsicum, Onion, Tomato)	99	149
BARBEQUE PANEER (Paneer Tikka, Onion)	109	159
VEG DELIGHT (Paneer, Mushroom, Capsicum, Onion, Tomato, Corn)	119	174

NON VEGETARIAN

SEEKH FIESTA (Seekh Kebab, Onion)	129	194
PATHAR DELIGHT Pathar Kebab, Capsicum	139	209
PIZZA-E-TIKKA (Murg Malai Kebab, Mushroom)	139	209
BARBEQUE EXTRAVAGANZA (Pathar Kebab, Murg Malai Kebab, Capsicum)	149	224

1X2 PIZZAS New

CHOOSE ANY TWO (VEG)	149	224
CHOOSE ANY TWO (NON VEG)	169	244

TANDOORI BURGERS New

TANDOORI ALOO BURGER	49
PANEER TIKKA BURGER	59

Food Prices are inclusive of all taxes

Location : LG 11 & 12,
Centre Point, Sushant Lok, Gurgaon (Haryana)
℗ 5044122, 5044133, 981003382

KEBAB KING

PATHAR KEBAB BURGER	89
SEEKH BURGER	69
CHICKEN TIKKA BURGER	79
CHICKEN SEEKH BURGER	79

KEBAB WRAPS

VEGETARIAN

TANDOORI ALOO WRAP	79/-
PANEER TIKKA WRAP	99/-
VEG SEEKH WRAP	109/-

NON VEGETARIAN

PATHAR KEBAB WRAP	159/-
SEEKH KEBAB WRAP	119/-
CHICKEN TIKKA WRAP	149/-
CHICKEN SEEKH WRAP	149/-

DUM BIRYANI

NON VEGETARIAN

GOSTH BIRYANI	149
MURG BIRYANI	149

VEGETARIAN

MIX VEG BIRYANI	129

(Biryani is Served with Raita)

DESSERTS

BROWNIE	34
PHIRNI	29
GULABJAMUN	29

The Best Omelettes on the Coast
Location: Costa Mesa, California (USA).

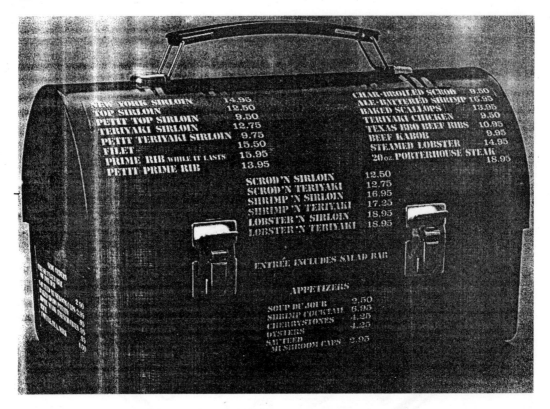

Courtesy: Scotch and Sirloin (USA)

POOL BAR & GRILL (ARIZONA)

SABINO'S CHAR-BROILED BURGERS
Plain; Chili & Cheese; Bleu Cheese;
Jack Cheese; Guacamole & Sprouts.
5.25

BALL PARK HOT DOG
2.75

DELI SANDWICHES
Ham, Turkey, Roast Beef, Swiss and Cheddar
on French, Whole-Wheat or Corn Rye.
4.95

FRESH PINEAPPLE BOAT
Fruit Salad with Cottage Cheese
or Soft Serve Yogurt.
5.25

SABINO SALAD
Deli Meats, Shrimp and Cheeses.
Choice of Dressing.
5.25

SOFT SERVE YOGURT
Regular 1.00   Large 1.50

ICE CREAM SANDWICHES
1.25

COFFEE, TEA, MILK, SOFT DRINKS
1.00

FRUIT JUICES
1.50

CANDY, NUTS, CHIPS
.75

SHIPMATES' PLATES

A special menu just for Skipper's Shipmates
(All Kids 12 or under)

Skipper's Clipper
One Fish Fillet with Fries,
Jell-O and Fun Surprise
$1.79

Chicken Ahoy
Three Chicken Breast Strips
with Fries, Jell-O
and Fun Surprise
$2.19

Chicken and Shrimp Trawler
Two Chicken Breast Strips
and Shrimp with Fries, Jell-O
and Fun Surprise
$2.79

Skipper's Bounty
(All-You-Can-Eat)
Fish Fillets, Fries, Chowder,
Jell-O and Fun Surprise
$3.29
(per Child)

Courtesy: Skippers Inn (USA)
Seattle, Washington

Courtesy: TGIF (USA)

INTRODUCTION ABOUT THE SPICES AND CONDIMENTS

ABOUT THE MASALAS

Spices and condiments both serve a common purpose, i.e. they add flavour to the food we eat. Although they have little food value, they serve the purpose of stimulating the appetite.

ESSENTIAL QUALITIES OF SPICES

With the exception of salt, which is a mineral, all spices and condiments are obtained from plants or vegetable substance, the majority of which grow best in tropical countries. The aromatic and flavouring characteristics of all spices and most condiments is attributable to the presence of every minute quantities of chemical substance found in the volatile essential oils which the plants contain. The spices that have been exposed to the atmosphere over a prolonged period of time will lose their essential oils and thus their aromatic and flavouring properties.

1. **All Spice (Pimento Officinalis)** : This spice is variously known as 'all spice'. The name all spices is given to it because its flavour and aroma resemble a mixture of cloves, nutmeg and cinnamon.
2. **Aniseed : (Pimpinalla anisum)**
3. **Capsicum** : The plants of the genus capsicum have many varieties which are widely distributed throughout the world, and they produce scarlet and green fruit pods of various sizes, the large long pods being known as capsicum or sweet peppers and the smaller ones as chillies, the smaller pods being much hotter than the large ones. Both types are used in the manufacture of pickles and the large ripe pods (capsicums or sweet peppers) are used fresh or canned for culinary purposes, either stuffed as a vegetable, as a garnish or as part of an *Hors d'Oeuvre*.
4. **Caraway seeds** : These are the fried, ripe seeds of an umbelliferous plant carum Carvi, a herb that is cultivated extensively in the UK and other European countries.
5. **Cardamoms** : The chief sources of supply are India and Sri Lanka, where the plant is also found growing wild.
6. **Cayenne pepper** : The hottest of all the peppers. It is prepared from the dried, red, fully ripened berries of one of the many types of capsicum plants.
7. **Chillies** : Chillies are also used in the manufacture of pickles and certain pungent sauces.
8. **Cinnamon** : The best cinnamon is light-yellow in colour and no thicker than thick pepper. It is gathered in May and again in November, and is allowed to ferment slightly before processing in order to develop the warm, sweet taste and pleasant, fragrant odour for which it is noted.
9. **Cloves** : These are the dried, unopened flower-buds of all tall, evergreen tree Eugenia Caryophyllata, which grows in most tropical countries, particularly Indonesia, West Indies, Sri Lanka, India, Africa and Brazil.
10. **Coriander (Coriandrum Sativum)** : These seeds have aromatic qualities similar to those of caraway seeds. They have a fragrant smell and sweet pleasant taste.
11. **Cumin (Cuminum Cyminum)** : The dried fruit of an umbelliferous annual plant and closely related to caraway. It

is used for much the same purpose but not as widely.

12. **Curry powder** : This condiment is a mixture of various spices and aromatic herbs and its ingredient vary considerably, depending upon the manufacturer. The main ingredients are ginger, cayenne pepper and turmeric and among the others are included cinnamon, nutmeg, mace, cloves, tamarind, lemon, grass, lime juice, salt cardamom, coriander, mango and black paper in varying proportions.

13. **Ginger** : Ginger is an aromatic and stimulating spice with important digestive properties. It is obtained from the underground stems or rhizomes of a plant that grows to a height of about three feet. These rhizomes are scalded with boiling water and then dried and stored at which stage they are known as black ginger. Sometimes, they are scrapped, washed and dried in the sun, after which they are called white ginger.

14. **Mace** : The kernel of the fruit produces nutmeg and this is covered by a bright crimson aril called mace.

15. **M.S.G. (Monosodium Glutamate)** : This is not a spice but a widely used chemical food additive commonly known as the fourth condiment, and sold under various names. A white crystalline, soluble substance, similar in appearance to coarse salt. It is a product of comparatively recent discovery and is, as yet, in more common use in food factories than in kitchens.

16. **Mustard** : The mustard commonly used in commercial catering is really a mixture of the ground seeds of two distinctly different plants, namely black mustard (Brassica Niger) and white mustard (Brassica albe), both of which are members of the cabbage family (brassica).

17. **Nutmeg** : This is the kernel of the fruit of the myristica tree.

18. **Paprika** : This is a spice of capsicum and is known as capsicum amum.

19. **Pimiento:** A species of capsicum is known as Pimiento or Spanish red pepper, which is not the same spice as is dried and ground to provide Cayenne pepper. The seeds are removed from the fleshy, ripe, red pods of the pimiento.

20. **Poppy seed** : Unlike the poppy of the Far Eastern countries (apaver somniferum) our garden poppy contain no trace of opium. The seeds of the poppy contain a high percentage of very palatable edible oil and for this reason are used in the making of a special type of bread.

21. **Salt (Sodium Chloride)** : This is the only condiment in regular use in the kitchen which is not a vegetable substance.

22. **Table Salt** : The type of salt usually sold and used as table salt contains a small proportion of a chemical substance, usually either calcium phosphate or magnesium carbonate which ensures that its free running properties are retained particularly during rainy season.

23. **Saffron** : A highly flavoured spice produced from the dried stigma of species of crocus are called crocus satives. Kashmir grows in plenty.

24. **Tabasco** : A liquid condiment known by the trade name of 'Tabasco' is manufactured from a mixture of the hottest peppers obtainable, and is marketed in a special type of bottle which dispenses the sauce a drop at a time.

25. **Turmeric (Curcuma Inga)** : An eastern plant closely related to ginger, which yields a spice of a bright yellow colour and pleasant aroma.

26. **Vanilla** : The fruit of a tropical climbing orchid (Vanilla planifolia) native to Asia and America. It is now cultivated mainly in the East and West Indies and in India.

27. **Charmagaj** : Dried seeds of fruits of melon family. Abundently available in India.

28. **Mixed spices** : Nowadays many companies have started marketing dried spices, to be used in various preparations like samabar, meat, chole etc. These are essentially trade mixtures of common Indian spices used for curry.

29. **Indian Garam Masala** : It is a mixture of clove, cinnamon and cardamon.

CULINARY HERBS

Unlike spices most herbs are easily cultivated and may be successfully grown in the garden with the minimum of attention.

1. **Bayleaf (Cerasus laurocerasus)** : The leaf of an evergreen shrub, known as the cherry laurel or green bay tree. Its flavour is very strong and must be used in very small quantities or the flavour of the dish to which it is added may be spoiled.

2. **Bouquet garni** : The indispensable 'Faggot' of herbs is used in the kitchen for flavouring soups, sauces, stews and braisings and consisting of a bayleaf, a few parsley stalks and a spring or pinch of thyme. Often with the addition of a few crushed pepper corns, all tied up with white cotton.

3. **Celery seed** : The dried seed of the celery plant (Apium graveolens) is used to impart the refreshing flavour of celery to a dish when fresh celery is not available. Used largely in soups, sauces, tomato juice, cocktails etc.

4. **Fennel (Faeniculum Vulgare)** : Related to and similar in appearance to celery Fennel is an important ingredient of the soup Bortsch.

5. **Garlic (Allium Sativum)** : A small bulbous rooted plant related to the onion, with extremely powerful aromatic and flavouring properties, Garlic should be used in the extreme moderation.

6. **Horseradish (Cobhelearia Armoracia)**: A very pungent root and very easy to cultivate, horseradish is usually made into sauces, creams and butter and used as one of the most common accompaniments for roast beef or grilled beef steaks.

7. **Mint** : A very useful herb, the kind used in the kitchen for making mint sauce and for adding to new potatoes, green peas etc.

8. **Coriander leaves** : Widely used in Indian kitchen.

9. **Onion green**: Used as herb also in rich and vegetable preparations. In addition to the above there are many well-known herbs used in may countries. They are Basil, Cheruil, Chives, Dil, Juniper, thyme etc. These are rarely used in Indian hotels. Available in winter time.

10. **Parsley (Petroselimum Sativum):** A commonly used umbelliferous plant easily grown in the herb-garden. The variety is easily chopped. It is indispensable in the kitchen, not only for its excellent flavouring properties but also as a garnish either chopper or in springs.

11. **Shallot (Allium ascalnicum):** A plant closely related to garlic, with bulbous-root very similar in forms but much milder in flavour. It is very widely used in the kitchen particularly in the making of sauces.

Following are some combined spices which can be pre-prepared for use in the kitchen:

1. CHAAT MASALA

Ingredients	Quantity
Dry mango powder or	
Pomegranate seeds or	To taste
Citric acid or	
Tartaric acid	
Powdered cloves, Cinnamon	To taste
Cardamom and pepper	
Red Chillies and coriander (roast separately and powder)	To taste
Rock Salt	To taste

Method

Mix all powders together and use as required

2. CHAAT MASALA

Ingredients	Quantity
Pepper	
Salt	
Rock Salt	
Black Salt (black crystals)	
Bay leaf	To taste
Cloves, cardamom, cinnamon, and dry ginger.	

Method

Powder together. Use as desired. Green chillies, fresh ginger, coriander and cumin can be grinded with the above ingredients if desired most.

3. SAMBHAR POWDER

Ingredients	Quantity
Fenugreek powder	150 gm.
Mustard powder	100 gm.
Turmeric powder	25 gm.
Asafoetida	10 gm.
Salt	100 gm.
Chilli powder	300 gm.
Oil	100 ml.

Method

Mix together fenugreek, mustard, turmeric, asafoetida and salt. Add to hot oil and roast. When roasted, remove from fire and add chilli powder. Mix well and use as required.

4. PANCH PHORAN

Ingredients	Quantity
Mustard seeds	1 teaspoon
Cumin seeds	2 gm.
Onion seeds	1/2 teaspoon
Fenugreek seeds	1/4 teaspoon
Fennel	1 teaspoon

Method

Mix all together and keep in a jar. Make more than required for a particular dish.

5. RASAM POWDER

Ingredients	Quantity
Coriander	150 gm.
Pepper	50 gm.
Split Bengal gram	15 gm.
Split red gram	35 gm.
Cumin	—
Turmeric	a small piece
Red chillies	15 gm.

Method

Dry and Powder.

6. CURRY POWDER

Ingredients	Quantity
Coriander	60 gm.
Pepper corns	10 gm.
Fenugreek	10 gm.
Cumin seeds	10 gm.
Whole wheat	10 gm.
Bengal gram	10 gm.

Method

Dry and powder.

7. CURRY PASTE

Ingredients	Quantity
Coriander	
Fennel	
Cloves	As required
Turmeric	
Cumin	
Fenugreek	
Black Pepper	

Method

Roast and powder. Use as desired.

8. GARAM MASALA

Ingredients	Quantity
Cardamom	15 gm.
Cloves	30 gm.
Cinnamon	30 gm.
Pepper corns	30 gm.
Mustard seeds	
(If to be used for beef double quantity)	
Garlic	3 Cloves
Onion	1 No.
Red Pepper	To taste

Method

Dry and Powder.

9. BIRYANI MASALA

Ingredients	Quantity
Cardamom (large variety)	
Cloves	
Cinnamon	15 gms.
Pepper corns	
Bayleaf	
Badyani	

Method

Dry and powder.

VINEGAR IN COOKERY

Vinegar is a versatile ingredient of all Kitchens. It has many varieties and uses.

Chemically vinegar is diluted acetic acid 4-6% (CH_3COOH) produced from ethyl alcohol (C_2H_5OH). It may be synthetic or natural. There are different types as under:

- **Fruit Vinegar** :- It is fruit flavoured vinegar used mostly in salads.
- **Herb Vinegar** :- Prepared by infusing herb flavours.
- **Malt Vinegar** :- Made from Barley malt, specially used in English fish dishes and pickles.
- **Rice Vinegar** :- Popular in Japanese dishes.
- **Wine Vinegar** :- Produced from the alcohol present in different wines.
- **Sherry Vinegar** :- Popular in Spanish market and Spanish Cookery.
- **Balsamic Vinegar** : This is a typical Italian vinegar prepared from grape must and not from wines This original and aged Vinegar is superb for use in Cookery.

CREAM IN COOKERY

- **Double cream** — Most versatile floats in soup and coffee.
- **Whipping cream** — Will whip to atleast double its volume.
- **Single cream** — Added to soups and sauces and sweets.
- **Soured cream** — It is ideal for salad dressings.
- **Clotted cream** — It is traditionally served with sauces and jam is suitable for spooning.

SALT IN COOKERY

One can not think of saltless cooking & eating Good foods.

Normal salt which is a chemical Compound of Sodium (Na) and chloride (Cl). Sodium Chloride is (NaCl). It is a Neutral compound. Table salt is mainly NaCl but at times little percentage (0.5%) Calcium Silicate is added to prevent absorption of moisture and dump. formation.

- **Iodised Salt** - In it iodine is added for enrichment of nutrients for goitre prevention.
- **Black Salt** - Is mined from the Ganges plain in India - especially suitable for chats.
- **Celtic Sea Salt** - Obtained from salt farm in marshlands in UK.
- **Rock salt** :- This is obtained from salt mine.
- **Kosher salt** :- Source from Kosher sea.
- **Milan red claysalt** : This is also known as Sadaren salt obtained from Salt mines of Mali, Africa.
- **Korean bamboo Salt (bio salt)** : It is made from sun - dried salt stuffed into bamboo hollows and sealed with clay. It is then backed 8-9 times for 3 hours each time. The resultant salt is red in colour sweet flavoured. It is some times used in special dishes.
- **Smoked Salt** :- Salt is smoked in different styles such as lickory smoked sea slat, oak smoked sea salt, Danish smoked salt is used in steak dishes.
- **Salt petre** : This is not a Sodium Compound but chemically it is potassium nitrate used in preservative.
- **Pink Peruvian lake salt** :- It is obtained from wells lined with rose quartz. It is said that the Incas and Mayans used this salt also for spiritual and healing purposes. Available in USA on premium price.
- **Sea Salt** :- It is the most common form of salt used globally. It has high mineral content.

COMMONLY USED THAI FRUITS, SPICES & HERBS

Mangosteen (Mangkut)

Dark purple skin protects a delicate white flesh.

Season : May through September.

Rambutan (Ngoh)

Rambut means hair in Malay, The hairy skin protects succulent white flesh.

Season : May through July.

Mango (Manuang)

Eaten when green and when ripened.

Season : April & May.

Rose Apple (Chomphu)

Pale green or soft pink, tastes vary according to variety. Popularity eaten with a lightly chilled soft and sugar dip. Harvested throughout the year.

Sapodilla (Lamut)

Resembles a hybrid kiwi fruit and small potato. Fruits taste like a mixture of figs and honey and are picked several times a year.

Durtan

Delicate creamy flesh makes this the most popular of Thai fruits.

Star Fruit (Mafuang)

Tastes vary from sour to very sweet. Often squeezed for juice and used as a food flavouring.

Pomelo (Sum - O)

Uniquely Thai fruit resembling large grapefruit. Succulent sweet - sour fruits

Crab Apple (phutsa)

Enjoyed mostly with a sugar / salt / chilli dip.

Lemon Grass (Ta-khrai)

Used as seasoning and flavouring in soups and curry pastes.

Coriander (Phak chi)

Leaves used as garnish. Roots used in curry pastes, seasoning and soup stocks.

Galanga (Kha)

Roots used in curry pastes and soups.

Krachai

Sometimes known as aromatic ginger.

Added to fish and game curries. Peeled tubers may be eaten with a dip.

Kaffir Lime (Ma - krut)

Leaves used as garnish in certain curries, soups and salads.

Peels are added to several curry pastes.

Pepper (Phrik Thai)

Customarily added to fish and game curries.

3

PREPARATION OF STOCKS, SAUCES, MARINADES, STUFFINGS AND GRAVIES

1. BOUILLON OR STOCK SPECIALLY MADE FOR SOUP

Following are some of the important stocks which one should know particularly for making continental dishes.

A. BROWN STOCK (FOR 5 LITRES)

Ingredients	Approx. Quantity
Beef, veal or mutton bones	2 kg.
Ham bone	200 gm.
Carrot	350 gm.
Onion	125 gm.
Water	7 litres.

Method

- Cut or break the bones into 8" × 4" pieces and place with fat in a roasting tray.
- Roast the bones until dip brown in hot oven. Remove bones from oven. Place in a stock pot.
- Cover with water and bring to boil.
- Add the fried carrots and onion, and the ham bone. The stock should simmer for six hours.
- Strain, reboil and use as required.

B. WHITE STOCK OR CHICKEN STOCK (FOR 5 LITRES)

Ingredients	Approx. Quantity
Water	7 litres
Chicken	
Chicken bones	2 kg.
Bay leaf	2 nos.
Leek	a few
Celery	a bunch

Method

- Blanch the bones.
- Saute the flesh so that it can be taken off the bones easily.
- Add bay leaves, leek, celery into water and cook for at least two hours.

C. FISH STOCK (FOR 5 LITRES)

Ingredients	Approx. Quantity
Water	7 litres
Fish bones	1.75 kg.
Onions	250 gm.
Margarine	60 gm.
Bay leaf	2 nos.
Lime	1/2 portion
Parsley stalks	A few
Pepper corns	6 nos.

Method

Add the sliced onions, fish bones and the remaining ingredients into melted margarine.

Cover with grease-proof paper arid a lid and sweat for 5 minutes. Remove grease proof paper.

Add the water, bring to boil, skim and simmer for 20 minutes. Strain it.

2. CONSOMME

Consomme are same as stock or bouillon specially clarified.

Example : To clarify four to six cups stock pull away inner skins from 2 egg shells; wash the egg shells and crush into 4 to 6 cups of hot stock. Add 2 egg whites. Beat with rotary beater, over moderate heat, for about 4 minutes or until thick foam forms on top.

Foam must be thick and high. Remove beater and bring mixture to a boil without stirring. Reduce heat to low and simmer for 10 minutes. Remove from heat and lit stand for 3 minutes. Place a piece of wet muslin in a large sieve. Pour the stock mixture slowly sieve. Pour the stock mixture slowly and steadily through the muslin, letting drain well. This procedure makes the stock sparkling clear for use in special aspics. Clarification is not a substitute for skimming, but an optional addition to it.

3. GLAZES

The glazes are used for meat, fish, chicken. The glazes are thicken reduced stock to syrup consistency and are widely used in cookery. The meat glaze is prepared by brown stock in the large pan and allowing it to reduce. After sometime the stock is strain into a small pan and the reduction process is continued. The reduction must be finished over a very moderate heat and in between skimming operation is to continue carefully to remove undesirable materials. Chicken glaze, fish glaze are also prepared in the same way with chicken and fish stocks instead of meat stock.

4. ROUX

Various kind of roux is used in cookery. These are basically thickening agents for their

Preparation. Three kinds of roux are used in cookery especially for continental items. They are:

a. Brown roux for brown sauces.
b. Blonde roux for veloute and cream sauces.
c. White roux for bechamel sauces.

It is advisable to cook roux slowly and carefully depending on the requirements. Use of clarified butter is recommended for the making of roux as the amount of cuisine which is present in culinary butter is detrimental to the making of good roux. A roux can also be made with pure stocks such as arrowroot, introduct flower.

5. PREPARATION OF DIFFERENT BASIC SAUCES

Sauces represents one of the most important component of cookery. This is absolutely essential to have mastery over preparation of sauces, particularly for french cuisine. The basic component used in production of sauce, is stock. So, production of perfect stock is essential for the production of good sauce. Following are some of the basic sauces of great importance for continental cookery.

A. ESPAGNOL SAUCE (FOR 600 ML.)

Ingredients	Quantity
Butter	50 gm.
Lean bacon	50 gm.
Carrot	
Mushrooms	40 gm.
Tomato pulp	150 gm.
Onions	125 gm.
Flour	50 gm.
Stock	600 ml.
Bouquet garni (Parsley, thymemarjoram, basil, bayleaf, lime, rind)	
Sherry (optional)	75 ml.
Salt	To taste (15-20 gm.)

Method

- Cut becon and vegetables into small pieces.
- Fry lightly in butter. Add flour and cook very slowly till golden brown.
- Add stock, tomato pulp and bouquet garni. Simmer for 30 minutes. Strain through a tammy. Reheat and add sherry.
- Derivatives of Espagnol sauces

1. **Demi-Glaze:** Refined espagnol made by simmering espagnol and brown stock and reducing by half.
2. **Sauce Chasseur:** Demi glaze + minced onion + tomato + white wine.
3. **Sauce Bordelaise:** Espagnole + Red wine + Shallots + Bone marrow.
4. **Bercy sauce:** Demi Glaze + White wine + Shallot + Parsley.
5. **Devilled sauce:** Demi glaze + shallots + Pepper corns + bay leaf + vinegar + white wine.

6. Madeira Sauce or Marsala sauce: Demi glaze + Madeira or Marsala

B. VELOUTE SAUCE

Ingredients	Approx. Quantity
Butter	1/4 cup
Flour	1/2 cup
Clarified basic chicken stock	6 cups

Derivatives of Veloute Sauce

1. *Caper Sauce/sauce aux Capers*
   M. Veloute + capers + cream
2. *Supreme sauce/sauce supreme*
   Ch. Veloute + butter + cream + trimming of mushroom.
3. *Chaud Froid*
   Veloute + gellatine
4. *Allemande sauce*
   Veloute + yolk + cream + lime + nutmeg.
5. *Nomande sauce*
   Fish veloute + mushrooms + egg yolks + cream.

C. BECHAMEL SAUCE

Ingredients	Approx. Quantity
Butter	3 tsps
Flour	3 tsps
Milk	2 cup
Salt	3/4 tsp.
White pepper	1/4 tsp.

Method

- Melt the butter in top of a boiler over boiling water; stir in the flour with a wooden spoon until smooth.
- Add the milk gradually, stirring constantly; cook until sauce is thick.
- Stir in salt and pepper.
- Remove top of double boiler from water.
- Strain sauce through a fire sieve; use as desired.
- Pour any remaining sauce into a small bowl.
- Cover top of sauce with a circle of wet waxed paper; refrigerate for future use. Yield : 2 cups.

D. TOMATO SAUCE

Ingredients	Approx. Quantity
Tomatoes	230 gm.
Bacon	5 gm.
Butter	20 gm
Carrot	25 gm.
Turnip	25 gm.
Onion	25 gm
Refined flour	20 gm.
White pepper	to taste
Stock or tomato liquid	300 ml.
Sugar	1 tsp.

Method

- Slice onion and tomatoes finely.
- Shred carrot and turnip.
- Put all into a pan with stock, bacon, butter and seasoning.
- Cook until tender.
- Rub through a sieve and blend in flour. Return to pan and stir until boiling. Boil for 4-5 minutes and remove.

Derivatives of Tomato Sauce

1. *Napolitaine*
   Tomato sauce + mint + orange
2. *Create*
   Tomato sauce + Basil + Tobasco + chilli
3. *Portogoese*
   Tomato sauce + onion + garlic + parsley.
4. *Barlsacne*
   Tomato sauce + ketchup + worcestes + Paparika
5. *Piquante*
   Onion + parsley + gherkins + tomato sauce

E. MAYONNAISE

Mayonnaise are widely used and enjoyed. Technically, mayonnaise is an uncooked emulsion prepared from egg (yolk or whole), oil, vinegar, lemon juice and spices. (An emulsion is a liquid mixture. Mixture in which a fatty substance is suspended in minute droplets).

Egg yolks are essential in making mayonnaise. They absorb oil and bind it into a thick, creamy mixture forming the basis of the mayonnaise. The tiny droplets of oil dispersed throughout the mixture are each surrounded by egg yolk, thus forming an emulsion. The maximum amount of oil that a large egg yolk will absorb is approximately 3/4 cup. When this limit is exceeded, the yolks become saturated and their binding properties break down. As a result the mayonnaise either thins out or separates. Be sure all the ingredients are at room temperature before beginning the mayonnaise.

MAYONNAISE

Ingredients	Approx. Quantity
Egg yolks	4 med.
Salt	1 tsp.
White pepper	1/8 tsp.
Vegetable oil	2 c
Wine vinegar	1 tsp.

Method

- Place the egg yolks, salt and pepper in a medium bowl. Beat with electric hand mixer at medium speed until thick, pale and fluffy.
- Add 5 ounces oil in very thin stream, beating constantly, until thickened and oil is absorbed. Beat in the vinegar.
- Add the remaining oil slowly, beating constantly, until all the oil is blended into the mixture. Mayonnaise will be very thick.
- Place in refrigerator container. Cut waxed paper to fit over top; rinse in cold water. Place over mayonnaise; cover and refrigerate until ready to use. Yield : 1¾-cups.

BASIC VANILLA SAUCE (FOR DESSERT)

Ingredients	Approx. Quantity
Milk	2 c
Vanilla pod	1 no.
Eggs	3 nos.
Sugar	4 tsps
Stiffy whipped Cream	3/4 c

Method

- Pour the milk in a small heavy saucepan; add the vanilla pod.
- Heat to just under boiling point.
- Remove vanilla pod; wipe pod dry and store. Beat the eggs until lemon coloured.
- Pour a small amount of hot milk over eggs, stirring constantly. Return to remaining hot milk in saucepan.
- Cook, stirring constantly, over low heat for about 20 minutes or until thick. Remove from heat; stir in sugar. Allow to cool.
- Fold in whipped cream gradually. One teaspoon vanilla extract may be substituted for vanilla pod.

    Add to custard after removing from heat.

Derivatives of Mayonnaise

1. **Cocktail sauce**
   Tamato ketchup + Tobasco + Cream
2. **Renoucade**
   Tartar sauce + Anchovi essence
3. **Tartar sauce**
   Mayonnaise + Gharkins + Parsley + Taragon + Chevil
4. **Sauce verte/Green sauce**
   Mayonnaise + Spinach + Tarragon + Cher
5. **Sauce Tyrolienne**
   Mayonnaise + Shallots + Oil + Tomato + Thyme + Parsley

BASIC HOLLAINDAISE SAUCE

Ingredients	Approx. Quantity
Butter	1/2 c.
Egg yolks (well beaten)	4 nos.
Lemon juice	2 to 2½ tbsp.
White pepper a pinch Salt	1/8 tsp.

Method

- Melt 2 tablespoons butter in the top of a double boiler, then pour gradually into the beaten egg yolks, stirring constantly.
- Return yolks to pan and place pan in or over hot water.
- Add the remaining butter by tablespoons; stir after each tablespoon until each is melted.

● Remove from the heat and stir in the lemon juice, pepper and salt.

BASIC MUSTARD SAUCE

Ingredients	Approx. Quantity
Dijon mustard	2 tbsps
Dry English mustard	2 tbsps
Whipping cream	1 cup

Method

● Combine mustards, mixing to a smooth paste.
● Whip the cream in a small bowl until soft peaks form. Stir a small amount of whipped cream into the mustard mixture, blending well.
● Beat the mustard mixture into the whipped cream just until blended. May serve as dip for vegetables or for meat fondues.

BASIC MORNAY SAUCE

Ingredients	Approx. Quantity
Basic white sauce	2 cup
Butter	1 tsp.
Parmesan cheese	1 c (grated)

Method

Prepare basic white sauce and remove from heat.

Cut the butter into small pieces. Stir the parmesan cheese and butter into white sauce, beating with wooden spoon until butter is melted.

The amount of salt in white sauce may be decreased if desired, because parmesan cheese sometimes imparts a salty flavour.

BASIC CHINESE SWEET AND SOUR SAUCE

Ingredients	Approx. Quantity
Sugar	3/4 c
Soy sauce	2 tbsp
Dry white wine	1 tbsp
Wine vinegar	3 tbsp
Catsup	3 tbsp.
Cornstarch	2 tbsp.
Water	1/2 c.

Method

● Combine the sugar, soy sauce, wine, vinegar and catsup in a saucepan and bring to a boil.
● Dissolve the cornstarch in the water and add to the sauce.
● Cook over low heat, stirring until sauce has thickened.
● This makes about 1 to 1¼ cups of sauce.

G. PREPARATION OF MARINADES

The word 'Marination' means "Preparing food items before cooking". In ancient cookery marination was not applied for cooking food. But now-a-days marination is applied for cooking food items especially meat, fish, seafood and vegetables, all over the world. The process of marination makes the food softer, tender and suitable for cooking.

Marination is an essential part of cooking. We use various types of marination to treat food items for cooking. The duration of marinating food items may be 10-15 minutes and over two hours and so on, depending on the nature of foods.

In Indian cuisine, marination is also applied for cooking food items. We use marination for making special dishes of rice, pulse, vegetables, meat and fish etc.

Types of Marinade (for Indian Cuisine)

For Indian cooking, following types of marinade are normally used :

1. *Curd and red chilli powder* (Nizam is a Urdu word, which is used for marinade): Beaten curd is used for marinating food items, especially for meat and fish.
2. *Paste of turmeric, salt and garlic:* A paste of turmeric, salt and garlic is generally used in Indian kitchen for making vegetables and also for meat and chicken.
3. *Papaya paste:* Green papaya paste is useful for softening food items.
4. *Mustard, green chilli and garlic paste:* Mustard, green chilli and garlic paste is also used for marination to cook vegetables and especially for cooking fish.

5. *Keora or rose water:* Water mixed with keora or rose water is a popular marination for making pulao, and other rice dishes.
6. *Curd, red chilli powder, ginger, garlic, onion paste (in small quantity) and salt:* This marination is used for tandoori dishes.
7. *Onion paste, green chilli, salt and lemon juice:* This is also a popular Indian marination.

MARINADES FOR CONTINENTAL CUISINE

Continental food preparation also need marination.

Following marinades are normally used in continental cooking:

1. Oil
2. Wine
3. Vinegar
4. Lemon juice
5. Herbs
6. Onions paste
7. Worchester sauce
8. Pepper powder and lemon juice.

In addition with these marinades, a mixture of the above ingredients are used with special need and choice.

a. Oil + Vinegar + Wine
b. Oil + Vinegar
c. Wine + Worchester sauce.

MARINADES FOR CHINESE CUISINE

The following marinades are used in Chinese cuisine

1. Soy sauce
2. Vinegar
3. Egg white + Corn flour

H. PREPARATION OF STUFFINGS

In cookery both in Continental and Indian as well as Chinese, stuffings are used. The stuffings should be vegetarian as well as non-vegetarian. The stuffing used in samosa is based on mashed potato mix with various masalas. It is a very common stuffing known to almost all Indians.

Apart from this creative mind in the kitchen can develop many useful stuffing for the purpose of stuffed food item like Murg Musallam, Stuffed Capsicum, Bhareli Aloo or Wantoon, Momo, are some stuffed chops. Some of the popular examples are: Forcemeat or keemas, fish eggs

Cheese are often used along with other minor food stuffs for stuffing or filling in the cookery.

I. PREPARATION OF GRAVY

The word 'Gravy" is actually applied to the liquid portion of the cooked food by the process of 'stewing'. It is very similar to that of the word called 'curry' used in Indian cookery in order to organise kitchen work for making food items as per order in restaurants and eatery. It is now a practice to pre-prepare certain basic gravies for making Indian dishes similar to that of sauces of western cookery. Following are some of the important recipes for basic gravies used in good class and star restaurants

1. WHITE OR SHAHI GRAVY

Ingredients	Approx. Quantity
Oil	50 gm.
Ginger	5 gm.
Garlic	5 gm.
Whole garam masala	5 gm.
Onion	500 gm.
Water	200 ml.
Cashew paste	25 gm.
Charmagaj paste (Paste of melon seed, cucumber seed, pumpkin seed and any other seed).	25 gm.
Sugar	To taste.
Poppy paste	25 gm.
Salt	To taste
Sugar	To taste.

Method

- Heat oil till it smokes.
- Add ginger paste and garlic paste and cook for sometime.
- Add whole garam masala.
- Fry it nicely so that ginger and garlic looses the raw flavour.

- Add boiled onion paste and add some water.
- Add cashew paste, charmagaj paste, poppy paste in water separately.
- Strain it and add the strained water to the gravy.
- Add salt and sugar.

2. Green Gravy

Ingredients	Approx. Quantity
Paste of spinach	300 gm.
Coriander powder	10 gm.
Paste of mint leaves	10 gm.
Oil	50 gm
Paste of green chillies	5 gm
Ginger paste	5 gm
Garlic paste	5 gm
Hot spices	5 gm.
Water	100 ml.
Salt	To taste.

Method

- Heat the oil.
- Add ginger paste and garlic paste and cook till the raw flavour is removed.
- Add the hot spices.
- Add the green paste.
- Add water.
- Add salt and sugar.
- When the gravy is done, add some more green paste. (If onion is added, then finely sliced onions are to be fried first and then added).

3. Makhani Gravy (Tomato gravy)

Ingredients	Approx. Quantity
Oil	50 gm.
Ginger paste	5 gm.
Garlic paste	5 gm.
Hot spices	5 gm.
Tomatoes	200 gms.
Water	200 ml.
Salt	to taste
Sugar	to taste
Corn flour or Arrowroot	25 gm.

Method

- Heat oil.
- Fry ginger paste and garlic paste.

- Add hot spices and chopped tomatoes.
- Fry for sometime.
- Add cornflour or arrowroot, salt and sugar.
- Pass it through a liquidizer.

4. Brown Gravy

Ingredients	Approx. Quantity
Oil	50 gm.
Onions	500 gm.
Red Chilli powder	5 gm.
Coriander powder	10 gm.
Cumin powder	10 gm.
Turmeric powder	a pinch
Ginger paste	5 gm.
Garlic paste	5 gm.
Water	200 ml.
Salt	to taste
Sugar	to taste.
Garam masala	5 gm.
Optional	
Sour curd	
Tomatoes	

Method

- Heat oil till it smokes.
- Add finely chopped onions and fry till golden brown.
- Add the paste of red chilli powder, coriander powder, cumin powder and turmeric powder.
- Add ginger paste and garlic paste.
- Fry all the above ingredients.
- Sprinkle water and go on stirring.
- Finally add salt and sugar. (If sour curd is added, then it must be beaten first and cooking is to be stopped as soon as the curd is added. If tomatoes are added, then cooking is to be continued).

5. Chilli Garlic Gravy

Ingredients	Approx. Quantity
Green chilli make paste.	100 gm.
Garlic	150 gm.
Boiled onion puree	100 gm.
Oil	As required
Water	As required.

Method

- Heat oil. Fry boiled onion puree for some time.

- Then add chilli-garlic paste and fry till oil comes out.
- Add water and cook till the gravy becomes thick for required consistency.

6. Bombay Gravy

Ingredients	Approx. Quantity
Onion	3 no.
Tomato	4 nos
Coconut	1/2 portion
Clove	8 nos.
Pepper corns	8 nos.
Coriander seeds	10 gm.
Red chilli powder	10 gm.
Turmeric powder	5 gm.
Garam Masala	5 gm.
Ginger-garlic paste	20-25 gm
Oil	30-35 ml.
Salt & sugar	to taste

Pre-Preparation

- Chop onion and tomatoes and coriander leaves.
- Grate coconut.
- Make ginger-garlic paste.

Method

- Heat oil in a pan. Add cloves, pepper corns and coriander seeds. After a few seconds, add chopped onion and fry till brown. Now add grated coconut and brown thoroughly. Grind this mixture to a fine paste.
- Heat oil. Add ginger-garlic paste and fry for some time. Then add coconut paste and mix well. Now add sufficient water for right consistency. Add salt sugar to taste.

- At the last step dust with garam masala powder.

LIQUID AND SOLID MEASURES FOR USE IN KITCHEN

Liquid Measures

Imperial	Metric
1 teaspoon (t)	5 ml.
1 tablespoon (T)	20 ml.
2 (1/4 cup)	62 ml.
4 (1/2 cup)	125 ml.
8 (10 cup)	250 ml.
1 pint (16 ounces) - 2 cups	500 ml

Solid Measures

Avoirdupois	Metric
1 ounce	30 gm
4 ounces (1/4 lb)	125 gm
8 ounces (1/2 lb)	250 gm.
12 ounces (3/4 lb)	375 gm.
16 ounces (1 lb)	500 gm.
24 ounces (1 1/2 lb)	750 gm.
32 ounces (2 lb)	1000 g (1 Kg)

OVEN TEMPERATURE GUIDE

Description	Gas		Electric	
	C	F	C	F
Cool	100	200	110	225
Very slow	120	250	120	250
slow	150	300	150	300
Moderately slow	160	325	170	340
Moderate	180	350	200	400
Moderately hot	190	375	220	425
Hot	200	400	230	450
Very hot	230	450	250	475

CONTINENTAL COURSE - ITEMS AND PREPARATIONS

A. APPETIZERS

1. Melon Cocktail
2. Tomato A La Monagesque
3. Salmon Mayonnaise
4. Cornets De Saumon Fuma Aux Oeifs De Poisson
5. Grape Fruit Cocktail
6. Prawn Cocktail
7. Frosted Tomato Cocktail
8. Scampi, Apple And Cheese Salad
9. Raw Vegetables with Hot Garlic Sauce
10. Pate De Foie

B. SOUPS

1. Cream of Tomato Soup
2. Cream of Asparagus Soup
3. Consomme Julienne
4. Consomme A La Royale
5. Scotch Broth
6. French Onion Soup
7. Vichssoise
8. Minestrone
9. Lobster Bisque
10. Chicken Chowder
11. Creamed Fish Soup

C. FISH COURSES

1. Sole Bonne Femme
2. Fish Vol-au-vents
3. Poached Haddock
4. Grilled Plaice
5. Sole Duglere
6. Goujons of Fish
7. Scampi Provencale
8. Poached Smoked Haddock
9. Fillets De Sole Veronique
10. Cold Poached Salmon
11. Truites A La Meuniere
12. Soused Fish
13. Fish and Bacon Whirls
14. Tuna Fish Provenacale

D. MAIN COURSES

1. Roast Leg of Lamb with Mint Sauce
2. Rolled Rib Roast of Beef With Yorkshire Pudding
3. Roast Saddle of Lamb, Mint Sauce
4. Roast Turkey
5. Roast Leg of Pork with Apple Sauce Seasoning
6. Entrecote A La Bordelaise
7. Sesame Chicken
8. Chicken Pie
9. Barbecued Chicken
10. Gammon with Pineapple and Corn Sauce
11. Beef Goulash
12. Braised Beef Neapolitan
13. Cold Loin of Pork Orientale
14. Lamb Shish Kebabs with Herbed Sauce

E. SWEETS

1. Charlotte Rousee
2. Strawberry Whip
3. Almond and Strawberry Gateaux
4. Apple Mousse
5. Trifle Pudding
6. Fresh Fruit Salad
7. Gateaux De Peaches
8. Frosted Coffee Gateau
9. Black Forest Cherry Gateau

PREPARATION OF APPETIZERS

1. Melon Cocktail

Ingredients	Approx. Quantity
Melon	
Ice	
Sugar	As required
Maraschino	
Kirsch	
Brandy or white port	

Pre-Preparation: Peel and cut melon.

Method

- Cut the flesh of ripe melon into 2 cm (3/4 in) cubes or into slices.
- Place the melon in a timbale on ice. Sprinkle with sugar and allow to chill well.

Serving

- Serve, sprinkled with maraschino, kirsch Arrange in raviers and decorate with brandy or white port according to taste in picked parsley, small glass coupes.

2. Tomato A La Monagesque

Ingredients	Approx. Quantity
Tomatoes (very small)	
Oil	
Vinegar	
Salt	
Pepper	
Tunna fish (finely chopped)	
Hard boiled egg	As required
Onion (chopped)	
Parsley	
Tarragon	
Chevil	
Mayonnaise	

Pre-Preparation: Cut a slice from the tops of tomatoes, remove pips from tomatoes.

Method

- Sprinkle the inside of tomatoes with a little oil, vinegar, salt and pepper to marinate.
- Fill dome shape with a mixture of equal quantities, finely chopped tunny fish and

hard boiled egg flavoured with chopped onion, parsley, tarragon and chervil mixed with a little mayonnaise.

Serving

- Arrange in raviers and decorate with picked parsley.

3. Salmon Mayonnaise

Ingredients	Approx. Quantity
Salmon (cooked)	
Salt	
Pepper	
Oil	
Vinegar or Lemon Juice	
Lettuce leaves	
Capers	As required
Anchovies	
Black olives	
Hard-boiled egg	
Mayonnaise	

Pre-Preparation: Cooking salmon, cut lettuce leaves.

Method

- Cut some cooked salmon into thin scallops and season with salt, pepper, oil and vinegar or lemon juice.
- Arrange the lettuce leaves in a bowl. Cover the lettuce with salmon escalopes, coat with mayonnaise, and garnish with capers, anchovies, black olives and quarters of hard boiled eggs.

Serving

Serve well chilled.

4. Cornets De Saumon Fuma Aux Oeifs de Poisson

Ingredients	Approx. Quantity
Salmon	
Cornets	
Fish roe	
Lettuce leaves	As required
Lemon	
Cream	
Lemon juice	
Horse radish	

Pre-Preparation: Smoke salmon, cut lettuce leaves. Mix cream with lemon juice. Grate horse radish. Make cornet.

Method

- Roll up some small slices of smoked salmon into cornets.
- Fill them with fish roe.
- Arrange them on a bed of shredded lettuce dressed with vinaigrette. Garnish with fluted lemon halves.

Serving

- Serve with mixed cream (cream, lemon juice, grated horse radish) in a sauceboat, with hot blinis.

5. Grape Fruit Cocktail

Ingredients	Approx. Quantity
Grapefruit	2-3 nos. (large)
Rum	15-20 ml.
Bananas	2 nos.
Brown sugar	10-12 gm.

Pre-Preparation: Cut grapefruits into halves. Remove the pips from grapefruit.

Method

- Mix the grapefruit with rum bananas and sugar.
- Spoon back into the grapefruit shells till done.

6. Prawn Cocktail

Ingredients	Approx. Quantity
Prawns (cooked)	200 gm.
Lettuce	As required

For Mary Rose Dressing

Ingredients	Approx. Quantity
Mayonnaise	60-65 ml.
Double cream	20-25 gm.
Lemon juice	15 ml.
Dry sherry	20-30 ml.
Tabasco sauce a little	
Fresh Tomato Puree	30-35 ml
Salt and pepper	To taste.

Garnish

Ingredients	Approx. Quantity
Lemon slices	
Prawns	As required

Pre-Preparation: Peel and cook the prawns. Shred the lettuce and chop into small pieces, as it has to be eaten with a teaspoon.

Method

- Blend together all the ingredients for the dressing.
- Add the prawns and allow to marinate in the dressing for atleast one hour in the refrigerator.
- Put the shredded lettuce into four individual glasses, top with the prawn mixture.

Serving

- Serve, garnished with the lemon and prawns.

7. Frosted Tomato Cocktail

Ingredients	Approx. Quantity
Tomatoes	1 kg. (Skinned & chopped and de-seeded)
Salt & pepper	To taste
Sugar One pine	
Lemon juice	
Worcestershire sauce	As required
Mint leaves	

Method

- Put the tomatoes, water, seasoning and sugar into a sauce pan and heat for a few minutes.
- Make puree and then add lemon juice Worcestershire sauce and any other seasoning, for example, celery salt cayenne pepper or chilli sauce.
- Freeze it slightly and then chop and spoor into chilled glasses.

Serving

- Serve, garnished with mint leaves.

8. Scampi, Apple and Cheese Salad

Ingredients	Approx. Quantity
Ricotta or cottage cheese	200 gm
Chopped toasted nuts	75 gm.
Escarole, batavian endive or lettuce	75 gm
Dessert apple (cared, sliced and brushed) with lemon juice	1 no.
Scampi or large shrimps (Shelled, fresh or frozen)	12-16 nos.

Dressing

Oil	3 tablespoons
Lemon juice	1 tablespoons
Salt and pepper	To taste
Avocado pear (mashed)	1/2 portion
Cream	1 tablespoon.

Method

- Roll the cheese into ball-shapes about the size of a walnut. (If cottage cheese is used, it should be sieved first).
- Roll the cheese balls in the chopped nuts and chill.
- Put some shredded escarole, endive or lettuce in four serving dishes and arrange the apple slices, scampi or large shrimps (prawns) and cheese balls on top.

Serving

- Combine all the dressing ingredients and pour over the individual salads, and serve.

9. Raw Vegetables With Hot Garlic Sauce

Ingredients	Approx. Quantity
Butter (Unsalted)	80 gm.
Olive oil	5 tablespoons
Can Anchovies in oil (Chopped)	1 small
Garlic cloves (chopped)	2-6 nos.
Celery stalks, (cut into 2 inch (5 cm. lengths)	4 nos.
Red pepper (pith and seeds removed, cut into thin strips)	1 no.
Green pepper (Pith and seeds removed, cut into thin strips)	1 no.
Carrots (peeled and cut into sticks)	4 nos
White cabbage (cut into fairly wide strips)	1/4 small

Method

- Cook butter, add oil, anchovies and garlic together stirring occasionally for 15 minutes.
- Place in a fondue pot and serve with raw vegetables.

10. Pate De Foie

Ingredients	Approx. Quantity
Butter	35 gm
Fat pork	70 gm.
Lean pork	70 gm.
Liver (chicken, lamb or pig)	200 gm.
Onion (chopped)	25 gm.
Garlic	1 flake
Thyme	1 sprig
Parsley	1 sprig
Salt-pepper	To taste
Fat bacon	30-40 gm.

Method

- Cut the liver in 2.5 cm. pieces and toss in garlic together, stirring occasionally for 15 butter for a few seconds with the onion, minutes, garlic and herbs.
- Cool it and after then mince twice with vegetables. lean pork and season it.
- Line an earthenware terrine with thin slices of fat bacon, put the mixture in it and cover with fat bacon.
- Put in a tray half-full of water and cook in a moderate oven for one hour.
- After getting cold, cut into small slices and serve on lettuce leaves on a silver flat.

PREPARATION OF SOUPS
1. Cream of Tomato Soup

Ingredients	Approx. Quantity
Tomato	200 gm.
Onions	20 gm.
Stock	1/2 cup
Butter	2 teaspoon
Bay leaf	1 no.
Pepper corns	1-2 nos.
Cornflour	1 teaspoon
Milk	1/4 cup
Salt	1/2 teaspoon
Pepper	1/8 teaspoon

For Garnish

Cream	1 tablespoon
Bread	1/4 slice
Fat	For frying

Pre-Preparation: Chop onions, make slices of tomatoes, prepare white sauce.

Method

- Melt 1 teaspoon butter in a sauce pan and saute chopped onion, sliced tomatoes and whole spices.
- Add stock or water, bring to a boil, reduce the heat and simmer for 10-20 minutes. Mix in a blender.
- Pass through a sieve and season. (Vol. of extract should be approx. 150 ml.)
- Prepare white sauce: Heat 1 teaspoon of butter in a pan, stir in the flour and cook for a few minutes. Remove from fire and gradually add milk with constant stirring to avoid lump formation. Return the mixture to heat and cook with constant stirring to avoid lump formation. Until smooth and thicken.
- Reheat tomato soup and whisk it into white sauce at the time of serving.

Serving

- Serve hot garnished with cream and bread croutons.
- Dilute with a few tablespoons of milk.

2. Cream of Asparagus Soup

Ingredients	Approx. Quantity
Asparagus	350 gm
Butter	30-35 gm.
Bechamel sauce and puree 1	1/2 pints.
Cream	150 gm.
Milk	60-70 ml.

Pre-Preparation: Shred and blanch the asparagus, prepare bechamel sauce. Make puree.

Method

- Cook the clean and blanch asparagus in butter in a covered pan.
- Add bechamel and puree in a food processor.

- Mix this bechamel with the cooked vegetable and simmer gently for 12-18 minutes.
- Heat and adjust the seasoning.
- Add fresh cream and stir while heating.

3. Consomme Julienne

(More than just a clear stock, consomme derives its special flavour from the vegetables used Egg whites and shells clarify this traditional and elegant appetizer soup).

Ingredients	Approx. quantity
Ordinary consomme	2 litres
Salt and sugar	
a pinch of each	

Ordinary Consomme (For 2 litres)

Ingredients		Approx. Quantity
White bouillon		2½ litres.
Beef (very lean, trimmed and chopped)		
	Chopped	750 gm
Carrots	into	50 gm.
Leek	pieces	100 gm.
Egg whites	2 nos.	

Method

- Put the chopped meat, vegetables and egg whites in a small stock-pot and mix well.
- Add the white bouillon and boil it, stirring time to time. Then simmer the heat for about 1 hour.
- At last strain the consomme through a clean cloth.

For Garnish

Ingredients	Approx. Quantity
Carrot	125 gm.
Turnip	125 gm.
White of leek	55 gm.
White of celery	55 gm.
Onion	30 gm.
Cabbage	70 gm.
Small peas	1 tablespoon
Chiffonade of sorrel and lettuce	
Pluches of chervil	l tablespoon

Pre-Preparation: Cut the carrot, turnip, leek and celery into even-size julienne, slice the onion.

Method

- Stew all the vegetables except the cabbage with a little butter, a pinch of salt and sugar.
- Moisten with one litre ordinary consomme.
- Add the blanched julienne of cabbage.
- Allow to cook gently and add the rest of the consomme (1½ litres) at the last moment.

Serving

- Serve, garnished with 1 tablespoon of small peas, 1 tablespoon chiffonade of sorrel and lettuce and pluches of chervil.

4. Consomme A La Royale

Ingredients	Approx. Quantity
Chicken or meat consomme with tapioca	3.5 to 4 litres.

For Garnish

4 dariole moulds of ordinary Royale.

Pre-Preparation: Make meat or chicken consomme. Prepare a plain or herb flavoured royale.

Method

- Thicken the consomme with tapioca and cool the royale completely.
- Unmould the cold royale on to a cloth (this will absorb any moisture), and cut it into small cubes.
- Add this garnish to the hot soup.

5. Scotch Broth

Ingredients	Approx. Quantity
Goat meat	125 gm.
Barley grain	35 gm.
Stock	300 ml.
Parsley	a few
Carrots	200 gm.
Turnip	50 gm.
Onion	50 gm.
Celery	50 gm.
Pepper	To taste
Salt	

Pre-Preparation: Wash barley. Clean and cut meat. Soak the meat in cold stock for 15 minutes.

Method

- Cook the meat for 1 hour.
- Skim off fat from broth and add diced vegetables barley, and seasoning and simmer for 2 hours.
- Remove meat and dice.
- Return to pan; add more seasoning if necessary.

Serving

- Remove all fat and serve hot garnished with chopped parsley.

6. French Onion Soup

Ingredients	Approx. Quantity
Onion	80 gm. (1 big)
Butter	1 tablespoon
Cornflour	1 tablespoon
Chicken stock	1 cup
Bay leaf	1 no.
Salt and pepper	to taste

For Garnish

Grated cheese	10 gm.

Method

- Heat butter and fry thinly sliced onion in foaming butter, till they are evenly browned all over.
- Stir in the flour and cook for two minutes, gradually add the stock and bring to boil. Add bay leaf and seasoning. Simmer for 30 minutes.
- Strain the soup to get approximately 150 ml. of extract.

Serving

- Serve hot, garnished with grated cheese.

7. Vichssoise

Ingredients	Approx. Quantity
Butter	50 gm.
Leeks	8 nos.
Potatoes	2 nos.
Chicken stock	750 ml.
Salt and pepper	to taste.
White wine	150 ml.
Double or whipping cream	150 ml.

For Garnish

Chives	2 tablespoons

Pre-Preparation: Chop leeks and potatoes.

Method

- Heat the butter in a large saucepan.
- Add the leeks and potatoes and turn in the butter for several minutes.
- Pour in the chicken stock and add a little salt and pepper to taste.
- Simmer the mixture gently for 20 to 25 minutes, until the vegetables and tender (don't overcook as this will darken the soup).
- Sieve or liquidize the ingredients with the wine and cream to give a velvet-like soup.

Serving

- Chill the soup well and top with the chives.

8. Minestrone

Ingredients	Approx. Quantity
Fresh belly of pork	60 gm.
Scraped fat pork	40 gm.
Onion	60 gm.
Shredded white of leek	150 gm.
White bouillon	13/4 litres.
Carrot	60 gm.
Turnip	60 gm.
Celery	30 gm.
Potato	100 gm.
Cabbage	100 gm.
Tomatoes	2 nos.
Peas	100 gm.
French beans	50 gm.
Rice	100 gm.
Garlic	8 gm.
Basil	a pinch
Chervil	a pinch

Pre-Preparation: Chop belly of pork, cabbage, tomato, leek and onion. Cut celery, turnip, carrot, potatoes and french beans into paysamme. Crush garlic.

Method

- Mix the belly of pork and scraped fat pork and place in a thick bottomed pan to heat and melt it.
- Add chopped onion shredded leek to it and cook together until lightly coloured.
- Moisten with i- litres white bouillon and add 15 gm. salt. Then add carrot, turnip, celery, potato, cabbage and tomatoes.
- Boil for about 25 minutes and after then add fresh peas, french beans, rice or spaghetti. Now cook the soup very gently for 1 hour. At last, add 6 gm. crushed garlic and a pinch of each of basil garlic and a pinch each of basil and chervil with scrapped pork fat.

9. Lobster Bisque

Ingredients	Approx. Quantity
Lobsters	1 kg.
For The Mirepoix	
Carrots	50 gm.
Onions	50 gm.
Butter	50 gm.
Thyme	1 sprig
Bay leaf	1 no.
Parsley stalks	3 nos.
Flamed brandy	1 small
White wine	2 ml.
For the Thickening and Moistening	
Rice	200 gm.
White bouillon	1 litre
For Finishing	
Cream	125 ml.
Butter	150 gm.

Pre-Preparation: Cut the carrots, onions, parsley stalks into very small dice. Wash the lobsters and remove the tails.

Method

- Cook the carrots, onion and parsley in the butter with thyme and bay leaf until light brown in colour. Cook the lobsters with the mirepoix until red in colour. Then season with salt and a little milled pepper, sprinkle brandy and wine over it and cook gently to reduce. Add white bouillon and allow to cook gently for 10 minutes.

- Cook the rice in white bouillon.
- Shell the lobsters and reserve all the tails and the heads.
- Finely pound the remainder of the shells, add the rice and its cooking liquid together with the cooking liquid from the lobster. Strain and dilute the puree with bouillon. Boil and again strain and then keep in the bain-marie.

Serving

Pour butter and cream over it and then serve.

10. Chicken Chowder

Ingredients	Approx. Quantity
Bacon rashers	3 nos.
Onion	1 no. (medium)
Butter or Margarine	for frying
Chicken stock	375 ml.
Root vegetables	300 gm.
Milk	250 ml.
Cooked chicken	150 gm.
Sweet corn	4 tablespoon
Salt and paprika	to taste
Parsley and paprika	as required

Pre-Preparation: Chop bacon rashers, onion and parsley. Dice root vegetables and cooked chicken.

Method

- Fry the onion in butter or margarine until the bacon is crisp and the onion soft and transparent.
- Stir in the stock and boil. Then add the vegetables and cook for about 10 minutes or until they are tender.
- Stir in the milk, chicken, sweet corn and seasoning to taste and cook for five minutes over low heat.

11. Creamed Fish Soup

Ingredients	Approx. Quantity
Fish fillets (Bhetki)	300 gm.
Fish stock	750 litre
Cornflour	30-35 gm.
Butter or margarine	25-30 gm.
Salt and pepper	to taste
Lemon (Grated rind of lemon)	1 no.
Plain yoghurt	250 gm.
Parsley	to garnish

Pre-Preparation: Skinned the fish fillets. Grate the rind of lemon. Chop the parsley.

Method

- Put the fish into a saucepan with about 1/3 of the fish stock. Bring to the boil and simmer gently until the fish is cooked and flakes easily.
- Remove the fish from the saucepan, leaving the stock behind.
- Blend the cornflour with the remaining fish stock and stir into the stock in the saucepan with the margarine, seasoning and lemon rind.
- Bring to the boil and simmer, stirring, until slightly thickened. Add the flaked fish and yoghurt and stir well. Heat for sometime and remove from fire before boiling.

Serving

- Serve, garnished with parsley.

PREPARATION OF FISH COURSES
1. Sole Bonne Femme

Ingredients	Approx. Quantity
Sole	1 kg
Mushrooms	60 gm.
Shallot	2-3 nos.
Parsley a few Butter	160-170 gm.
Thin fish veloute	1 1/4 dl
White wine	1 1/4 dl

Pre-Preparation: Prepare the sole. Slice, mushrooms. Chop, shallot and parsley.

Method

- Butter a dish and sprinkle the bottom with sliced mushrooms, shallot and parsley.
- Place the sole on top, add white wine thin fish veloute and shallow poach in a moderate oven.
- When the sole is cooked, drain off the cooking liquid, reduce and enrich and thicken it with butter.
- Pour the sauce over the sole and glare quickly under the salamander.

2. Fish Vol-au-vents

Ingredients	Approx. Quantity
Vol-au-vents	8 nos. (medium)
Cooked or corned fish	350 gm.
White sauce (thick)	150 gm.

Pre-Preparation: Prepare vol-au-vents. Cook the fish. Prepare white sauce.

Method

- Roll out the puff pastry until 1.5 cm in thickness.
- Cut into 13 rounds about 6 to 7.5 cm. in diameter.
- Put on to a slightly damp baking tray.
- Take a 3.5 cm. cutter, press halfway through the pastry.
- Brush the rim of the pastry with beaten egg for savoury vol-au-vents and with lightly whisked egg white and a sprinkling of caster sugar for sweet case. Flake the sides of the rounds so the pastry rises well.
- Chill before cooking.
- Bake just above the centre of a hot oven for about 10 minutes.
- Lower the heat slightly and cook for further 3 to 4 minutes or until firm.
- With the tip off a knife lift out the centres of the cases. If necessary, return the cases to the oven for a few minutes to dry out.

White Sauce

Ingredients	Approx. Quantity
Butter or Margarine	25 gm.
Flour	25 gm.
Milk	300 ml.
Salt & pepper	to taste.

Method

- Heat the butter in the pan.
- Stir in the flour. Cook for 2-3 minutes and then blend in the milk.
- Stir as the sauce comes to the boil and continue stirring until thickened.
- Season to taste.

Method for hot serving

- Blend the fish with the hot sauce and put into the hot vol-au-vents just before the meal.

Method for cold serving

- Add the fish to the cold sauce or mayonnaise and put into the cold pastry. (Freeze pastry cases and filling separately).

3. Poached Haddock

Ingredients	Approx. Quantity
Haddock	
Cold milk	
Butter	As required
Lemon juice	
Parsley	
Boiled potatoes	

Pre-Preparation: Smoke, haddock and soak in cold milk for 2-3 hours. Melt the butter.

Method

- Bring the milk to the boil.
- Add the haddock and poach without boiling, for 6-10 minutes, depending on the thickness of the fish.

Serving

- Serve with melted butter strongly flavoured with lemon juice and chopped parsley, accompanied by boiled potatoes.

4. Grilled Plaice

Ingredients	Approx. Quantity
Fillets of Plaice	As required.
Oil	

Method

- Incise the fillets with shallow cuts in a criss-cross pattern.
- Season, the fillets.
- Brush them well with oil and grill gently.

Serving

- Serve, placed on a suitable compound butter or accompanied with a sauce boat of sauce saint-malo.

5. Sole Duglere

Ingredients	Approx. Quantity
Sole	—
Onion	20 gm.
Shallot	20 gm.
Tomato	120 gm.
Parsley	a little
Salt	to taste
Pepper	to taste
Fish veloute	1/2 dl
Butter	30 gm
Lemon juice	a few drops
White wine	1 dl

Pre-Preparation: Prepare the sole Chop, tomato and parsley.

Method

- Place the sole in a buttered dish which has been sprinkled with chopped onion and shallot, roughly chopped flesh of tomato, a little roughly chopped parsley and a little salt and pepper.
- Add white wine and shallow poach in the oven.
- Drain off the cooking liquid and reduce by half.
- Thicken with fish veloute and at last pour over butter and a few drops of lemon juice.

Serving

Coat the fish with the sauce and serve.

6. Goujons of Fish

Ingredients	Approx. Quantity
White fish	450 gm
Oil or fat	For deep frying
Coating	
Salt and pepper	To taste
Flour little	
Grist breadcrumbs	50-100 gm

Method

- Skin the fish and cut into narrow ribbons.
- Coat in seasoned flour and then in beaten egg and crisp breadcrumbs.
- Fry in hot oil or fat until crisp and golden.

7. Scampi Provencale

Ingredients	Approx. Quantity
Cooked scampi	450 gin.
Water	150 ml
Salt, Pepper	to taste
Parsley	One bunch
Oil	1 tablespoon
Garlic (crushed)	1 clove
Onions (chopped)	2 small Tomatoes
(skimmed & chopped)	4 medium.
Dry white wine	4 tablespoons
Black olives	few
Parsley (chopped)	2 tablespoons

Pre-Preparation: Peel the scampi. Put the shells into a saucepan, add the water, a pinch of salt, a shake of pepper and the parsley. Cover the pan and simmer for 10 minutes, Then strain the liquid and measure out 3 tablespoons.

Method

- Heat the oil in a pan and fry the garlic and onions for 2 to 3 minutes. Add the tomatoes and cook for a further 2 to 3 minutes then add the reserved stock and wine.

- Add the scampi, the olives and half the pastry. Heat for a few minutes and top with remaining parsley.

Serving

- Serve with cooked rice.

8. Poached Smoked Haddock

Ingredients	Approx. Quantity
Smoked haddock	1 large or 2 smaller.
Water or milk and	as required.
Water Butter	50 gm.

Pre-Preparation: Cut away the fins and tail, divide the haddock into neat pieces.

Method

- Put the haddock into simmering water or milk and poach gently for 10 minutes or until just tender.

Serving

- Serve, garnished with butter.

9. Fillets De Sole Veronique

Ingredients	Approx. Quantity
Sole	
Lemon juice	
White wine	As required
Water	
Butter	
Grapes	

Pre-Preparation: Remove the fillets from a nice sole, trim them, lightly flatten and fold.

Method

- Place the fillets of sole in a buttered dish which has a cover and season.
- With the trimming and bones of the sole and the usual flavourings, lemon juice, white wine and water, prepare approximately 1 dl of fish stock.
- Strain this over the prepared fillets, cover with the lid and shallow poach gently.
- Carefully drain the cooked fillets, reduce the cooking liquid to the consistency of a light syrup and mix in butter.

- Replace the fillets, overlapping in a circle in the dish in which they were cooked, coat with the sauce and quickly glaze.

Serving

- Place in the centre of the fillets a nice bouquet of very cold, skinned and depipped muscated grapes; cover the dish with the lid and serve immediately.

10. Cold Poached Salmon

Ingredients	Approx. Quantity
Salmon	
Court bouillion	
or	
Fish fumer	
As required	

For Garnishing: Lettuce hearts, hard boiled eggs or stuffed vegetables.

Method

- Poach a whole salmon in a court bouillon or a fish fumet and leave to cool in the liquid.
- Drain the fish, wipe it and arrange on a large dish.
- Garnish with lettuce hearts and hard boiled eggs or stuffed vegetables.

Serving

- Serve with andalouse sauce or mayonnaise.

11. Truites A La Meuniere

Ingredients	Approx. Quantity
Turbot	
Butter	
Flour	
Lemon	As required
Salt	
Pepper	
Parsley	

Pre-Preparation: Cook the slices or fillets of fish in a frying pan in very hot butter, lightly coated with flour. Place it on a very hot serving dish and squeeze a little lemon juice over the fish

Method

- Season the fish with a little salt and pepper and sprinkle with blanched and chopped parsley.
- At last step, coat the fish with some butter and cook until brown in colour. Serve hot.

12. Soused Fish

Ingredients	Approx. Quantity
Herring (Backbone removed)	6 nos.
Onion	1 no. (Medium size)
Vinegar	
Water	As required
Bay leaves	4 nos.
Cloves	2 nos.
All spice berries	12 nos.
Mace blades	2 nos.
Salt	1 teaspoon

Pre-Preparation: Slice the onions.

Method

- Lay the herrings, skin side down, on a working surface and place sliced onion on the centre of each fish.
- Roll up the fish from head to tail and secure with wooden toothpicks.
- Place the fish rolls in an oven proof dish and add vinegar and water to cover in the proportion of three parts vinegar to one part water. Add the herbs, spices and salt.
- Cover the dish and cook in a low oven 300°F, gas mark 2, for 3 hours or until the fish is cooked. The liquid must not boil. Transfer the fish to a serving dish and strain the cooking liquid over. Chill until the liquid becomes jelly.

Serving

- Serve, garnished with black olives and pickled cucumber and with potato and cucumber salads.

13. Fish And Bacon Whirls

Ingredients	Approx. Quantity
Frozen fish fingers in	
Breadcrumb coating	8 nos.
Oil or fat	For frying
Streaky bacon rashers	8 nos.
Tomatoes	4 nos.

Pre-Preparation: Cut the bacon rashers into long strips. Cut the tomatoes into halves.

Method

- Fry the fish fingers in oil or fat until golden brown.
- Remove them from the pan and wrap the bacon strips around them and secure them with cocktail sticks if necessary.
- Return to the pan with the tomatoes and continue frying until the bacon and fish fingers are cooked.

14. Tuna Fish Provencale

Ingredients	Approx. Quantity
Cans tuna	175 gm.
Lemon juice	1/2 lemon
Salt & pepper	to taste.
Anchovy fillets	4 nos.
Onion oil	1 tablespoon
Tomatoes	4 nos.
Garlic cloves	1 no.
Bouquet garni	1 no.
White wine	125 ml.
Parsley	a little.

Pre-Preparation: Crop the onion, tomato and parsley. Crush garlic. Remove the tuna from the cans.

Method

- Place tuna, side by side on ovenproof dish. Sprinkle with lemon juice and season lightly. Arrange the anchovy fillets on top.
- Fry the onion in the oil until soft. Add the tomatoes, garlic, bouquest garni and wine and bring to the boil. Boil rapidly until this

sauce is reduced and thickened. Pour the sauce over the tuna, cover and bake in a moderate oven, 350°F, gas mark 4, for 15 minutes. Remove the bouquet garni.

Serving

- Serve sprinkled with parsley.

PREPARATION OF MAIN COURSES
1. Roast Leg of Lamb with Mint Sauce

Ingredients	Approx. Quantity
Lamb leg	As required
Mint sauce	

Pre-Preparation: Score the covering of leg fat with the point of a small knife.

Method

- Roast in a hot oven allowing approximately 25-30 minutes, per 1 Kg.

Serving

- Serve with mint sauce.

Mint Sauce

Ingredients	Approx. Quantity
Mint leaves	150 gm.
Sugar	1-2 tablespoons
Vinegar	3-4 tablespoons

Method

- Chop the leaves with a little sugar on the board.
- Put into a sauce boat.
- Add the rest of the sugar and the vinegar.

2. Rolled Rib Roast of Beef with Yorkshire Pudding

Ingredients	Approx. Quantity
Rolled rib roast of beef	1 nos.
Salt and freshly ground	
Black pepper	To taste
Dry mustard	1 teaspoon

Yorkshire pudding

Flour	1 cup
Salt	a pinch
Egg	1 no. (large)
Milk	1 cup

Method

- Rub all the surfaces of the roast beef with the salt and pepper and dry mustard.
- Place on a rack in a roasting pan and cook in a moderate over 350°F (180 C) for 25 minutes per pound (55 minutes per 1 Kg). Keep warm, after removing from the roasting pan.
- Make a gravy from the pan drippings and cook Yorkshire pudding.
- Make a well in the centre in the flour and salt mixed together. Break the egg into the well and gradually stir in the flour. Add half the milk gradually until a smooth batter is formed. Beat with the back of a spoon facing upwards for 10 minutes until bubbles form on the surface. Allow the batter to stand covered for 30 minutes.
- Stir in the rest of the milk just before cooking.
- Grease a large cake pan with the fat from the roast and pour the batter into the pan and cook in a very hot oven 450°F, for 20 minutes or until golden brown and puffed up and crispy.

Note: The saddle should not be boned out or larded.

3. Roast Saddle of Lamb, Mint Sauce

Ingredients	Approx. Quantity
Saddle of lamb	As required

Pre-Preparation: Score the covering of saddle fat with the point of a small knife and then tie up with string.

Method

- Roast in a hot oven allowing approximately 15-18 minutes per 1 Kg.

Serving

- Serve with mint sauce.

4. Roast Turkey

Ingredients	Approx. Quantity
Turking	As required

For stuffing

Sage	
Butter	
Onion	As required
White breadcrumbs	
Milk	
Veal suet	

Pre-Preparation: Prepare the sage and onion stuffing. Remove the tendons from the legs.

Serving

- Sage and Onion stuffing

Method

- Stuff the bird with sage and onion stuffing and roast on slow fire.
- Place on a dish and surround with either grilled sausages or grilled rashers of bacon.

Method

- Bake 4 large unpeeled onions and when soft, peel and chop them finely.
- Melt some butter in a pan, add the onion, a pinch of chopped fresh or rubbed dry sage and cook gently for a few minutes.
- Add the same weight of white breadcrumbs. Soaked in milk and chopped veal suit.

5. Roast Leg of Pork with Apple Sauce

Ingredients	Approx. Quantity
Leg of pork	
Oil	As required
Salt	

Method

Score the rind of the pork at 1/2 cm (1/4 in.) intervals and rub well with oil and salt.

Place on a rack in a roasting tin at a temperature of 220°C (425°F) and cook allowing 25 minutes.

Apple Sauce

Ingredients	Approx. Quantity
Cooking apples	2 nos.
Butter	
Sugar	
Lemon juice	

Method

- Peel, core and slice the apples and cook to a pulp in 2 tablespoons of water.
- Beat until smooth and add the butter. A little sugar may be added, if wished, but a tart sauce is the best accompaniment for pork.

6. Entrecote A La Brodelaise

Ingredients	Approx. Quantity
Sauce Bordelaise	
Sirloin steaks	
Butter	As required
Beef bone marrow	

Pre-Preparation: Prepare sauce Brodelaise

Method

- Season and shallow fry the sirloin steaks in butter and arrange them on a long oval hot dish.
- Place an overlapping line of poached slices of beef bone marrow along the centre of each steak.

Serving

- Serve with sauce Bordelaise separately.

Method of Sauce Brodelaise

Ingredients	Approx. Quantity
Red wine	3 dl
Chopped shallot	30 g.
Ground pepper	a little
Bayleaf	1/2 no.
Thyme	One sprig
Espagnole	5 dl
Melted meat glare	—
Lemon	1/4 portion
Bone marrow	50 gm.

Method

- Place red wine into a small pan with chopped shallot; a little coarsley ground pepper, bayleaf and thyme.
- Reduce it by three quarters.
- Add espagnole and cook for 15 minutes, on slow fire, skimming necessary.
- Pass through a fine strainer and finish the sauce with melted meat glaze, the lemon juice and bone marrow cut into small slices and poached.

7. Sesame Chicken

Ingredients	Approx. Quantity
Chicken breasts, boned	2 nos.
Butter or margarine	50 gm.
Soya sauce	1 tablespoon
White wine	1 tablespoon
Dried tarragon	a pinch
Dry mustard	1/2 teaspoon
Sesame seeds	As required

Pre-Preparation : Put the chicken breasts in a shallow dish and marinate with a mixture of butter or margarine, soya sauce, wine, tarragon and mustard for 3 hours. Drain and reserve the marinade.

Method

- Grill (broil) the chicken for 4 to 6 minutes on each side. Remove from the heat, brush with the reserve marinade and roll in sesame seeds.
- Return to the heat and grill until the sesame seeds are golden brown.

8. Chicken Pie (For 6 portions)

Ingredients	Approx. Quantity
For Pastry	
Flour	200 gms.
Salt	a pinch
Butter or Margarine	150 gms.
Water	As required
Beaten egg	
Filling	
Chicken	1 1/2 Kg.
Onion	1 nos. (Medium size)
Bouquet garni	1 (medium size)
Mushrooms	200 gms.
Butter or Margarine	60 gms.
Flour	30 gms. (1 oz.)
Parsley	1 tablespoon
Salt & Pepper	to taste
Double cream	4 tablespoons
White wine (optional)	2 tablespoons

Pre-Preparation: Chop the onion and parsley. Make the pastry. Shift the flour and salt into a bowl. Add the butter or margarine and cut into small pieces. Add enough water to make a soft dough. Roll out the dough to an oblong on a lightly floured board. Fold the dough in three like an envelope. Roll out again, fold and turn. Repeat the rolling, folding and turning once more and chill well.

Method

- Put the chicken onion and bouquet garni into a sauce pan. Add enough water to cover and bring to the boil. Cover with a tight-fitting lid and simmer for about 1 hour or until the chicken is tender. Remove the chicken from the stock and allow to cool. Strain the stock and reserve about 1/2 pint (250 ml.)
- Fry the mushrooms in the butter or margarine until just tender. Stir in the flour and cook. Stirring, for 1 minute gradually add the reserved chicken stocks, stir constantly. Bring to the boil and simmer for 2 to 3 minutes, stirring, or until the mixture thickens. Stir in the parsley, seasoning, cream and wine if used. Remove from the heat and keep aside.
- Take the chicken meat off the carcass, remove the skin and cut the meat into bite-sized pieces. Put the chicken meat, in alternating layers with the mushrooms mixture, in a 1 litre or 5 cup pie dish. Let it cool.
- Roll out the dough to about 1/4 inch thickness and large enough to cover the pie dish with a 1/2 inch border. Cut 1/2 inch border from the dough, dampen the rim of the pie dish and press the border strip on to it. Place a pie funnel in the centre of the pie dish and lay the dough

over the top, pressing firmly on to the border strip to seal. Crimp the edge and use the dough trimming to decorate the top. Brush with beaten egg. Bake in a hot oven, 425 F, gas mark 7, for 25 to 30 minutes or until the pastry is risen and golden brown.

9. Barbecued Chicken

Ingredients	Approx. Quantity
Oil or melted butter or Margarine	2 tablespoons
Prepared mustard	1 tablespoon
Worcestershire sauce	few drops
Chicken drumsticks	6 nos.

Pre-Preparation: Mix together the oil or melted butter or margarine, mustard and Worcestershire sauce.

Method

● Brush the drumsticks with this mixture and cook them over the barbecue, with sausages, tomatoes, and jacket potatoes.

10. Gammon with Pineapple and Corn Sauce

Ingredients	Approx. Quantity
Lean gammon	2 slices
Butter or Margarine (melted)	50 gm.
Canned pineapple rings (halved)	3 to 4
Sauce	
Butter or margarine	12 1/2 gms.
Flour	12 1/2 gms.
Milk	125 ml (1/4 pint)
Salt and pepper	to taste
Onion	1 no. (small)
Cooked sweet corn	4 tablespoons
Parsley	2 tablespoons
Watercress	
Syrup from the can of pineapple	2 tablespoons.

Pre-Preparation: Chop the onion and parsley. Melt the butter or Margarine.

Method

● Strip the fat off the gammon. Brush it with melted butter or margarine and grill (broil) for several minutes on one side. Turn, brush with more butter or margarine and continue cooking. When the gammon is nearly ready, add the pineapple rings to the grill (broiler) pan. Brush them with the remainder of the melted butter or margarine and heat thoroughly.

For sauce

● Melt the butter or margarine in a saucepan and stir in the flour. Cook, stirring for 1 minute. Gradually add the milk, stirring constantly, and simmer until the mixture is thick. Add seasoning, the onion, sweetcorn, and parsley and warm gently.

Serving

● Place the gammon and pineapple on a plate and garnish with watercress; and whisk the pineapple syrup into the sauce.

11. Beef Goulash

Ingredients	Approx. Quantity
Chuck steaks (cut into cubes)	3/4 Kg.
Onions	3 nos.
Butter or Margarine	50 gm.
Stock	250 ml.
Paprika	1 tablespoon
Tomatoes	1/2 Kg.
Salt & pepper	To taste
Potatoes	1/2 Kg.
Soured cream or plain Yogurt	As required
Parsley	

Pre-Preparation: Cut the chuck steak into cubes. Slice the onions. Chop the tomatoes & parsley. Cut the potatoes into pieces.

Method

● Brown the meat and onions in the butter or margarine.
● Mix together the stock and paprika and add to the pan with the tomatoes and

seasoning to taste. Simmer gently for hours, then add the potatoes. Continue cooking for another 45 mins.

Serving

● Serve, topped with soured or yogurt and parslev.

12. Braised Beef Neapolitan

Ingredients	Approx. Quantity
Braising steaks	150 to 200 gms.
Salt and pepper	to taste
Tomatoes	1/2 kg
Onion	1 no.
Garlic clove	1 no.
Bay leaf	1 no.
Mixed dried herbs	1/2 teaspoon

Pre-Preparation: Chop the onion and the tomatoes. Crush, garlic.

Method

● Season the steaks and grill (broil) them for 5 minutes on each side.
● Mix together the remaining ingredients.
● Place the steaks in a casserole and spoon over the tomato mixture.
● Braise in *a* moderate oven, 350°F, gas mark 4, for 1 hour.

13. Cold Loin or Pork Orientale

Ingredients	Approx. Quantity
Loin of pork, (boned and rolled)	2 1/2 kg.
Dry mustard sherry	100 ml.
Soya sauce	100 ml.
Fresh ginger or	1 tablespoon
Ground ginger	2 tablespoons
Garlic cloves	2 nos.
Red currant jelly	200 gm.

Pre-Preparation: Grate the ginger. Crush the garlic. Rub the pork with mustard. Mix together sherry and soya sauce, ginger and garlic. Pour this mixture over the pork, and leave to marinate for 2 hours, turning occasionally.

Method

● Place the pork on a rack in a roasting pan and roast in a moderate oven, 350°F, gas mark 4, for 2 to 3 hours or until the meat is cooked. Paste with the marinate from time to time during the roasting.
● Melt the red currant jelly in a saucepan. Stir in the remaining 2 tablespoons each of sherry and soya sauce and heat for 1 minute. Spoon this mixture over the pork and leave in a cold place. Serve at room temperature.

14. Lamb Shikh-kebabs with Herbed Sauce

Ingredients	Approx. Quantity
Lean lamb (from the leg) cut into 1 inch (2½ cm.) cubes	1/2 kg.
Green pepper (pith and seeds removed, cut into chunks)	1 no.
Button mushrooms	8 to 12
Tomatoes	4 nos.
Onions	12 nos.
Butter or margarine	25 gms.
Salt and pepper	To taste.
Sauce	
Tomato juice	225 ml.
Prepared mustard	2 teaspoons
Plain yoghurt	125 ml.
Cayenne pepper	a pinch
Fresh mint	4 teaspoons
Chives or spring onions	4 teaspoons
Salt and pepper	to taste
Ground cinnamon	1/2 teaspoon

Pre-Preparation: Chop mint and chives. Mix together all the ingredient for the sauce in a shallow dish. Put the lamb cubes into the sauce and leave to marinate for 3-4 hours, turn several times. Lift the cubes out of the sauce and thread on to four skewers with the green pepper and mushrooms, tomatoes and onions. Brush the vegetables not the meat with the melted butter or margarine and season.

Method

- Grill, lamb cubes until tender. Brush the meat once or twice with the sauce.

Serving

- Serve with gently heated sauce.

PREPARATION OF SWEETS

1. Charlotte Rousee

Ingredients	Approx. Quantity
Pineapple	4 small slices
Syrup	100 ml.
Red jelly	25 gm.
Gelatin	ii teaspoons
Lemon juice	2 teaspoons
Sponge fingers	7 to 8 nos.
Cream	100 gm.
Powdered sugar	30 gm.
Cherries	2-3 nos.

Method

- Melt the jelly in 125 ml. of boiling water. Cool and pour into a wet mould. Put to set in a refrigerator.
- Cut sponge fingers and keep aside the trimmings and arrange them as a border over the jelly.
- Chop the pineapple slices.
- Add gelatin to syrup and heat. Then add lemon juice to gelatin mixture.
- Beat the cream with sugar and mix with chopped pineapple and gelatine in a bowl and place this bowl in ice cubes, stirring continuously until the mixture thickens.
- Now add the trimmings of the sponge fingers and pour this mixture over the jelly and put to set in a refrigerator.
- Unmould it in hot water for a few seconds and invert on a serving plate and garnish with whipped cream and cherries.

2. Strawberry Whip

Ingredients	Approx. Quantity
Milk	3/4 litres
Strawberries	1/2 Kg.
Vanilla Ice cream	4 tablespoons
Sugar	50 gms.
Vanilla essence or brandy	1 tablespoon
Ice cubes	
Whipping cream (whipped)	125 ml. (1/4 pint).
Strawberries	To garnish

Method

- Blend the milk, strawberries, ice-cream, sugar and vanilla or brandy together in a liquidizer.
- Pour on to the ice cubes in serving glasses.

Serving

- Serve, top with whipped cream and whole straw-berries.

3. Almond and Strawberry Gateau

Ingredients	Approx. Quantity
Blanched almonds	50 gm.
Egg whites	2 nos.
Vinegar	1/2 teaspoon
Castor sugar	100 gms

Glaze

Red currant jelly	6 tablespoons
Lemon juice	1 tablespoon
Arrowroot	1/2 teaspoon
Water	3 tablespoons

Topping

Strawberries	450-700 g (1-1 1/2 lb.)
Double cream (whipped)	150 ml/1/4 pint

Pre-Preparation: Chop almonds and brown the almonds under the grill cool it. Whisk the egg whites, until stiff, add the vinegar and the sugar.

Method

- Line a 20 cm/8 inch sandwich tin with oiled paper or silicone paper. Spread the meringue over this and allow to set for about 1 hour in the centre of a very slow oven (130-140°C/250-275°F).
- Put the jelly and lemon juice into a pan. Blend the arrowroot and water and add to the pan. Stir over a low heat until the

jelly melts and continue stirring until clear. Allow it to cool and then brush a little over the meringue base, top with the strawberries then the rest of the glaze. Before serving decorate with cream.

4. Apple Mousse

Ingredients	Approx. Quantity
Apples	1 large plus 1 small
Lemon	1/4 portion.
Gelatin	1½ teaspoons
Egg	1 nos.
Cream	50 gms.
Sugar	15 gm.

Pre-Preparation: Peel one large apple. Cut it into small pieces.

Method

- Add 1 Tablespoon water and lemon rind to apples and cook.
- Sieve and get the puree.
- Take out lemon juice and melt gelatin in it (and water if required).
- Add to apple puree.
- Whisk the egg and sugar into a bowl over boiling water until thick and creamy.
- Add egg and sugar to apple puree.
- Beat the cream and fold in the apple mixture.
- Pour into a suitable size wet mould and set in refrigerator.
- When set, unmould it.

Serving

- Serve, decorated with water thin slices of red apple

5. Trifle Pudding

Ingredients	Approx. Quantity
Sponge cake	of 1 egg.
Fruit cocktail	½ small can.
Sugar	15 gm.
Milk	150 ml.
Custard powder	1½ teaspoons
Cream	100 ml.
Castor sugar	1 teaspoon

Pre-Preparation: Prepare sponge cake of one egg.

Prepare custard: Dissolve custard powder in a small amount of milk. Bring the rest of the milk to boil, add custard mixture to it with constant stirring, add sugar and cook till the custard coats the back of the spoon.

Method

- Take a glass dish, place the sponge in it and soak it with syrup from fruit cocktail.
- Arrange the fruit around the cake in the dish.
- Pour custard over it and set in refrigerator.
- Beat the cream with 1 t castor sugar till stiff and spread 3/4 of the cream over custard layer.
- Colour the rest of the cream.

Serving

- Serve, decorated with coloured cream.

6. Fresh Fruit Salad

Ingredients	Approx. Quantity
Water	250 ml.
Oranges	2 nos.
Lemon	1 no.
Sugar	75-100 gm.
Mixed prepared fresh fruit	1 Kg.

Method

- Put the water with thin strips of the orange and lemon rind into a saucepan.
- Simmer for 5 minutes.
- Add the sugar, stir until dissolved, then add the orange and lemon juice.
- Strain over the fruit and allow to become cold.

7. Gateaur De Peaches

Ingredients	Approx. Quantity
Light sponge cake	of 4 eggs.
Whipped cream	1/2 tin
Peaches	1 tin
Jam	100 gm.
Pista	30 gm.

Method

- Sandwich sponge with whipped cream and chopped peaches.
- Smear strawberry jam on top and sides.
- Arrange peaches on top and centre.
- Pipe cream in between peaches, in centre and on sides.

Serving

- Serve, sprinkled with pista on top.

8. Frosted Coffee Gateau

Ingredients	Approx. Quantity
Butter (softened)	75 gm.
Egg (large)	3 nos.
Castor sugar	150 gm.
Instant coffee powder	3 teaspoons
Boiling water	3 tablespoons
Sponge finger biscuits	225 gms.
Walnuts	50 gm.

Decoration: Take the butter out of the refrigerator and leave in a warm place. Crumble the sponge biscuits into fine crumbs. Chop the nuts. Blend the biscuits and nuts with the coffee mixture.

Method

- Whisk the eggs and sugar in a heatproof bowl over a pan of very hot water until thick and creamy. Gradually whisk in the butter. Remove from the heat. Dissolve the coffee in the boiling water and whisk into the egg mixture. Allow to cool.
- Line a loaf tin with waxed paper. Spoon in the mixture and freeze until firm. Turn out. Whip the cream until it just stands in peaks. Spoon over the top of the coffee gateau.

Serving

- Serve, decorated with the halved walnuts.

9. Black Forest Cherry Gateau

(This magnificient gateau is always served with afternoon coffee, but it also makes served chilled from the refrigerator)

Ingredients	Approx. Quantity
Cherries	
Morello cherries	4 cups
Sugar	1/2 cup plus 2 tablespoons
Pastry Base	
Flour	1 cup
Butter	1/4 cup
Sugar	35-40 gms.
Almonds	10-12 gms.
Rind of lemon	1/4 portion
Egg yolk	1 no.
Chocolate Sponge Cake	
Flour	30-35 gm.
Cornstarch	30-35 gm.
Baking powder	5 gm.
Egg yolks	4 nos.
Cocoa	30-35 gm.
Butter	1/4 cup
Filling	
Heavy cream	21/2 cup
Sugar	40-45 gm.
Kirsch	30-35 gm.
Grated semirsweet chocolate	45 ml.

Pre-Preparation: Greate the rind of lemon. Melt and cool butter. Toss the cherries lightly with the sugar and put them aside.

Method

- To make the pastry base, sift the flour into a bowl and rub in the butter until the mixture resembles fine breadcrumbs. Stir in the sugar, ground almonds and grated lemon rind. Add the egg yolk and knead the ingredients to a firm dough. Shape it into, a ball Wrap it in foil and leave it in a cool place for at least 30 minutes.
- Preheat the oven to 350°F and butter a spring-form pan.
- Roll the dough thinly and line the base of the prepared pan with it. Bake for 20 minutes. Let the baked pastry rest in the pan for a few minutes before transferring it to a wire rack to cool.
Wipe the cake pan clean and grease it with more butter.

- To make the cake, sift the flour, cornstarch and baking powder together. Beat the egg yolks with the sugar and 4 tablespoons of hot water until the mixture is thick and foamy. Beat the egg whites until stiff but not dry.
- With a large metal spoon, fold the sifted flour, cornstarch and baking powder into the egg yolk mixture, and at last add sifted cocoa. Then, fold in the beaten egg whites and finally, the melted butter.
- Pour the butter into the prepared pan. Bake for 35 to 40 minutes, or until the cake is well risen and has shrunk slightly from the sides of the pan. Let the cake stand for a few minutes before turning it out on to a wire rack to cool.
- Put the sugared cherries together with their juices in a heavy saucepan. Bring them to a boil over low heat. Drain the cherries, return the juice to the pan and boil until it is reduced to a thick syrup. Pour this over the cherries and keep aside to cool.
- To make the filling, whisk the cream lightly. Add the sugar and kirsch, and continue to whisk the cream until stiff.
- To assemble the gateau, cut the chocolate cake in half horizontally. Place the pastry base on a flat serving dish, spread it with one-third of the kirsch cream and spoon half of the cherries and the syrup evenly over the top cover with a layer of chocolate cake. Spread it with half of the remaining cream, after then spread the remaining cherries and syrup. Put the second layer of chocolate cake on top. Spread it with the remaining cream and decorate the top with a sprinkling of grated chocolate.
- Chill until ready to serve.

CHINESE COURSE—
ITEMS AND PREPARATIONS

A. Appitizers

1. Fried Wonton
2. Ham and Chicken Rolls
3. Barbecued Spareribs
4. Chicken and Banana Squares
5. Hors d'Oeuvre Rolls
6. Stuffed Mushrooms

B. Soups

1. Crab Combination Soup
2. Long Soup
3. Szechuan Soup
4. Hot and Sour Soup
5. Wonton Soup
6. Velvet Corn Soup
7. Chicken Noodle Soup
8. Sweet Corn Chicken Soup
9. Vegetable Soup
10. Egg Drop Soup

C. Pork

1. Spiced Pork
2. Barbecued Pork Spareribs
3. Trotters with Ginger
4. Sweet and Sour Pork
5. Pork Ribs With Chilli Plum Sauce
6. Garlic Pork Rashers
7. Mu-shu-jou (Egg Flower Pork)
8. Twice-cooked Pork

D. Fowl

1. Garlic Chicken
2. Almond Chicken
3. Lemon Chicken

4. Szechwan Duck
5. Eight-jewel Duck
6. Peking Duck
7. Honey Chilli Chicken
8. Beggar's Chicken
9. Chicken With Asparagus
10. Snow White Chicken
11. Cashew Chicken

E. Chow Mein

1. Beef chow mein
2. Chicken chow mein
3. Vegetable chow mein

F. Rice

1. Fried rice
2. Stir-fried rice stick noodles with shrimp and vegetables
3. Ham and egg fried rice
4. Hunan steamed rice

G. Sea Food

1. Seafood combination
2. Scallop and vegetable combination
3. Sute prawns
4. Crab claws
5. Abalone in oyster sauce
6. Shrimp with green peas
7. Barbecue prawns
8. Squid with broccoli
9. Bamboo prawns
10. Chinese bream
11. Braised prawns with vegetables
12. Steamed sea bass with fermented black beans

13. Deep fried shrimp balls
14. Stir Fried sea scallops and pork kidneys

H. Beef

1. Saute beef
2. Braised star anise beef
3. Curried beef
4. Beef with celery
5. Beef with cashews
6. Ginger beef

7. Pepper steak
8. Beef with black bean sauce

I. Vegetables

1. Stir-fried spiced cabbage
2. Stir-fried string beans and water Chestnuts
3. Chinese vegetables
4. Stir-fried snow peas with Chinese Mushrooms and bamboo shoots
5. Braised bean curd with mushroom and hot meat sauce

PREPARATION OF APPETIZERS
1. Fried Wonton

Ingredients	Approx. Quantity
Wonton wrappers	1/2 Pkt.
Lean minced pork	500 Gm
Finely chopped uncooked spinach	1 Cup
Dried sherry, salt, pepper	1 tablespoon
Dried mushrooms	30 gm.
Oil for deep frying	

Pre-Preparation: Put dried mushrooms in hot water for 30 minutes. Then squeeze dry and chop finely. Put into bowl with pork mince spinach, sherry salt and pepper. Mix well.

Method

- Put a teaspoon of mixture in centre of each wonton wrapper.
- Gather edges of wonton wrapper around filling, press together firmly at top, above filling.
- Heat oil in pan or wok, deep fry wonton until golden brown, drain on observant paper.

Serving

- Serve with sweet and sour sauce over wontons.

Sweet and Sour Sauce

Ingredients	Approx. Quantity
White vinegar	1/2 cup
Canned pineapple juice	1 cup
Soya sauce	2 teaspoons
Tomato sauce	3 teaspoons
Sugar	1/2 cup
Corn flour	2 tablespoons
Water	1/4 cup
Chinese mixed pickle	184 gm.

Method

- Put vinegar, pineapple juice, soy sauce, tomato sauce and sugar in sauce pan and boil them.

- Add combined cornflour and water, stir until sauce boils and thickens, reduce heat, and cook for three minutes.
- Add drained and sliced pickle, cook further three minutes.

2. Ham and Chicken Rolls

Ingredients	Approx. Quantity
Chicken breasts	2 whole
Ham	4 slices
Salt	1 teaspoon
Pepper	1/2 teaspoon
Five spice powder	1/4 teaspoon
Garlic	1 clove
Wrapper flour	4 sprig roll
Egg	1 no.
Milk	2 tablespoons
Oil	for deep frying

Pre-Preparation: Remove skin from chicken breasts. Remove chicken meat from bones and make four individual pieces. Separate the fillets which runs along the bone on either side.

Method

- Pound breast pieces and fillet pieces out separately until very thin. Lay fillet piece on top of each large breast, pound lightly. Spread chicken pieces with combined salt, pepper, five spice powder and crushed garlic. Roll each slice of ham and place on top of chicken, roll up firmly.
- Dip chicken rolls in flour, then in combined beaten egg and milk. Place chicken roll diagonally across spring roll wrapper. Fold in ends and roll up squarely. Seal end with a little of the egg mixture.
- Deep fry rolls in hot oil until golden brown and cooked through about three minutes. After then drain on absorbent paper.

Serving

- Cut the rolls into diagonal slices and serve.

3. Barbecued Spareribs

Ingredients	Approx. Quantity
Spare ribs (in one piece)	2 pound
Marinade	
Soy sauce	1/4 cup
Honey	2 teaspoon
Hoisin sauce	2 teaspoon
White vinegar	2 teaspoon
Chinese rice wine	
or	
Pale dry sherry	1 tablespoon
Finely chopped garlic	1 teaspoon
Sugar	1 teaspoon
Chicken stock, fresh or canned	2 tablespoons
Canned plum sauce	

Pre-Preparation: Trim fat from the spare ribs. If the breaststone is still attached, use a cleaver to chop it away from the ribs and discard it. Place the spare ribs in a long, shallow dish. In a small bowl, combine the soy sauce, honey, hoisin sauce, vinegar, wine, garlic, sugar and chicken stock. Stir until they are well mixed. Pour the sauce over the spare ribs, baste them thoroughly and let them marinate for 3 hours at room temperature, turning them over in the marinade and basting them every hour or so.

Method

- Pre-heat the oven to 375°C. Insert the curved tips of two or three S-shaped hooks—such as curtain hooks or 5-inch lengths of heavy-duty wire or even unpainted coat hangers bent into shapes— at each end of the spare ribs.
- As if hanging a hammock, use the curved ends of the hooks to suspend the ribs from upper-most rack of the oven directly for 45 minutes. Then raise the oven heat to 450° and roast about 15 minutes longer, or until the spare ribs are crisp and a deep golden brown.

Serving

- To serve, place the ribs on a chopping board and with a cleaver, separate the strip into individual ribs. If the ribs are large, chop them and serve hot or cold with plum sauce.

4. Chicken and Banana Squares

Ingredients	Approx. Quantity
Slice bread	6 squares
Chicken breasts	2 nos.
Bananas	2 nos.
Eggs	3 nos.
Milk	3 tablespoons
Flour	As required
Fresh Breadcrumbs	2 cups
Oil	for deep frying

Pre-Preparation: Remove crusts from bread, and cut each slice into four squares. Steam or boil chicken in usual way until tender, allow to cool in water and then remove skin from chicken. Carefully remove chicken meat from bones and make four pieces of chicken. Cut each piece of chicken in half horizontally and make eight slices of chicken; cut each slice into three. Peel bananas, cut in half horizontally. Cut each length of banana into pieces the same as the chicken. Brush one side of each piece of bread with combined beaten egg and milk. Arrange a piece of chicken on top of the egg glazed side. Arrange a piece of banana on top of the chicken. Coat chicken and banana squares lightly with flour, holding chicken and banana firmly on to the bread. Dip in combined beaten egg and milk, coat well with breadcrumbs. Repeat once more with egg mixture and breadcrumbs.

Method

- Deep-fry in hot oil until golden brown.
- Drain on absorbent paper.

Serving

- Serve with sauce.

5. Hors d'Oeuvre Rolls

Ingredients	Approx. Quantity
Puff pastry	375 gm.
Butter	30 gm.
Minced pork	125 gm.
Mushrooms	60 gm.
Shallots	6 nos.
Cooked prawns	250 gms.
Hard boiled egg	1 no.
Egg noodles (roughly broken)	1/2 cup fine
Salt, pepper	to taste
Dry sherry	1 tablespoon
Egg (for glazing)	1 no.
Oil	for deep frying

Pre-Preparation: Cook noodles in boiling salted water for three minutes or until tender, rinse under hot water, drain. Shell prawns. Chop mushrooms, shallots, prawns, egg and noodles.

Method

- Heat butter in pan, add pork mince, saute until well browned. Add mushrooms and shallots, saute further two minutes. Remove from heat, add shelled prawns, egg, noodles, sherry,' salt and pepper. Mix well.
- Cut pastry in half, roll each half into rectangle 40 cm x 33 cm (16 x 13 inch); with sharp knife, trim to 38 x 30 cm (15 x 12 inch). Cut each piece into five 8 cm. (3 inch) strips, then each strip into four 8 cm. (3 inch) squares.
- Put a heaped teaspoonful of mixture in centre of each square. Leave edges free. Glaze edges with lightly beaten egg.
- Roll up pastry lightly, securing edges together with beaten egg. Deep fry in hot oil until golden brown. Drain on absorbent paper.

Serving

- Serve hot with soy sauce or sweet and sour sauce.

6. Stuffed Mushrooms

Ingredients	Approx. Quantity
Mushroom (mid.)	500 gm.
Flour	As required
Salt & Pepper	
Oil (for deep-frying)	
Stuffing	
Pork mince	250 gm.
Shallots	4 nos.
Red Pepper	
Celery	
Water chestnuts	
Green ginger	2.5 cm (1 inch) piece
Dry sherry	
Soy sauce	
Egg white	
Hoisin sauce	1 teaspoon
Salt	1/4 teaspoons
Cornflour	2 teaspoons
Batter	
Cornflour	
Plain flour	
Baking powder	1/2 teaspoon
Salt	
Water	1/4 cup
Milk	1/4 cup

Pre-Preparation: Remove stems from mushrooms. Finely chop stems, add to prepared stuffing; mix well. To prepare the stuffing put mince, chopped shallots, seeded and finely chopped pepper, finely chopped celery, water chestnuts, peeled and grated green ginger, sherry, any sauce, egg white, hoisin sauce, salt and corn flour in a bowl; Mix well. Fill stuffing into cavity of mushrooms. Mound the filling in the centre. To make the batter, sift dry ingredients into bowl, make a well in the centre and gradually add milk and water. Mix to a smooth batter. Coat mushrooms with flour seasoned with salt and pepper. Dip in prepared batter.

Method

Put mushrooms a few at a time into deep hot oil. Fry until golden brown and cook for approximately five minutes. (Do not have oil too hot or mushrooms will brown too quickly and not cook through).

PREPARATION OF SOUPS

1. Crab Combination Soup

Ingredients	Approx. Quantity
Chicken stock	1/2 litres
Oil	1 teaspoon
Egg	1 no.
Shallots	8 no.
Dried mushrooms	30 gms.
Can bamboo shoots	1/2 * 230 gm.
Grated green ginger	1/2
Can crab meat	150 gm.
Scallops	125 gm.
Cornflour	
Water	
Chicken stock cubes	
Soy sauce	
Dry sherry	as required
Salt, pepper	
Egg whites	
Water (extra)	

Pre-Preparation: Cover mushrooms with boiling water, 30 minutes. Drain, remove stalks and slice thinly. Chop shallots, cut bamboo shoots into fine strips. Wash scallops; and slit them along back and remove dark vein; slice scallops thinly. Drain and flake crab. Lightly beat egg with fork.

Method

- Heat oil in small frying pan, add egg, swirl egg in pan to coat sides and base of pan evenly. Loosen edges of pancake with spatula turn and cook other side. Remove from pan, roll up, slice into thin strips.
- Put chicken stock into large pan, bring to boil. Add mushrooms, bamboo shoots, shallots, ginger, crab meat, scallops, salt and pepper. Bring to boil, reduce heat and cook for two minutes. Remove from heat, stir until soup comes to boil, reduce heat, cook uncovered for two minutes.
- Beat egg whites and extra water lightly, add to soup and mix well.

2. Long Soup

Ingredients	Approx. Quantity
Lean pork	500 gm.
Shallots	200 gm.
Cabbage (small)	250 gm.
Oil	2 tablespoons
Chicken stock	3 litre (12 cups)
Grated green ginger	1 teaspoon
Chicken stock cubes	4 no.
Soy sauce	3 teaspoons
Salt, pepper	to taste
Fine egg noodles	200 gm.
Shallots (extra)	6 nos.

Pre-Preparation: Peel shallots and cut in thin slices. Slice pork into fine shreds. Shreds cabbage finely.

Method

- Heat oil in large pan or wok, add pork and cabbage, fry quickly a few minutes. Stir constantly.
- Add stock, salt, pepper, crumbled stock cubes, soy sauce and ginger. Bring slowly to the boil, reduce heat, add shallots and cook for 10-15 minutes.
- Cook noodles in boiling salted water until tender, and drain well.

Serving

Place a spoonful of noodles in soup bowls. Pour the hot soup over, sprinkle a few extra chopped shallots on top.

3. Szechuan Soup

Ingredients	Approx. Quantity
Lean pork	200 gm
Ham	125 gm.
Dried mushrooms	8 nos.
Red pepper	1/2 no.
Chinese pickles	30 gm.
Can water chestnuts	500 gm.
Shallots	8 nos.
Prawns	250 gm.
Chicken stock	if litres
Dry white wine	1/2 cup
Soy sauce	1 tablespoon

Ingredients	Approx. Quantity
Chilli sauce	1/2 teaspoon
Salt	1/2 teaspoon
Cornflour	2 tablespoons
Water	1/4 cup
Sesame oil	1 teaspoon
Vinegar	2 teaspoons
Egg	1 no.
Water (extra)	1 tablespoon
Bean curd	250 gm.

***Pre-Preparation*:** Put mushrooms with 1/2 cup of warm water for 30 minutes. Discard the water. Cut away and discard the rough stems of mushrooms, and shred the caps by placing one at a time on a chopping board. Cut them horizontally into paper-thin slice, and then into thin strips. Drain the pieces of bamboo shoot and bean curd, and rinse them in cold water. Shred them as fine as the mushrooms. With a cleaver or sharp knife, trim the pork of all fat. Then shred it, too by slicing, the meat as thin as possible and cutting the slices into narrow strips about 1 to 2 inches long.

Method

- In a heavy 3-quart saucepan combine the stock, salt, soy sauce, mushrooms, bamboo shoots and pork. Bring to a boil over high heat, then immediately reduce the heat to low, cover the pan and cook for 3 minutes. Drop in the bean curd, and the pepper and vinegar. Bring to a boil again. Give the cornstarch mixture a stir to recombine it and pour it into the soup. Stir for a few seconds until the soup thickens, then slowly pour in the beaten egg, stirring continuously.

Serving

- Remove the soup from the heat and put it into a tureen or serving bowl. Stir in the sesame-seed oil and sprinkle the top with scallions. Serve at once.

4. Hot and Sour Soup

Ingredients	Approx. Quantity
Chinese mushrooms	4 nos. (1 to 1/2" inch in diameter)
Fresh Chinese bean curd	2 squs., 3" each.
Canned bamboo shoots	1 cup
Boneless pork	1/4 pound
Chicken stock	1 quart
Salt	1 teaspoon
Soy sauce	1 teaspoon
Ground white pepper	1/4 teaspoon
White vinegar	2 tablespoons
Cold water	3 tablespoons
Egg (lightly beaten)	1 no.
Sesame-seed oil	2 teaspoons
Scallion, (including the green top)	1 no.

***Pre-Preparation*:** Soak mushrooms in hot water for 30 minutes; drain, squeeze dry, remove stems and slice thinly. Cut pork, ham, and pickles into fine shreds. Remove seeds from pepper, slice into thin strips. Chop shallots, slice water chestnuts. Shell prawns, remove dark vein.

Method

- Put chicken stock, wine, soy sauce, chilli sauce and salt into large saucepan, bring to boil, boil uncovered for five minutes. Remove pan from heat. Put water and cornflour into bowl, stir until combined. Gradually add cornflour mixture to chicken stock. Stir until combined.
- Heat pan, stir until soup comes to boil, reduce heat, add ham, mushrooms, pork, pickles, water chestnuts and red pepper, stir until combined. Cook uncovered for five minutes.
- Stir in vinegar and sesame oil. Beat egg and extra water lightly with a fork. Gradually add to chicken stock. Stir constantly. Add shallots, bean curd cut into 1 cm (1/2 inch) cubes and prawns. Cook for one minute and serve.

5. Wonton Soup

Ingredients	Approx. Quantity
Wonton wrappers	1/2 pound
Lean boneless pork	3/4 pound
Soy sauce	4 teaspoons
Ginger root (finely chopped peeled)	3/4 teaspoons
Salt	3/4 teaspoons
Spinach	3/4 pound
For the soup	
Thicken stock (fresh or canned)	6 cups
Fresh spinach	1 cup

Pre-Preparation

To make the filling: In a large bowl, combine the pork, soy sauce, ginger and salt and mix them thoroughly. Then mix in the spinach.

To assemble the wontons: Place 1 teaspoon or so of the filling just below the centre of each wrapper. Fold one side over the filling and tuck its edge under the filling. Then, moisten the exposed sides of the wrapper and roll up the filled cylinder, leaving 1/2 inch of wrapper unrolled at the top. Now take the two ends of the cylinder in the fingers of both hands and pull them down beneath the roll until the ends meat and overlap slightly. Pinch the ends firmly together. Place them on a plate and cover with a dry towel.

Method

- In a 4 to 5 quart saucepan, bring 2 quarts of water to a boil, and drop in the wonton. Return to a boil, reduce the heat to moderate and cook uncovered for 5 minutes, or until tender but still a little resistant to the bite. Drain the wontons through a colander. Pour the stock into the pan and bring to a boil, add the spinach and the wontons, and again boil it.

Serving

- Serve at once.

6. Velvet Corn Soup

Ingredients	Approx. Quantity
Fresh ears of corn, shucked	2 nos. (large)
Egg whites	2 nos.
Milk	2 tablespoons
Chicken stock (fresh or canned)	3 cups.
Salt	1 teaspoon
Cornstarch	1 tablespoon (dissolved in 2 tablespoons cold chicken stock fresh or canned or cold water)
Smithfield ham slice (1/8 inch)	about 1 cup. (finely chopped)

Pre-Preparation: Slice the kernels of fresh corn from their cobs into a bowl. In a small bowl beat the egg whites with a fork until frothy. Then beat in the 2 tablespoons of milk.

Method

- In a 2 quart saucepan, bring the chicken stock to a boil over high heat. Add the corn and salt, and stirring constantly, bring to a boil again.
- Stir the cornstarch mixture to recombine it and pour it into the soup. Cook, stirring constantly, until the soup has thickened and immediately pour in the egg white mixture, stir only once.

Serving

- Pour the hot soup into a tureen or individual bowls, sprinkle with the chopped ham and serve.

7. Chicken Noodle Soup

Ingredients	Approx. Quantity
Dried Chinese mushrooms	4 nos.
Cooked Chicken	1/2 cup (slice 1/8 inch thick and cut into 1 inch squares)
Roast pork	
Smithfield ham	
Canned bamboo shoots	1/4 cup thinly sliced

Ingredients	Approx. Quantity
Loosely packed watercress leaves	1/2 cup
Fresh Chinese egg noodles	1/2 pound
Salt	1 teaspoon
Chicken stock (fresh or canned)	4 cups

Pre-Preparation: Cover the mushrooms with half cup of warm water and for 30 minutes. Discard the water. Cut away and discard the tough stems of the mushrooms and cut the caps in half.

Method

- In a 3 or 4 quart pot, bring 2 quarts of water to a boil over high heat. Drop in the noodles and boil the vigorously, uncovered, for 2 minutes stirring occasionally.
- Drain the noodles through large sieve and pour cold water over them to stop their cooking.
- Now bring the stock to a boil. In the same pot add the mushrooms, bamboo shoots, water-cress, salt and noodles and reduce the heat to low. Cook uncovered, for about 2 minutes.

Serving

- Lift the noodles and vegetables out of the simmering soup with a bamboo strainer or slotted spoon, or serving bowl. Arrange the chicken, pork and ham on top of them. Pour in the soup stock down one side of the bowl and serve at once.

8. Sweet Corn Chicken Soup

Ingredients	Approx. Quantity
Chicken	50 gm.
Sweet corn	50 gm.
Chicken stock	1½ cup
Corn flour	1½ teaspoons
Egg white	1/2 portion
Salt	1/4 teaspoon
Pepper powder	1/8 teaspoon
Soy sauce and chilli sauce	to taste

Method

- Boil and shred the chicken.

- Boil the stock, add sweet corn and shredded chicken to it and bring to a boil again.
- Make a paste of cornflour and add to boiling soup with constant stirring. Add seasoning and cook for 2-3 minutes or till it thickens and then add egg whites.
- Add soy sauce and chilli sauce before serving.

9. Vegetable Soup

Ingredients	Approx. Quantity
Spring onions	2 nos. (large)
Cabbage	1/2 cup
French beans	1/2 cup
Carrots	1/2 cup
Flowerettes of cauliflower	1/2 cup
Oil	30 ml.
Ajinomoto	1 gm.
Water	5 cups
White pepper	5 gms.
Sugar	5 gms.
Soy sauce	5 gms.
Salt	to taste
Cornflour (mixed with 1 cup water)	50-55 gm.

Pre-Preparation: Peel the onions and chop into 8 long pieces.

Method

- Heat the oil and add the spring onions, cabbage, French beans, carrots, cauliflower, ajinomoto, pepper and salt. When starts boiling, slow the fire and cook for 2 minutes.
- Now add cornflour and bring to boil. Then slow the fire and cook again for 2 minutes.

10. Egg Drop Soup
(Egg drop soup is an appetizing first course)

Ingredients	Approx. Quantity
Celery	1/4 cup
Mushrooms	25 gm.
Onion (green)	1 no.
Chicken stock	3 cups.
Salt	1/2 teaspoon (2 gm.)
Pepper	few grains
Egg	1 no.

Pre-Preparation: Slice celery, mushroom and onions thinly. Beat egg.

Method

- Combine vegetables and chicken stock in a saucepan. Stir in salt and pepper, bring to boil and cook for 5 minutes.
- Reduce heat and drizzle egg slowly into stock while stirring. Stir until egg separates into shreds. Cook 1 minute before serving.

PREPARATION OF PORK

1. Spiced Pork

Ingredients	Approx.
Lean pork chops	1.5 kg.
Five spice powder	1/2 teaspoon
Sweet sherry	tablespoon
Cornflour	tablespoons
Salt, pepper	To taste
Soy sauce	2 tablespoons
Green ginger	1 teaspoon
Water	1/4 cup
Chicken stock cube	1 no.
Soy sauce (extra)	2 teaspoons
Oil	for frying

Pre-Preparation: Trim chops, discard remaining ingredients in bowl, except chicken stock cube, water and extra soy sauce; add chops, and mix well. Keep aside for two hours. Stir occasionally.

Method

- Pour oil into wok or pan (oil should be 2.5 cm (1 inch) in depth in wok). When hot add marinated pork chops, fry quickly on both sides until golden brown and cook through.
- Remove pork chops from pan, cut into serving size pieces, keep warm.
- Combine water, crumbled stock cube and extra soy sauce, in the pan add boil, pour over pork.

Serving

- Serve with Chinese mixed pickle.

2. Barbecued Pork Spareribs

Ingredients	Approx. Quantity
Pork spareribs	1/2 kg (2 Lb.)
Barbecue sauce	4 tablespoons
Honey	4 tablespoons
Brown vinegar	4 tablespoons
Chinese chilli sauce	1 tablespoon
Five spice powder	1/4 teaspoon
Dry sherry	1/3 tablespoon
Soy sauce	2 tablespoons
Garlic	1 clove
Green ginger	2.5 cm (1 inch) piece

Pre-Preparation: Put pork spareribs in large saucepan of water. Boil and reduce heat, and cook covered for 20 minutes.

Method

- Combine the barbecue sauce, honey, vinegar, chilli sauce, five spice powder, dry sherry, soy sauce, crushed garlic and grated ginger and mix well. Put pork spareribs into baking dish, pour sauce over, leave to stand one hour; turn occasionally.
- Bake in moderately hot oven for one hour, or until pork is tender, baste frequently.

3. Trotters with Ginger

Ingredients	Approx. Quantity
Pig's trotters	4 nos.
Green ginger	250 gm.
Sugar	11 cups
Brown vinegar	1 - cups
Chinese turnips	24 nos.

Pre-Preparation: Place trotters into large bowl, cover with cold water, for 15 minutes. Drain, cover with fresh water, allow to stand for 15 minutes. Drain, place trotters in large saucepan or small boiler. Cover well with cold water. Place over heat, bring to boil for one minute, drain. Cover again with cold water, bring to boil for one minute, drain. Scrape skin from ginger, and cut into chunky pieces, approximately, cut into 2.5 cm (1 inch) lengths.

Method

- Return trotters to pan, add vinegar and sugar. Add prepared ginger, stir until combined. Place pan over heat and when starts to boil, reduce heat, cover and cook two hours. Stir occasionally.
- Add prepared turnips to pan, cover and cook for a further 60 minutes. During last 15 minutes of cooking time, remove lid, increase heat slightly. Ginger sauce should be reduced enough to coat pig's trotters in a thick glaze. Stir occasionally during the last 15 minutes of cooking time.

4. Sweet and Sour Pork

Ingredients	Approx. Quantity
Lean pork chops	1.25 Kg
Sugar	2 teaspoons
Soy sauce	3 teaspoons
Dry sherry	1 tablespoon
Egg yolk	1 no.
Cornflour	2 teaspoons
Oil	For deep frying
Onion	1 (large)
Shallots	8 nos.
Red pepper	1 no.
Mushrooms	125 gm.
Cucumber	1 medium
Celery	2 sticks
Oil	3 tablespoons
Canned pineapple pieces	475 gms.
Tomato sauce	2 tablespoons
White vinegar	1/4 cup
Water	1 cup
Chicken stock cube	1 no.
Cornflour	1 - tablespoons.

Pre-Preparation: Combine sugar, 11/2 tablespoons soy sauce, sherry and egg yolk, stir well. Cut meat into 2.5 cm cubes, place into soy sauce mixture and stir until meat is coated. Cover, leave one hour, stir occasionally. Drain meat from marinade, reserve liquid. Toss meat lightly in cornflour.

Method

- Heat oil, cook meat until golden brown colour for about seven minutes and then drain.
- Peel and slice onion; slice shallots diagonally; slice pepper thickly, remove seeds; slice mushroom and celery, cut the cucumber into quarters, lengthwise, remove seeds, cut cucumber into slices.
- Heat three teaspoons oil in large pan, add all the prepared vegetables, and saute for three minutes. Drain pineapple and add pineapple syrup to pan with marinade from meat, remaining soy sauce, tomato sauce, vinegar and crumbled stock cube. Blend extra cornflour and water, add to pan, stir until sauce boils and thickens, add pineapple pieces, season with salt and pepper. Add pork, stir until combined.

5. Pork Ribs with Chilli Plum Sauce

Ingredients	Approx. Quantity
Pork ribs	750 gm.
Oyster sauce	1 tablespoon
Dry sherry	2 tablespoons
Soy sauce	1 tablespoon
Black beans	3 tablespoons
Five spice powder	1½ teaspoons
Pepper	1/2 teaspoon
Salt	1 teaspoon

Pre-Preparation for pork ribs: Remove excess fat from ribs. Cover black beans with water, leave 15 minutes, drain, mash with fork. In a bowl combine oyster sauce, sherry, soy sauce, black beans, five spice powder, pepper and salt.

Method

- Coat each rib with black bean mixture. Put under grill for 10 minutes. Turn occasionally.
- Remove pork ribs from grill, brush on both sides with chilli plum sauce. Return pork to grill, continue to cook five to ten

minutes or until golden brown and cooked through.

Serving

Serve with chilli plum sauce.

Chilli Plum Sauce

Ingredients	Approx. Quantity
Oil	2 teaspoons
Garlic	1 clove
Green ginger	1½ teaspoons
Shallots	2 nos.
Plum sauce	170 ml.
Chilli sauce	1 teaspoon
Chicken stock cube	1 nos.
Water	1/3 cup
Soy sauce	2 teaspoons
Cornflour	2 teaspoons

Method for Sauce

Heat oil in a small sauce pan, add crushed garlic, ginger and chopped shallots. Cook over gentle heat for 1 minute. Remove from heat, add plum sauce and chilli sauce, stir until combined. Add combined water, crumbled stock cube, soy sauce and cornflour. Return pan to heat. Stir until sauce boils and thickens.

6. Garlic Pork Rashers

Ingredients	Approx. Quantity
Pork rashers	750 gms.
Oil	2 tablespoons
Canned black beans	2 tablespoons
Water	1 cup
Soy sauce	2 teaspoons
Green ginger (grated)	2 teaspoons
Garlic	2 cloves
Cornflour	2 teaspoons
Water (extra)	2 tablespoons
Sherry	2 teaspoons

Pre-Preparation: Chop rashers into 5 cm (2 inch) pieces with sharp knife or cleaver. Soak washed black for 10 minutes. Place in blender with remaining water, blend on high speed one minute, or mash beans well with the water.

Method

- Saute pork pieces in hot oil until golden brown.
- Combine soy sauce, ginger and crushed garlic, stir in black bean mixture. Place sauted rashers in pan, pour sauce over, bring to boil, reduce heat, simmer covered, one hour.
- Combine cornflour, extra water and sherry, stir until smooth. Add to pan, stir until sauce boils and thickens, reduce heat and cook one minute.

7. Mu-Shu-Jou (Egg flower pork)

Ingredients	Approx. Quantity
Vegetable oil	45 ml.
Lean boned pork	225 gm.
Dried Chinese mushrooms (medium sized)	5 nos.
Dried tree ears	30 gm.
Scallion stalks	2 nos.
Soy sauce	20 ml.
Stock	30 ml.
Lard	10 gm.
Sesame oil	25 ml.
Eggs	4 nos.
Dry sherry	30 ml.

Pre-Preparation: Slice and shred pork. Soak mushroom for 30 minutes drain, remove stalks and slice Soak tree ears for 30 minutes and drain. Cut scallions into lengths. Soak golden needles for 30 minutes, drain and cut into lengths. Beat eggs with 1 teaspoon salt.

Method

- Heat the oil in a deep frying pan. Add the pork and stir-fry over high heat for 2 minutes. Add the mushrooms, tree-ears, scallions and golden needles if used, and stir-fry for 2 minutes. Add the soy-sauce and stock and stir-fry for a further il minutes. Remove the pan from the heat and keep hot.
- Heat the lard and oil in a small frying pan. When the lard has melted, pour in the beaten eggs. Swird the eggs around so that they cover the bottom of the pan

completely. Cook the mixture over low heat until the eggs have set in a thin, flat omelette.

- Remove the pan from the heat. Take out the omelette and cut into thick strips. Add the strips to the pork and mushroom mixture and return the pan to the heat. Stir in the sherry and gently mix the ingredients over high heat until hot.
- Turn the mixture out on to a warmed serving dish and serve immediately.

8. Twice-Cooked Pork

Ingredients	Approx. Quantity
Water	6 cups
Pork belly or leg	875 gm.
Salt	10 gm.
Onion (large)	1 no.
Vegetable oil	15 gm.
Scallions	2 nos.
Fresh ginger	5 gm.
Garlic cloves	2 nos.
Fermented salted black beans	10 gm.
Soy sauce	25 ml.
Chinese chilli sauce	10-15 gm.
Tomato paste	10-12 gm.
Beef stock	20 gm.
Sugar	10 gm.
Dry sherry	20 gm.
Sesame oil	10 gm.

Pre-Preparation: Chop scallion, ginger and garlic. Soak beans in water for 30 minutes, drain and mash.

Method

- Heat the water in a large saucepan. Add the pork, salt and onion. Bring the water to a boil, cover the pan, reduce the heat and simmer gently for 40 minutes. Remove the pork. Discard the liquid and the onion. Cut the pork into thin slices by about 10 cm by 15 cm.
- Heat the oil in a large, heavy frying-pan. Add the scallions, ginger and garlic and stir-fry over medium heat for 1 minute. Add the black beans and continue to stir fry for 2 minutes. Add the soy sauce,

chilli sauce, sugar and sherry. Stir and mix for 2 minutes. Add the sliced pork. Turn the slices in the sauce until every piece is well coated. Sprinkle with the sesame oil. Serve on a heated serving platter.

PREPARATION OF FOWL

1. Garlic Chicken

Ingredients	Approx. Quantity
Chicken	1.5 kg
Cornflour	As required
Oil	2 cups
Onions	2 large nos.
Green ginger	5 cm piece
Garlic	4 cloves
Chilli powder	1 teaspoon
Water	1/2 cup
Chicken stock cubes	1 cup
Salt	to taste
Dry sherry	2 tablespoons
Soy sauce	1 tablespoon
Vinegar	1 tablespoon
Sugar	2 teaspoons
Cornflour (extra)	2 teaspoons
Shallots	3 teaspoons
Chinese egg noodles	185 gms.
Soy sauce (extra)	2 teaspoons.

Pre-Preparation: Add noodles to large quantity of boiling salted water, stir well to separate noodles. Boil uncovered three to five minutes or until noodles are tender; drain, rinse under cold water. Make sure that noodles are well drained. Cut chicken into small serving-sized pieces. Coat chicken pieces lightly with cornflour. Peel and chop onions, ginger and garlic.

Method

- Heat oil in frying pan or a wok. Fry pieces of chicken until golden brown and for approximately five minutes; drain well.
- Drain off all oil from pan, return three tablespoons of oil to pan, add noodles and extra soy sauce; toss in pan until heated. Spread on serving plate; keep warm.

- Place peeled and roughly chopped onions, peeled and chopped ginger, peeled garlic and chilli powder into electric blender. Blend on medium speed for 30 seconds or until mixture is very finely chopped. Return 2 tablespoons of the oil to pan or wok, add onion mixture, cook for three minutes over low heat. Add chicken, toss well for 2 minutes over medium heat. Add combined water, crumbled stock cubes, salt, sherry, soy sauce, vinegar, sugar and extra cornflour. Toss mixture over a high heat until sauce boils and thickens. Continue tossing mixture until sauce thickly coats the chicken. Spoon chicken over the noodles.

Serving

- Serve, garnished with finely shredded shallots.

2. Almond Chicken

Ingredients	Approx. Quantity
Chicken breasts	4 nos.
Salt	1 teaspoon
Cornflour	1 tablespoon
Egg white	1 no.
Dry sherry	1½ tablespoons
Oil	6 nos.
Shallots	6 nos.
Mushrooms	125 gm.
Large carrot	1 no.
Can bamboo shoots	225 gms.
Celery	3 sticks
Grated green ginger	1 teaspoon
Oil (extra)	2 tablespoons
Blanched almonds	60 gm.
Sauce	
Cornflour	1 tablespoon
Water	II cup
Soy sauce	1 tablespoon
Chicken stock cube	1 no.
Dry sherry	1 tablespoon

Pre-Preparation: Slice mushrooms and celery roughly into 2.5 cm pieces. Slice bamboo thinly. Cut into 1 cm strips. Peel and dice carrot. Bone chicken breasts, remove skin; cut meat into 2.5 cm pieces, combine with salt, cornflour, lightly beaten egg white and sherry. Mix well.

Method

- Deep fry chicken pieces in hot oil, drain well. Fry almonds and then drain on absorbent paper.
- Add grated ginger and diced carrots to pan. Fry gently for one minute, add remaining and saute until tender, stirring occasionally. Then add chicken mix well and stir in almonds.

Method for sauce

- Blend cornflour with water soy sauce, sherry and crumbled stock cube. Stir over medium heat until sauce boils and thickens.

3. Lemon Chicken

Ingredients	Approx. quantity
Chicken breasts	4 nos.
Cornflour	1/2 cup
Water	3 tablespoons
Egg yolks	to taste
Salt, pepper	to taste
Shallots	6 nos.
Oil	For deep frying.
Lemon sauce	
Lemon juice	1/2 cup
Chicken stock cubes	2 nos.
Cornflour	2 tablespoons
Honey	2 tablespoons
Brown sugar	2½ tablespoons
Green ginger	1 tablespoon
Water	3½ cups

Pre-Preparation: Wash the chicken thoroughly under cold running water, then pat it completely dry, inside and out, with paper towels. Place the chicken on a table or chopping board, breast side up. Press down hard on the breastbone to break it and flatten it.

Method

- Prepare batter with cornflour, water, beaten egg, salt and pepper. Dip chicken breasts into this batter, drain well. Fry chicken in hot oil until lightly golden brown and cooked through.

- Slice each cooked chicken breasts across into three or four pieces. Arrange in a plate and decorate with chopped shallots.

Serving

- Serve, garnished with hot sauce.

Lemon sauce preparation

- Combine lemon juice, crumbled stock cubes, cornflour, honey, brown sugar, ginger and water in a pan. Cook over low heat until sauce boils and thickens.

4. Szechwan Duck

Ingredients	Approx. quantity
Duck	4 to 5 pound
Salt	2 tablespoons
Whole szechwan peppercorns	2 tablespoons (crushed with a cleaver or with a paste in a mortar)
Fresh ginger root (peeled)	8 Slices tops (1 inch in diameter and 1/4 inch thick)
Scallions (including the green tops)	2 nos.
Soy sauce	2 tablespoons
Five spice powder	1 teaspoon
Peanut oil	3 cups
Salt and pepper (Roasted)	To taste
Steamed flower-roll	As required

Pre-Preparation: Remove skin from duck breasts, debone and make eight pieces. Pound duck breasts out lightly.

In a small bowl, combine the salt, crush peppercorns, scallions and ginger. With a large spoon, rub the seasonings together to release their flavours. Rub the duck inside and out with the mixture, finally pressing the ginger and scallions firmly against the skin and inside cavity of the duck to make them adhere. Place the duck on a platter and refrigerate it covered with aluminium foil or plastic wrap for atleast 6 hours or overnight.

Before cooking, mix the soy sauce and five-slice powder thoroughly together in a small bowl, and rub it over the skin and inside the cavity of the duck. Pour enough boiling water into the lower part of a steamer to come to within an inch of the cooking rack. Place the duck on its back on a deep, heat proof platter 1/2" smaller in diameter than the pot so that steam can freely circulate around the duck. Place the pot securely and bring the water in the steamer to a rolling boil, keeping the water at a continuous boil, steam the duck for 2 hours. Keep a kettle of water at *a* boil all the time, the duck is steaming, and use this to replenish the water in the steamer as it boils away. Turn off the heat. Let the duck rest in the tightly covered steamer for 30 minutes, then turn the bird over on its breast. Recover the steamer and let the duck rest for 30 minutes longer. Transfer the duck from the steamer to a platter lined with a double thickness of paper towels. Brush off and discard the scallion pieces and ginger slices, and place the duck in a cool, airy place to dry for 3 hours or longer.

Method

- Pour 3 cups of oil into a 12 inch wok or heavy deep-fryer and heat it until a baze forms above it or it reaches a temperature of 375°C on a deep-frying thermometer. With two large spoons, carefully lower the duck into the hot oil on its back and fry it for about 15 minutes. Keep the 375°C temperature and move the duck about from time to time with chop sticks or two slotted spoons to prevent it from sticking to either the bottom or sides of the pan. Then turn the duck over on its breast and deep-fry it, moving it in the same fashion for another 15 minutes. When the duck is a deep golden brown on all sides, carefully transfer it to a chopping board. With a sharp knife, cut off the wings, legs and thighs of the duck and chop them across the bone in 2-inch pieces. Then cut away and discard the backbone and chop the breast, bone and all, into 2 inch squares.

Serving

● Arrange the duck pieces attractively on a large heated platter and serve at once with roasted salt and pepper and steamed flower-roll buns.

Roasted Salt and Pepper

● Set a heavy 5 or 6 inch skillet over high heat, and pour in the salt and all the peppercorns. Turn the heat down to moderate and cook, stirring constantly, for 5 minutes, or until the mixture browns lightly. Crush it to a fine powder. Shake the crushed a fine sieve or strainer into a small bowl and serve it as a dip for szechwan duck.

5. Eight-jewel Duck

Ingredients	Approx. Quantity
Glutinous rice	1 cup
Dried Chinese mushrooms	2 nos.
Dried shrimps	10 nos.
Duck	4-5 pound
Canned whole water-pack. French or Italian chestnuts	1 cup
Peanut oil	2 tablespoons
Lean boneless pork	1/4 pound
Sugar	1/2 teaspoon
Chinese rice wine or Pale dry sherry	1 tablespoon
Soy sauce	2 tablespoons
Canned whole gingko nuts	1/4 cup
Fresh water chestnuts (peeled)	3 nos.
Cook smithfield ham	1/4 inch thick slice
Salt	2 teaspoons
Chinese parsley	1 spring

Pre-Preparation: Soak rice with cold water for 2 hours. Then pour enough boiling water into the lower part of a steamer to come within an inch of cooking thickness of paper towels. Now drain the rice and spread it evenly over the lined rack. Over high heat, bring the water in the steamer to a rolling boil. Cover the pan tightly and steam the rice for 30 minutes, or until the rice is tender.

Keep a kettle of boiling water on the stove to replenish the water in the steamer if necessary. Remove the rice from the pot, place it in a bowl and cover it with aluminium foil to keep warm. In a small bowl, cover the dried shrimp with 1/4 cup of warm water and allow them to soak for atleast 30 minutes. Don't drain the shrimps or discard the water. In a small bowl, cover the mushrooms with 1/2 cup of warm water and let them soak for atleast 30 minutes. Then remove them with a slotted spoon and discard the water. With a sharp knife cut away and discard the tough stems of the mushrooms and chop the caps fine. Meanwhile, bone the duck.

Method

● Set a 12 inch Wok or 10 inch skillet over high heat for 30 seconds. Pour in the 2 tablespoons of oil, swirl it about in the pan and heat for another 30 seconds, turning the heat down to moderate if the oil begins to smoke. Add the pork and stir. Fry for 2 or 3 minutes until the pork losses its reddish colour. Stir in the wine and soy sauce, then add the mushrooms, gingko nuts, water chestnuts, rice, ham, shrimp and soaking water. Mix them together thoroughly and gently fold in the chestnuts. Transfer the entire contents of this stuffing mixture from the pan to a bowl and cool to room temperature.

● Preheat the oven to 400°C. Rub the inside surfaces of the duck with the 2 teaspoons of salt, then close up the neck opening very securely with cups. Pack the stuffing loosely into the cavity of the duck and close up the tail opening. Pat, shape and mold the body of the duck back into its original shape and place it, breast side up, on a rack set in a deep roasting pan. Add about 1 inch of water to the pan. Roast in the centre of the oven for 30 minutes, reduce the heat to 350°C and roast the duck for 1½ hours longer.

● When done, remove its clips. Place the duck on a heated serving platter.

6. Peking Duck

Ingredients	Approx. Quantity
Duck	A5 pound
Water	6 cups
Honey	1/4 cup
Peeled fresh ginger root	4 pieces
Scallion	2 nos.
For Sauce	
Hoisin sauce	1/4 cup
Water	1 tablespoon
Sesame seed oil	1 teaspoon
Sugar	2 teaspoons
Scallions	12 no.
Mandarin pan cakes	

Pre-Preparation: Wash the duck in cold water then pat dry. Tie one end of a 20-inch length of white cord around the neck skin. Place the bird in a cool airy place for 3 hours to dry the skin. In a wok, combine water, honey, ginger root and scallions and boil over high heat. Holding the duck by its skin is moistened with the liquid. Remove the duck and hang it again in the cool place. Put a bowl beneath it to catch any drippings. Make the sauce by combining hoisin sauce, water, sesame-seed oil and sugar in a small pan and stirring until sugar dissolves. Bring to a boil, then reduce heat to its lowest point and simmer uncovered for 3 minutes. Pour into a small bowl, cool and reserve until ready to use. To make scallion brushes, cut scallions down to 3-inch lengths and trim off roots. Standing each scallion on end, make four intersecting cuts 1 inch deep into its stalk. Repeat at other end. Place 1 inch deep into its stalk. Repeat at other end. Place scallions in ice water and refrigerate until cut parts curl into brushlike fans.

Method

● Preheat oven to 375°C. Untie the duck and cut off any loose neck skin. Place duck, breast side up, on a rack and set in a roasting pan just large enough to hold the bird. Roast the duck in the middle of the oven for one hour. Then lower the heat to 300°C, turn the duck on its breast and roast for 30 minutes longer. Now raise the heat to 375°C, return the duck to its original position and roast for a final half hour. Place the duck to a carving board. Remove the crisp skin from the breast, sides and back of duck. Cut skin into 2/3 inch rectangles and arrange them in a single layer on a heated platter. Cut the wings and drumsticks from the duck, and cut all the meat away from breast and carecass. Slice meat into pieces 2½ long and ½" wide, and arrange them with the wings and drumsticks on another heated platter.

Serving

● To serve, place the platters of duck, the heated pancakes, the bowl of sauce and the scallion brushes in the centre of the table.

7. Honey Chilli Chicken

Ingredients	Approx. Quantity
Chicken	1.5 Kg
Salt	To taste
Oil	for deep frying
Green finger	2.5 cm (1 inch) piece.
Honey	2 tablespoons
Water	1/3 cup
Chinese chilli sauce	1 tablespoon
Lemon juice	1/2 cup
Soy sauce	4 teaspoons
Shallots	6 nos.
Flour	As required

Pre-Preparation : Cut chicken into serving size pieces. Coat chicken pieces lightly with flour, which has been seasoned with salt.

Method

● Fry the chicken in deep hot oil until golden brown. Reduce heat, cook approximately five minutes, or until chicken is done. Remove from oil, drain on absorbent paper. Pour off excess oil, leaving 1 tablespoon of oil in pan.

- Add peeled and grated green ginger to pan, saute gently one minute. Add honey, stir for one minute. Add combined cornflour, water, chilli, sauce, lemon and soy sauce. Stir until sauce boils and thickens.
- Add chicken toss in sauce for three minutes or until chicken is heated through. Add sliced shallots, cook for a few minutes again.

8. Beggar's Chicken

Ingredients	Approx. Quantity
Chicken	1.5 kg
Shallots	3 nos.
Green ginger	2.5 cm (1 inch) piece
Sugar	2 teaspoons
Soy sauce	3 tablespoons
Dry sherry	2 tablespoons
Water	1 tablespoon
Five spice powder	1/4 teaspoon

Ingredients	Approx. Quantity
Soy sauce (extra)	2 tablespoons.
Oil	As required
Clay Dough	1 kg
Cooking salt	4 cups
Plain flour	1 cups
Water	1/2 cups

Pre-Preparation

To make the dough: Place unsifted flour and salt into bowl; mix well. Gradually stir in water. Mix to a firm dough. Place two sheets of aluminium foil on the table, brush the chicken in the middle of foil. Place roughly chopped shallots, sugar, peeled and sliced ginger, soy sauce, sherry, water and five spice powder in a bowl and mix well. Rub chicken all over with extra soy sauce, then rub with the 2 tablespoons of oil. Rub well into the skin. Pull skin at neck end down under chicken, tuck wing tips under chicken and over neck skin. Carefully pour soy sauce mixture into chicken cavity, holding chicken up slightly so that no sauce runs out. Secure end of chicken with small skewer. Wrap aluminium foil around the chicken and secure like a parcel. Roll dough out to approximately 1 cm (1/2 inch) thickness, so that it will completely encase the chicken, fold dough over the chicken. Press edges and ends together.

Method

- Place chicken into lightly oiled baking dish. With wet fingers, smooth out all joints, making sure there are no holes in the pastry, for the steam to escape.
- Bake in a hot oven for one hour. Reduce heat to moderately slow, cook further three hours.
- Remove chicken from oven, break open pastry clay with mallet or hammer and remove chicken.

Serving

- Lift foil wrapped chicken into serving plate, carefully remove the foil and serve.

9. Chicken With Asparagus

Ingredients	Approx. Quantity
Celery	3 sticks
Red pepper	1 no.
Shallots	6 nos.
Green ginger (grated)	1 teaspoon
Can asparagus tips	250 gms.
Can whole baby corn	225 gms.
Chicken breasts	2 (whole)
Egg white	1 no.
Cornflour	1 tablespoon
Oil	2 tablespoons
Chicken stock cubes	2 nos.
Soy sauce	1 tablespoon
Dry sherry	1 tablespoon
Cornflour (extra)	2 teaspoons
Oil (extra)	if cup

Pre-Preparation: Cut celery diagonally into 2.5 cm. (1 inch) pieces. Cut pepper in half, remove seeds, cut into large pieces. Slice shallots diagonally. Drain asparagus, cut in half, reserve liquid. Skin chicken breasts, and remove meat from bones. Cut meat into 2.5 cm (1 inch) pieces and combine with lightly beaten egg white, cornflour and oil, mix well.

Method

- Heat extra oil in pan or wok, add chicken pieces, fry gently until chicken is cooked through. Drain on absorbent paper. Drain excess oil from pan, leaving two tablespoons in pan.
- Heat this reserved oil in pan, add grated ginger, celery and pepper; cook one minute.
- Stir in chicken pieces, shallots and drained corn. Combine extra cornflour, reserved asparagus liquid, crumbled stock cubes, soy sauce and dry sherry. Pour over chicken and vegetables, stir until sauce boils; add asparagus, fold through lightly and cook to two minutes.

10. Snow-white Chicken

(This food item is coated with rice and steamed so it is called snow-white chicken).

Ingredients	Approx. Quantity
Chicken breasts	2 pieces
Salt	To taste
Black pepper	
Dry sherry	3 tablespoons
Glutinous rice	225 gm
Egg whites	2 nos.

Pre-Preparation: Skin and bone the chicken. Soak the rice in cold water for 1 hour and drain. Beat egg whites with 1 tablespoon cornstarch.

Method

- Cut the chicken breasts into 1/4 inch-thick slices. Using the point of a sharp knife, score criss-cross lines across both sides of the meat. Cut the meat into 1 inch squares and place them in a shallow bowl. Add salt, pepper and the sherry and toss well.
- Keep aside for 5 minutes.
- Spread the rice out on a baking sheet or tray. Dip the chicken pieces into the egg-white mixture and then press them into the rice to coat them fully.

- Arrange the rice-covered chicken pieces on a heatproof dish and place the dish in a steamer, for about 30-45 minutes before serving.

11. Cashew Chicken

Ingredients	Approx. Quantity
Chicken breast meat	200 gm.
Cashew nuts	100 gm.
Dried mushroom	5 pieces.
Green pepper	1 no.
Carrot	50 gm.
Onion	1 no.
Garlic	2 cloves
Soy sauce	1 teaspoon
Cornflour	1 teaspoon
Salt	1 teaspoon
Pepper	One pinch
Ginger	2 slices
Cooking Oil	1 tablespoons

Pre-Preparation: Dice chicken mushrooms, pepper, carrot and onion. Roast cashew nuts. Crush garlic.

Method

- Season the chicken meat with cornflour and soy sauce for 10 minutes:
- Heat cooking oil, fry garlics, ginger and dried mushroom.
- Now add chicken meat, green pepper and onion to fry for few minutes and add salt and pepper to taste.
- Place the ingredients to a plate and mix with the prepared roasted cashewnuts.

PREPARATION OF CHOW-MEIN

1. Beef Chow-Mein

Ingredients	Approx. Quantity
Thick rump steak	750 Kg
Soy sauce	2 tablespoons
Chilli sauce	1 tablespoon
Sate sauce	1 tablespoon
Dry sherry	1 tablespoon
Egg noodles	250 gm.
Oil	2 tablespoons

Ingredients	Approx. Quantity
Small mushrooms	125 gm.
Bean sprouts	125 gm.
Red pepper	1 no.
Celery	3 sticks
Onions	2 no. (medium)
Oil (extra)	2 tablespoons
Oyster Sauce	
Sugar	1 teaspoon
Cornflour	3 tablespoons
Water	3/4 cup
Chicken stock cubes	2 nos.
Dry sherry	1 tablespoon
Oyster sauce	2 tablespoons
Soy sauce	1 tablespoon
Dry sherry (extra)	1 tablespoon

Pre-Preparation: Remove all fat from meat, cut meat into very thin strips, approximately 5 cm × 5 mm strips. Place meat into bowl, add 1 tablespoon soy sauce, chilli sauce, sate sauce and sherry. Mix well and keep for 60 minutes. Peel onions, cut into wedges, separate layers of onion out. Seed pepper, cut into strips, slice mushrooms slice celery.

Method

- Add egg noodles to enough boiling salted water, boil uncovered for five minutes or until noodles are tender. Stir noodles occasionally to separate; drain well. Heat 1 tablespoon oil in pan or wok, add noodles and one tablespoon soy sauce, toss for two minutes, remove from pan, keep warm.
- Heat remaining oil in a pan, add onions, saute for one minute. Add remaining vegetables, toss for two extra oil in wok, add half the meat, fry quickly until meat just changes colour; remove from pan. Add remaining meat, work in the same way, return all meat to pan, fry. Combine all ingredients for oyster sauce, add to meat, toss until sauce is boiling, add vegetables, toss for a further two minutes over high meat.

Serving

- Place noodles on to serving plate, top with meat mixture.

2. Chicken Cow-Mein

Ingredients	Approx. Quality
Egg noodles	250 gm.
Oil	4 cups
Chicken	2 kg
Lean pork	250 gm.
Green king prawns	500 gm.
Onions	2 medium
Red Pepper	1 no.
Celery	2 sticks
Cabbage	1/4 portion
Shallots	8 nos.
Soy sauce	2 teaspoons
Dry sherry	2 teaspoons
Cornflour	2 teaspoons
Oil (extra)	4 teaspoons
Garlic	1 clove
Green ginger	2.5 pieces
Salt	To taste
Water	1/2 cup
Cornflour (extra)	2 teaspoons
Soy sauce (extra)	1 teaspoon
Chicken stock cubes	2 nos.

Pre-Preparation: Boil noodles in salted water uncovered for four minutes, drain rinse noodles well under hot water. Place a clean tea towel or two layers of absorbent paper on wire rack, spread noodles out on towel. Keep at room temperature for three hours, or until noodles are almost dry. Remove skin and bones from chicken and cut into 2.5 meat. Shell prawns, remove back vein, leaving tail intact. Peel and chop onion, seed and slice pepper, slice celery and cabbage. Chop shallot and ginger. Place chicken and pork in a bowl and mix with sherry, soy sauce and cornflour. Keep aside for 1 hour.

Method

- Heat oil (about 2 cups) and fry noodles until golden brown. Drain it and remove oil from pan.

- Heat extra oil, ginger and garlic and saute for one minute. Then add chicken and pork and toss constantly till done over high heat. Now add prawns and toss for 2-3 minutes. Add last vegetables and combined salt, water, extra cornflour, cubes, extra sherry and toss until sauce boils and thickens.

Serving

- Place fried noodles around edge of serving plate, spoon chicken and vegetable into the centre before serving.

3. Vegetable Chow-Mein

Ingredients	Approx. Quantity
Raw noodles	50 gm
Water	6 cups
Salt	1 teaspoon
Oil	7 teaspoons
Capsicum	1 no.
Carrot	1 no.
French beans	16 nos.
Spring onions	2 nos.
Shredded cabbage	1/2 cup
Oil	4 tablespoons
Flowerettes of cauliflower	1/2 cup
Bean sprouts	1 cup
White pepper	1 teaspoon
Sugar	1 teaspoon
Ajinomoto	1/4 teaspoon
Salt	To taste
Water	1 cup
Soya sauce	1½ tablespoons
Cornflour (mixed with 1/4 cup of water)	1½ tablespoons
For the noodles	

Pre-Preparation: Cook the noodles : Boil the water and add noodles and salt. Cook, uncovered, over a high flame for about 8 minutes and then drain and add 1/2 teaspoon oil. Cool it. Fry the noodles till light brown colour. Drain and keep warm in a serving dish. Prepare the vegetables Boil the cabbage, carrot and french beans in

salted water for 1 minute and drain and cool. Shred the capsicum, carrot, french beans and onions.

Method

- Heat 4 tablespoon oil in the pan, used for frying the noodles. Add the cauliflower and bean sprouts and fry for two minutes over high flame. Now add the remaining vegetables, pepper, sugar, ajinomoto and salt and stir fry, for 2 minutes.
- Now add the water and soy sauce. When starts boiling add cornflour (mixed with 1/4 cup water) and stir cook until thickened.
- Pour this mixture over the fixed fried noodles and serve.

PREPARATION OF RICE

1. Fried Rice

Ingredients	Approx. Quantity
Long grain rice	375 gm.
Bacon	3 rashers
Cooked pork	250 gm.
Eggs	3 nos.
Salt	To taste
Pepper Grated green ginger	2 teaspoons
Shallots	8 nos.
Prawns	500 gm.
Oil (extra)	2 tablespoons
Soy sauce	2 teaspoons.

2. Stir-fried Rice Stick Noodles with Shrimp and Vegetables

Ingredients	Approx. Quantity
Rice stick noodles	1/3 pound
Celery cabbage	1/2 pound
Uncooked shrimp	1 pound
Peanut oil	4 tablespoons
Chinese rice wine	1 tablespoon
Salt	1/2 teaspoon
Soy sauce	1 tablespoon
Chicken stock (fresh or canned)	1/2 cup.

Pre-Preparation: In a large bowl, cover the rice stick noodles with cold water. Soak for 5 minutes then dry thoroughly in a colander. With a cleaver or sharp knife, trim off any wilted top leaves of the cabbage and the root ends. Separate the stalks, wash well and slice each stalk lengthwise into 1/8" wide strips. Shell the shrimp, and, with a small, sharp knife make a shallow incision down the back and lift out the black or white intestinal vein. Wash the shrimp, dry with paper towels and cut each in half lengthwise.

Method

- Put large saucepan of water on to boil, add two teaspoons salt. When at full rolling boil, add rice gradually. Boil rapidly, uncovered 10 to 12 minutes. When rice is tender, drain immediately. Put colander or strainer under cold running water to remove any starch; drain well again.
- Spread rice evenly over two large shallow trays, refrigerate overnight. Stir occasionally to allow rice to dry completely.
- Finely dice bacon, fry until crisp, drain; slice pork thinly. Beat eggs lightly with fork, season with salt and pepper. Heat a small quantity of oil in pan, pour in enough of egg mixture to make one pan cake; turn, cook other side. Remove from pan, repeat with remaining egg mixture. Roll up pancakes, slice into smaller pieces. Heat extra oil in pan or wok. Saute ginger for one minute, stir in rice, five minutes. Add bacon, pork, shallot, egg strips and prawns, mix lightly.

Serving

- Serve hot, with soy sauce.

3. Ham and Egg Fried Rice

Ingredients	Approx. Quantity
Fresh peas	1/2 cup
Peanut oil	6 tablespoons
Eggs	2 no.
Chinese boiled rice	3 cups
Salt	1 teaspoon
Boiled ham (slice 1/4" thick and cut into 1/4" pieces)	2 oz.
Scallion	1 no.

Pre-Preparation: Blanch fresh peas and boil uncovered for 5 to 10 minutes, or until tender. Then drain and cool it to stop their cooking and set their colour.

Method

- Set a 12" wok over high heat for 30 seconds. Pour in 2 tablespoons of oil. Add the shrimp and stir fry for 1 minute, or until they turn pink. Add 1/2 teaspoon salt and wine, stir once or twice, then transfer the contents of the pan to a plate and keep aside. Pour 2 more tablespoons of oil into the pan, heat it for 30 seconds and in it, stir fry the cabbage for 2 minutes. Then add the salt, sugar and noodles, and cook, stirring, for 1 minute. Pour in the soy sauce and stock, and boil briskly for 3 minutes, or until the liquid has evaporated. Return the shrimp to the pan and stirring constantly, cook for 30 seconds.

Serving

- Transfer the entire contents of the pan to a heated platter and serve at once.

4. Hunan Steamed Rice

Ingredients	Approx. Quantity
Long grain rice	1 cup
Water	2½ cups

Pre-Preparation: Wash and drain rice.

Method

- Set a wok or skillet over high heat for 30 seconds. Heat oil and add beaten eggs, (which will form a film on bottom of the pan). Remove this film and push it to the back of the pan so that the liquid eggs can spread across the bottom of the pan to cook.
- As soon as the egg set, place them to a small bowl and break them up with a fork.
- Pour and heat the remaining oil. Add the rice and stir fry for 2-3 minutes until all the grains are coated with oil. Add salt, peas and ham and stir-fry for a few

seconds. Put again the eggs to the pan, add scallions and cook till the eggs done and serve hot.

PREPARATION OF SEAFOOD

1. Seafood Combination

Ingredients	Approx. Quantity
Scallops	250 gms.
Squid	250 gms.
Green king prawns	250 gms.
Fish fillets	2 nos.
Canned water chestnuts	275 gms.
Canned bamboo shoots	273 gms.
Shallots	8 nos.
Celery	3 sticks
Cornflour	1 teaspoon
Water	1/2 cup
Chicken stock cube	1 no.
Dry sherry	2 teaspoons
Sesame oil	2 teaspoons
Soy sauce	2 teaspoons
Oil	2 teaspoons

Pre-Preparation: Clean and prepare scallops, squid and prawns. Skin fish and cut into large pieces. Slice celery and shallots diagonally. Drain water chestnuts, cut in half. Drain bamboo shoots, slice thinly.

Method

- Bring the water to a boil in a saucepan.
- Add rice and boil it again and cook for 5 minutes, stirring continuously. Now drain the rice.
- Spread the rice on a large heatproof dish and steam in a steamer for 25 to 30 minutes or as required to be very tender.

2. Scallop and Vegetable Combination

Ingredients	Approx. Quantity
Scallops	500 gms.
Dried mushrooms	30 gms.
Onions	2 nos.
Celery	2 nos.
Beans	250 gms.
Green ginger (grated)	2 teaspoons

Ingredients	Approx. Quantity
Garlic	1 clove
Cornflour	1 tablespoon
Water	1 cup
Dry sherry	2 tablespoons
Chicken stock cubes	2 nos.
Soy sauce	2 tablespoons
Baby corn	As required

Pre-Preparation: Make slit along dark vein of scallops. Wash well, pat dry. Cover dried mushrooms with hot water, for 15 minutes or until softened. Drain, slice thinly. Peel and quarter onions. Slice celery diagonally; string beans, slice diagonally; slice shallots diagonally.

Method

- Heat 2 tablespoons of the oil in pan, add the prepared vegetables, saute two minutes, remove from pan.
- Add remaining oil to pan, heat. Add scallops, squid, prawns and fish, saute two minutes. Mix cornflour with a little of the water until smooth, add remaining water, crumbled stock cube, sherry, sesame oil and soy sauce. Add sauce to pan, stir until boiling, add vegetables to pan, toss until cooked through.
- Divide prawn mixture into ten equal portions and make balls. Place meat end of crab claw into centre of prawn meat, wrap prawn meat around crab meat. Coat crab claws lightly with cornflour.
- Dip crab claw, into prepared batter, then place into deep hot oil, dry until golden brown and cooked through, approximately four minutes. (Don't have oil too hot or batter will brown too quickly and crab claw will not cook right through).

Serving

- Serve with sweet and sour sauce.

Method

- Heat oil in a pan add onions, celery, beans, ginger and crushed garlic, saute two minutes. Mix cornflour with a little of the water until smooth, add remaining

water, dry sherry, crumbled stock cubes, salt and soy sauce.
- Add sauce to the pan, stir until boiling. Add scallops, drained baby corn, mushrooms and shallots and cook three minutes or until scallops are tender.

3. Saute Prawns

Ingredients	Approx, Quantity
Green king prawns	1 kg. (2 lb)
Onions	3 nos. (medium)
Oil	3 tablespoons
Water	1 tablespoon
Marinade	
Five spice powder	1/4 teaspoon
Chilli powder	1/4 teaspoon
Sate sauce	2 tablespoons
Salt	Two pinch
Curry powder	1/2 teaspoon
Cornflour	1 teaspoon
Sugar	1½ teaspoons
Soy sauce	1 teaspoon
Dry sherry	1 teaspoon

Pre-Preparation: Shell prawns; cut each prawns down back and remove back vein. With sharp knife, make deep slit down back of prawn (taking care not to cut right through). Combine marinade ingredients in bowl, add prawns, mix well, and keep aside two hours. Peel and cut onions.

Method

- Heat oil in large pan or wok, add onions, saute until transparent, approximately two minutes.
- Add prawns and marinade mixture to wok, saute until prawns have turned light pink and prawns are cooked, approx. three minutes. Then add water and mix well.

Serving

- Arrange lettuce leaves around edge of plate, spoon prawns over.

4. Crab Claws

Ingredients	Approx. Quantity
Crab claws (thick)	10 nos.
Green king prawns	1 kg
Shallots	6 nos.
Celery	2 sticks
Green ginger	2.5 cm (1 inch) piece
Salt	1/4 teaspoon
Cornflour	As required
Oil	For deep-frying
For Batter	
Cornflour	1/2 cup
Plain flour	1/2 cup
Baking powder	1/2 teaspoon
Water	1 cup
Salt	1/2 teaspoon
Sweet Sour Sauce	
Canned Chinese mixed pickles	175 gms.
Water	1 cup
Chinese chilli sauce	1 teaspoon
Tomato sauce	1 tablespoon
Soy sauce	1 teaspoon
Sugar	1 tablespoon
Cornflour	2 teaspoons

Pre-Preparation

Make the batter : Sift dry ingredients into bowl, gradually and water, mix to a smooth batter.

Make sauce: Drain pickles, place liquid into pan. Shred pickles finely. Place pickles, water, chilli sauce, tomato sauce, soy sauce, sugar and cornflour into pan with reserved liquid, stir until combined and sauce boils. Reduce heat, and cook for three minutes. Remove the shell from fat end of claw and leave shell on largest nipper. Shell prawns, remove back vein. Chop prawn meat very finely, until prawn meat comes together in a thick mass. Finely chop shallots, celery and peeled ginger. Place prawn meat, shallots, celery ginger and salt into bowl; mix well.

5. Abalone in Oyster Sauce

Ingredients	Approx Quality
Can abalone	450 gms.
Dried mushrooms	30 gms.
Red pepper	1 no.
Shallots	6 nos.
Cucumber	1/2 portion
Oyster sauce	2 tablespoons
White vinegar	1 tablespoon
Sugar	1/2 teaspoon
Chicken stock cube	1 no.
Dry sherry	1 tablespoon
Soy sauce	2 teaspoons
Cornflour	3 teaspoons
Sesame oil	1/4 teaspoon
Green ginger	1 teaspoon
Oil	4 tablespoons

Pre-Preparation: Drain liquid from can of abalone. Cut abalone into thin slice. Put dried mushrooms in hot water for 15 minutes and remove tough stalks and slice thinly. Cut shallots into slice. Remove seeds and cut pepper in half. Peel and cut cucumber.

6. Shrimp with Green Peas

Ingredients	Approx. Quantity
Raw shrimp in their shells	1 pound
Fresh peas (Shelled)	1 pound
Cornstarch	2 teaspoon
Egg white	1 no.
Chinese rice wine	2 teaspoons
Salt	1 teaspoon
Peanut oil	3 tablespoons
Scallion	1 tablespoon
Fresh ginger root (peeled)	3 slices 1"

Pre-Preparation: Shell the shrimp and, devein them by making a shallow incision down the back and lifting out the black or white intestinal vein with the point of knife. Wash the shrimp under cold running water and pat them thoroughly dry with paper towels. Split each shrimp in lengthwise, then cut each of the halves in two, cross-size. Blanch the freshly shelled peas by dropping them into a quarter of rapidly boiling water and letting them boil uncovered for 5 to 7 minutes, or until just tender when tasted. Then drain the peas and place in cold water for a few seconds to stop their cooking and set their colour. In a large mixing bowl, combine the shrimp and cornstarch, and toss them together with a spoon until each shrimp piece is lightly coated with cornstarch. Add the egg white, wine and salt, and stir them with the shrimp until they are thoroughly mixed together. Keep the mixture aside for at least one hour.

Method

- Heat a little oil in a pan, Add abalone and toss for one minute. Remove and keep warm.
- Heat remaining oil in pan, add ginger, mushrooms, pepper, shallots and cucumber. Toss in pan for 1 minute and then add combined oyster sauce, vinegar, sugar, crumbled stock cube, dry sherry, soy sauce, water, cornflour and sesame oil. Toss this mixture over high heat until sauce boils and thickens. Add abalone and cook till done.

7. Barbecue Prawns

Ingredients	Approx. Quantity
Green king prawns	500 gms.
Cornflour	2 teaspoons
Salt	1 teaspoon
Egg white	1 no.
Curry powder	1 teaspoon
Onion	1 no.
Sugar	1/4 teaspoon
Sate sauce	2 teaspoons
Cream	3 teaspoons
Red pepper	1/2 teaspoon
Oil	1 cup

Method

- Set a wok over high heat for 30 seconds. Pour in the 3 tablespoons of oil and heat. Add the scallions and ginger slices, and stir fry for 30 seconds to flavour the oil, then remove them with a slotted spoon and discard. Immediately drop the shrimp into the pan and stir fry them for 2 minutes, or until they turn pink. Don't let the shrimp over cook. Then drop in the peas and stir fry about 1 minute to heat the peas through.

Serving

- Transfer the entire contents of the pan to a heated platter and serve at once.

8. Squid with Broccoli

Ingredients	Approx. Quantity
Squid	1 Kg
Onions	2 nos.
Celery	2 sticks
Broccoli (fresh)	1 Kg
Shallots	4 nos.
Oil	1/2 cup
Green ginger (grated)	2 teaspoons
Cornflour	1 tablespoon
Water	1/2 cup
Dry sherry	2 tablespoons
Chicken stock cubes	2 nos
Oyster sauce	3 tablespoons
Soy sauce	1 tablespoon
Sesame oil	2 tablespoons
Sugar	2 tablespoons
Salt	1 tablespoon

Pre-Preparation: Pull out head and inside of the body of squid. Remove bone which will be found at open end of squid. Clean squid under cold running water, then rub off the outer skin. Cut squid lengthwise down centre. Spread squid keeping inside facing upwards. With sharp knife make shallow cuts across squid in diamond shape. Cut onions into quarters; slice celery diagonally; cut broccoli, including stalks. Slice shallots diagonally.

Method

- Heat oil in pen or wok, add squid, cook until it curls, remove from pan, drain on absorbent paper. Then add onions, celery, broccoli and ginger to pan and fry for 3 minutes.
- Blend cornflour with a little of the water until smooth, add remaining water, dry

sherry, scrambled stock cubes, oyster sauce, soy sauce, sesame oil, sugar and salt. Mix well. Add to pan, stir until sauce boils.

- Return squid to pan, cook until done. Put on to serving dish.

Serving

- Put on to serving dish, top with shallots and serve.

9. Bamboo Prawns

Ingredients	Approx. Quantity
Green king prawns	500 gm.
Oil	3 tablespoons
Green ginger (grated)	1 teaspoon
Bamboo shoot	
Celery	
Ham	
Water	
Chicken stock cube	As required
Cornflour	
Dry sherry	

Pre-Preparation: Shell prawns. Remove back vein; rinse and pat dry. With sharp knife, make deep slit along the back of each prawn. Put cornflour, salt and unbeaten egg white into bowl, and keep aside for 1 hour. Chop onion finely and slice pepper.

Method

- Heat oil in frying pan or wok, add prawns; fry quickly for 2 minutes or until prawns are just cooked, remove from pan, drain well.
- Drain off oil from pan, leaving approx. 1/4 cup oil. Add peeled and chopped onions to pan, saute 2 minutes. Add curry powder and sugar, stir for 1 minute. Add sate sauce and cream, bring to boil, reduce heat and cook for 1 minute, stirring constantly. Add seeded and sliced pepper. Remove from heat.

Serving

- Line serving dish with lettuce leaves, spoon prawn over. If desired, place small metal bowl in the centre of prawns. Fill bowl with warmed brandy and keep side. Pick up a prawn with chop sticks, hold over the brandy flame to heat and flavour prawns before serving.

10. Chinese Bream

Ingredients	Approx. Quantity
Bream	2 × 500 gms. (1 Kg)
Water	As required
Salt	To taste
Green ginger	2.5 cm. (1 inch)
Soy sauce	3 tablespoons
Shallots	6 nos.
Green ginger (extra)	2.5 gm (1 inch) Piece
Oil	3 tablespoons

Pre-Preparation: Clean and scale fish, remove back vein inside fish. Fill the pan with water. Add salt and crushed ginger; bring to boil for five minutes. Reduce heat, put fish in water, cover, cook 10 minutes or until cooked.

Method

- Remove and drain fish well and put on heated serving plates. While fish cooks, peel extra ginger, cut in thin slices, then into thin strips. Peel shallots, cut in thin diagonal slices.
- Now heat oil until nearly boiling.

Serving

- Before serving soya sauce over fish, sprinkle with ginger and shallots. Pour heat oil over fish and serve.

11. Braised Prawns with Vegetables

Ingredients	Approx. Quantity
Green king prawns	500 gms.
Canned Bamboo shoots	250 gms.
Broccoli	250 gms.
Canned mushrooms	475 gms.
Oil	1 tablespoon
Chicken stock	1/2 cup
Cornflour	1 teaspoon
Oyster sauce	1 teaspoon
Salt, pepper	To taste
Sugar	Two pinch
Green ginger (grated)	1 teaspoon.

Pre-Preparation: Shell and cut prawns, out remove back vein. Cut broccoli into thick pieces. Drain mushrooms and bamboo shoots and cut into thin slices.

Method

- Heat oil in pan or wok, add prawns, saute quickly until tender and light pink in colour, approx. 3 minutes.
- Now add the bamboo shoots, broccoli and mushrooms, toss well. Blend cornflour with chicken stock, oyster sauce, salt, pepper sugar and ginger. Bring to boil, Stir continuously and cook one minute.

12. Steamed Sea Bass with Fermented Black Beans

Ingredients	Approx. Quantity
Sea Brass (Cleaned but with head and tail left on)	450 gm
Salt	1 teaspoon
Fermented black beans	2 teaspoons
Soy sauce	1 tablespoon
Chinese rice wine or	
Pale dry sherry	1 tablespoon
Ginger root (peeled & finely shredded)	1 tablespoon
Scallion (Including the green top, cut into 2 inch lengths)	1 no.
Peanut oil	1 tablespoon
Sugar	1/2 teaspoon

Pre-Preparation: Wash the bass under cold running water and pat it dry inside and out with paper towels. With a sharp knife, lightly score the fish and by making diagonal cuts. Then sprinkle the fish, inside and out, with the salt. Chop the fermented beans, then combine them in a bowl with the soy sauce, wine, oil and sugar. Mix well. Lay the fish on a heat proof platter 1/2 inch smaller in diameter than the pot you plan to steam it in. Pour the bowl of seasoning over the fish, and arrange the pieces of ginger and scallion on top.

Method

- Pour enough boiling water into the lower part of a steamer.

- Bring the water in the steamer to a rolling boil and place the platter of fish on the rack. Cover the pot securely.
- Keep the water in the steamer at a continuous boil and steam the fish for about 15 minutes, or until it is firm to the touch.

Serving

- Serve at once, on its own steaming platter placed on top of a serving dish.

13. Deep-fried Shrimp Balls

Ingredients	Approx. Quantity
White bread (fresh)	1 slice
Chicken Stock (cold)	2 tablespoons
Shrimps (Uncooked in their shells)	1 pound
Fresh pork fat	1/4 cup
Fresh water chestnuts, or Drained canned water chestnuts	4 nos.
Salt	1 teaspoon
Ginger root	1/2 teaspoon
Egg yolk	1 no.
Egg white	1 no.
Peanut oil	3 cups
Roasted salt and pepper	To taste

Pre-Preparation: Trim crust from the bread and tear bread into small pieces. Place them in a bowl and sprinkle with the stock and or water. Shell the shrimp and lift out the intestinal vein with the point of the knife. Wash the shrimp under cold water and pat them dry with paper towels. Chop the shrimp and pork fat together until they form a smooth paste. In a bowl, combine the soaked bread, shrimp mixture, water chestnuts, salt, ginger and egg yolk and mix thoroughly. Beat the egg white to a froth, and stir it into the shrimp mixture.

Method

- Preheat the oven to its lowest setting. Pour 3 cups of oil into a wok or large deep fat fryer and heat until a haze forms above it or it reaches 350° on a deep-frying thermometer.
- Take a handful of the shrimp mixture and make a ball about the size of a walnut, use a spoon to scoop off the ball and drop it in the hot oil, till golden brown.
- Transfer the fried balls to the paper-lined baking pan to drain and keep warm in the oven.

Serving

- Place the finished shrimp balls to a heated platter and serve with roasted salt and pepper dip.

14. Stir-fried Sea Scallops and Pork Kidneys

Ingredients	Approx. Quantity
Pork kidney	4 nos.
Fresh or thoroughly defrosted Frozen sea scallops	1/2 pound
Peanut oil	1/4 cup
Chinese rice wine or pale Dry sherry	1 tablespoon
Fresh ginger root (Peeled and chopped)	1 teaspoon
Scallion, chopped (Including the green top)	1 no.
Soy sauce	2 tablespoons
Salt	1/2 tablespoon
Sugar	1 tablespoon
Cornstarch (dissolved in 1 tablespoon chicken stock)	1 tablespoon

Pre-Preparation: Peel of the thin outer membrane covering the kidneys. Split the kidneys up half lengthwise and cut away the small knobs of fat and any tough membrane surrounding them. Place the kidney halves flat side down on a chopping board and score their surfaces, cutting about two-thirds of the way down into them and spacing the cuts about 1/4 inch apart. Then cut the slices into strips about 2 inches long. Wash the scallops under cold running water, pat them dry with paper towels and cut them horizontally into slices 1/4 inch thick.

Method

- Set a wok or skillet over high heat for 30 seconds. Pour in 2 tablespoons of oil, heat for another 30 seconds.
- Add the scallops and stir-fry for only 1 minute. Then pour in the wine and add the salt, stir well, and with a large spoon, transfer the scallops to a plate.

- Pour the remaining 2 tablespoons of oil into the pan, heat for about 30 seconds, and add the ginger and scallions. Stir for a few seconds and drop in the kidneys. Stir fry over high heat for 2 minutes or until their edges begin to curl. Then add the soy sauce and sugar.
- Return the scallops and their accumulated juices to the pan, and mix with the kidneys for a few seconds.

Serving

- Recombine cornstarch mixture and add it to the pan. When the kidneys and scallops are coated with a light, clear glaze—(a few seconds)—transfer the entire contents of the pan to a heated platter and serve at once.

PREPARATION OF BEEF

1. Sate Beef

Ingredients	Approx. Quantity
Fillet steak (in one piece)	500 gms.
Soy sauce	I - teaspoons
Pepper	To taste
Sesame oil	2 teaspoons
Cornflour	1 teaspoon
Water	1 tablespoon
Oil	2 tablespoons
Sauce	
Garlic	1 clove
Onion	1 (medium) no.
Sate sauce	3 teaspoons
Dry sherry	2 teaspoons
Curry powder	1 teaspoon
Salt	To taste
Water	2 tablespoons
Soy sauce	2 tablespoons
Sugar	1 - tablespoons

Pre-Preparation: Trim all fat and sinew from meat. Cut meat into 5 mm (1/4 inch) slices. Gently pound each slice to flatten slightly. Put meat in bowl. Add soy sauce, pepper sesame oil cornflour and water, mix well and keep for 20 minutes.

Method

- Heat oil in wok or pan, saute meat until brown, and remove from pan.
- Peel and roughly dice onion, add to pan with crushed garlic and saute for 2-3 minutes. Combine sate sauce, sherry,

sugar, curry powder, salt, water and soy sauce. Add to onions in pan. Stir until boiling. Return beef to pan, cook until beef is tender.

2. Braised Star Anise Beef

Ingredients	Approx. Quantity
Boneless beef	2 pounds
Cold water	3-4 cups
Soy sauce	5 tablespoons
Chinese rice wine or pale dry sherry	2 tablespoons
Sugar	2 tablespoons
Peeled fresh ginger root	4 slices
Star anise	1 (whole)
Sesame seed oil	1 tablespoon

Method

- Place the beef in a heavy 3 to 4 quart saucepan and pour in to just cover the meat. Bring to a boil over high heat and, as the scum begins to rise to the surface of the water, skim it carefully. Then, stir in the soy sauce, wine, sugar, ginger and star anise and partially cover the pan. Reduce the heat to moderate and for to 3 hours, or until it shows no resistance when pierced with the tip of a sharp knife. Add the sesame seed oil and simmer slowly for another 10 minutes.

3. Curried Beef

Ingredients	Approx. Quality
Fillet Steak	500 gms.
Potatoes	3 nos.
Onions	2 nos.
Curry powder	2 teaspoons
Oil	2 tablespoons
Oil (extra)	2 tablespoons
Curry powder (extra)	3 tablespoons
Sate sauce	2 tablespoons
Chinese chilli sauce	1 tablespoon
Soy sauce	1 tablespoon
Water	1/3 cup
Chicken stock cube	1 no.
Cornflour	3 teaspoons
Dry sherry	1 tablespoon

Pre-Preparation: Slice fillet steak thinly. Peel and cut potatoes, and onion into cubes.

Method

- Heat oil in pan or wok, add potatoes, cook five minutes or until just tender but still crisp. Toss occasionally. Add onions and curry powder, cook further for two minutes; remove it from pan.
- Heat extra oil in pan, add steak, cook until golden brown on both sides and through. Add potato, onions and extra curry powder, toss for two minutes.
- Add combined sate sauce, chilli sauce, soy sauce, water, crumbled stock cube, cornflour and sherry. Toss until sauce boils and thickens. Reduce heat, simmer three minutes.

4. Beef with Celery

Ingredients	Approx. Quantity
Rump steak	500 gms.
Vinegar	1 teaspoon
Soya sauce	2 teaspoons
Egg white	1 no.
Oil	3 tablespoons
Shallots	6 nos.
Green ginger	2.5 cm. (1 inch) piece
Cornflour	3 teaspoons
Water	1/2 cup
Soya sauce (extra)	1 tablespoon
Dry sherry	1 tablespoon
Oyster sauce	2 teaspoons
Garlic	1 clove

Pre-Preparation: Remove excess fat from meat, cut meat into strips 2.5 cm (1 inch) long, combine with vinegar, soy sauce and lightly beaten egg-white. Cover and keep aside for one hour, stir occasionally. Peel ginger, chop finely, chop shallots into 2.5 cm (1 inch) lengths, slice celery diagonally. Put celery into boiling salted water, boil two minutes, drain, rinse under cold running water, drain well.

Method

- Heat 2 tablespoons of the oil in pan or wok, add meat, till brown and then remove from wok.

- Heat remaining oil in wok, add celery, shallots, ginger and crushed garlic and saute for one minute.
- Add meat to pan, toss well. Combine cornflour with water, extra soya sauce, sherry and oyster sauce, mix well. Before serving add to wok, stir until boiling and well combined.

5. Beef with Cashews

Ingredients	Approx. Quantity
Rump steak	500 gms.
Unsalted roasted cashews	100 gms.
Shallots	8 nos.
Garlic	2 cloves
Green ginger	2.5 cm. (1 inch) piece
Oil	3 tablespoons
Cornflour	1 tablespoon
Water	1/2 cup
Sate sauce	1 teaspoon
Soya sauce	1 tablespoon

Pre-Preparation: Remove fat from meat and cut into thin slices. Chop shallots into 2.5 cm (1 inch) pieces; peel ginger, chop finely; crush garlic.

Method

- Heat two tablespoons of the oil in pan or wok, add the beef, and cook until well browned.
- Heat remaining oil in pan, add garlic, shallots, ginger and cashew nuts, saute one minute.
- Add meat to pan with vegetables, toss well, combine cornflour, water, sate sauce, sesame oil and soya sauce, mix well. Add to pan, stir until boiling and well combined.

6. Ginger Beef

Ingredients	Approx. Quantity
Fillet steak (in one piece)	500 gms.
Cornflour	2 teaspoons
Oil	2 teaspoons
Soya sauce	1 teaspoon
Sugar	1 teaspoon
Salt	1 teaspoon

Ingredients	Approx. Quantity
Green ginger	125 gms.
White vinegar	2 tablespoons
Oil (extra)	2 tablespoons
Green pepper	1 tablespoon
Shallots	6 nos.
Red chilli	1 no.

Pre-Preparation: Trim all fat and sinew from meat, slice meat into 5 mm slices. Put meat in bowl, combine with cornflour, oil and soy sauce. Mix well, marinate 20 minutes. Clean, peel and thinly slice green ginger, combine with vinegar, sugar and salt in separate bowl, marinate 20 minutes or longer. Cut pepper in half, remove seeds, chip into 2.5 cm. cubes.

Method

- Heat extra oil in wok or pan, add meat slices gradually spreading out in pan, when browned on one side, turn to brown other side; don't overlap slices or meat, will not brown well. Cook quickly and only until meat is tender then from pan.
- Add ginger with liquid to pan with chopped pepper and shallots, cook quickly stirring for two to three minutes. Return meat to pan, continue cooking for a further minute. Stir constantly.

Serving

- Serve, garnished with thinly sliced chilli or sliced shallots.

7. Pepper Steak

Ingredients	Approx. Quantity
Flank steak	1 pound
Chinese rice wine	1 tablespoon
Soya sauce	3 tablespoons
Sugar	1 tablespoon
Cornstarch	2 tablespoons
Green pepper (Seeded, deribed and cut into 1/2" sauce)	2 tablespoons
Fresh ginger root (Peeled)	4 slices
Peanut oil	4 cups

Pre-Preparation: With a sharp knife, cut the flank steak lengthwise into strips 1-wide, then crosswise into 1/4 inch slices. In a large bowl, mix the wine, soya sauce, sugar and cornstarch. Add the steak slices and toss with a large spoon to coat them thoroughly. The steak may be cooked at once, or marinated for as long as 6 hours.

Method

- Set a 12" wok over high heat for about 30 seconds. Pour in a tablespoon of the oil, swirl it about in the pan and heat for another 30 seconds, turning the heat, down to moderate if the oil begins to smoke. Immediately add the pepper squares and stir-fry for 3 minutes, or until they are tender but still crisp. Scoop them out with a slotted spoon and reserve. Pour 3 more tablespoons of oil into the pan and heat almost to the smoking point. Add the ginger, stir for a few seconds, then drop in the steak mixture. Stir-fry over high heat for about 2 minutes, or until the meat shows no sign of pink. Discard the ginger. Add the pepper and cook for few minutes.

Serving

- Transfer the contents of the pan to a heated platter and serve.

8. Beef with Black Bean Sauce

Ingredients	Approx. Quantity
Rump Steak	750 gms.
Egg white	1 no.
Dry sherry	1 tablespoon
Soya sauce	2 tablespoons
Cornflour	1 tablespoon
Canned black beans	1 tablespoon
Cornflour (extra)	2 tablespoons
Water	1/3 cup
Sugar	Two pinch
Curry powder	1 teaspoon
Bamboo shoots (Sliced)	1/3 cup
Red pepper	2 nos.
Shallots	4 nos.
Oil	1/2 cup

Pre-Preparation: Trim away any fat from steak. Cut steak into 5 cm x 5 mm strips. Combine in bowl with egg white, sherry, soya sauce and cornflour, mix well. Stand 30 minutes. Put beans in bowl, cover with water, stand fifteen minutes, drain and rinse under cold running water. Put on to plate, add sugar and one teaspoon water, mash well. Chop shallots into 2.5 cm pieces, cut pepper in half, remove seeds, cut each half into thin strips.

Method

- Add two tablespoons oil to pan, add shallots, red pepper, bamboo shoots, and curry powder and saute for two minutes. Remove it. Now heat remaining oil in wok, add meat and marinade and cook until browned.
- Put vegetable again in a pan with bean mixture and combine well. Blend extra cornflour with remaining water, add to wok, stir until mixture boils and thickens.

PREPARATION OF VEGETABLES

1. Stir-fried Spiced Cabbage

Ingredients	Approx. Quantity
Chinese cabbage	500 gms
Sugar	2 tablespoons
White vinegar	2 tablespoons
Soya sauce	1 tablespoon
Salt	1 tablespoon
Cayenne pepper	1/4 tablespoon
Peanut oil	1 tablespoon

Pre-Preparation: With a sharp knife, trim the top leaves of the cabbage and the root ends. Separate the stalks and wash them under cold running water. Cut each stalk, leaves and all, into 1 by il inch pieces. In a small bowl, combine the sugar, vinegar, soya sauce, salt and cayenne pepper, and mix thoroughly.

Method

- Set a 12 inch wok or 10 inch skillet over high heat for 30 seconds. Pour in the 2 tablespoon of oil, swirl it about in the pan and heat for another 30 seconds, turn

the heat down to moderate if the oil begins to smoke. Drop in the string beans and stir-fry for 3 minutes.
- Add the salt, sugar, water chestnuts, and stir once or twice before pouring in the stock.
- Cover the pan and cook over moderate heat for 2 to 3 minutes until the beans are tender but still crisp. Now give the cornstarch mixture a stir to recombine it and add it to the pan. Cook stirring until the vegetables are coated with a light, clear glaze.

Serving

- Transfer the entire contents of the pan to a heated platter and serve at once.

2. Stir-fried String Beans and Water Chestnuts

Ingredients	Approx. Quantity
Fresh string beans	400 nos.
Peanut oil	4 tablespoons
Salt	2 tablespoons
Sugar	2 tablespoons
Water chestnuts (Cut into 1/4 inch slices)	2 nos.
Chicken stock	1/2 cup
Cornstarch (Dissolved in 1 tablespoon chicken stock, freshor canned)	2 teaspoons

Pre-Preparation: Snap off and discard the ends of the beans, and with a small knife, remove any strings. Cut the beans into 2 inch pieces.

Method

- Set a 12 inch wok or 10 inch skillet over high heat for 30 seconds. Pour in the oil swirl it about in the pan and heat for another 30 seconds, then turn, the heat down to moderate. Immediately add the cabbage and stir fry for 2-3 minutes. Make sure all the cabbage is coated with the oil.
- Remove the pan from the heat and stir in the soy-vinegar mixture.

Serving

- Transfer the cabbage to a platter and let it cool to lukewarm before serving, or serve it chilled.

3. Chinese Vegetables

Ingredients	Approx. Quantity
Broccoli	500 gms.
Finely chopped green ginger	1 tablespoon
Onions	2 nos.
Celery	4 sticks
Mustard cabbage or spinach	1 bunch
Snow peas	250 gms.
Shallots	8 nos.
Oil	1/4 cup
Chicken stock cubes	2 nos.
Water	3/4 cups

Pre-Preparation: Peel and quarter onions, string celery and slice diagonally, take the leaves from the stalks of the cabbage, slice the stalks diagonally, slice leaves roughly, trim stalks from broccoli, cut stalks into even diagonal lengths, cut broccolli tops into flowerets; string snow peas; slice shallots diagonally.

Method

- Heat oil in wok or large frying pan, add ginger, sliced cabbage stalks, broccoli stalks and onion; stir gently to coat all vegetables with oil, cook for one minute.
- Add remaining vegetables, toss together lightly.
- Stir in water and crumbled stock cubes, bring to boil. Cover and cook until vegetables are just tender, about three minutes. Remove lid to stir occasionally.

Serving

- Serve, garnished with sliced shallots.

4. Stir-fried Snow Peas with Chinese Mushrooms and Bamboo Shoots

Ingredients	Approx. Quantity
Dried Chinese mushrooms	6 nos.
Fresh snow peas	1 pound
Canned bamboo shoots (sliced, 1/8" thick and cut into 1-by-1 inch triangular tree shaped pieces)	1/2 cup
Salt	1½ teaspoons
Sugar	1 - teaspoons
Peanut oil	2 tablespoons

Pre-Preparation: In a small bowl, cover the mushrooms with 1/2 cup of warm water and let them soak for 30 minutes. Remove them with a slotted spoon. With a cleaver or sharp knife, cut away and discard the tough stems of the mushrooms and cut each cap into quarters. Strain the soaking water through a fine sieve and reserve 2 tablespoons of it. Snap off the tips of the fresh snow peas and remove the strings from the pea pods.

Method

- Set a 12 inch wok on 10 inch skillet high heat for 30 seconds. Pour in the 2 tablespoons of oil. Swirl it about in the pan and heat for another 30 seconds, turning the heat down to moderate if the oil begins to smoke. Immediately drop in the mushrooms and bamboo shoots and stir fry for two minutes. Then add snow-peas, salt and sugar reserved mushrooms—soaking water at cook stirring constantly at high heat for about two minutes or until the water evaporates.

Serving

- Place the contents of the pan to a heated platter and serve at once.

5. Braised Bean Curd with Mushrooms and Hot Meat Sauce

Ingredients	Approx. Quantity
Vegetable oil	30 ml.
Onion (medium sized)	1 no.
Garlic clove	1 no.
Pork or beef	110 gm.
Chinese dried mushroom	4 nos.
Beef stock	90 ml.
Soya sauce	30-35 gms.
Black pepper Chinese chilli sauce or	
Tabasco sauce	I - gm.
Dry sherry	30 ml.
Bean curd	5 cubes.
Cornstarch	10-12 gm.
Sesame oil	7 ml.

Pre-Preparation: Slice onion thinly. Cruch garlic. Soak mushrooms for 30 minutes drain, remove stalk and slice cap. Cut bean curd cake in 20 pieces. Mix cornstarch with 2 tablespoons cold water.

Method

- Heat the oil in a large heavy frying pan. Add the onion and garlic and stir-fry over moderate heat for 2 minutes. Add the meat and mushrooms and continue to stir-fry for 5 minutes.
- Pour in the stock and add the soy sauce, pepper, chille or tabacco sauce and sherry. Cook stirring frequently for 3 more minutes. Add the bean corn and mix with the ingredients.
- Pour the cornstarch mixture evenly over the ingredients and cook stirring constantly for 1 minutes. Sprinkle with sesame oil serve immediately.

N.B.: Both the spelling Soy sauce and Soya sauce are used in cooking.

INDIAN COURSE - ITEMS AND PREPARATIONS

A. Indian Starters and Soups
Starters
1. Achari Salad
2. Cuchumber
3. Chaat Papri
4. Achari Winglets

Soups
5. Winter vegetable soup
6. Mushroom soup
7. Sweetcorn soup
8. Cream of winter potato soup
9. Boula-boula
10. Tomato coconut shorba

B. Indian Non-veg. items

I. Egg
1. Ande Ka Salan.

II. Fish
1. Fresh water fish curry.
2. Red tomato fish.
3. Goan styled fish curry.
4. Fish kundan kalia.
5. Chingree (prawn) malai curry.
6. Kerala styled fried fish.
7. Machchi ka kalia.

III. Mutton
1. Mutton curry.
2. Meat do pyaz.
3. Mutton kasa (Dry bhuna meat).
4. Meat masala.
5. Luckhnawi meat korma.
6. Nilgiri korma.
7. Achari ghost.
8. Dal meat.
9. Murg mussallam.
10. Sunday meat curry.

IV. Chicken
1. Butter chicken.
2. Dahi chicken.
3. Methi chicken.
4. Peshawari bharawan murg
5. Handi chicken.
6. Murg sagwala.

C. Indian Vegetarian Items

I. Paneer Ki Subji
1. Pea-paneer
2. Paneer sagwala
3. Sahi paneer
4. Kadahi paneer
5. Paneer durbar

II. Other Vegetable Items
1. Cashew potato curry
2. Dum aloo
3. Vegetable Tak-a-tin
4. Hare chane ke sabji
5. Sauted winter vegetables

(a) Cauliflower + Capsicum + Mushroom.
(b) Cabbage + Potato + Capsicum + Green peas.
(c) Aloo + Gobi + Beans
(d) Patna Kadoo

6. Brinjal with chilli garlic gravy
7. Vegetable augratin
8. Shyaamgadda Pulusu

III. Dal

1. Dal Maharani
2. Dal Panchmahal
3. Moti Mahal dal
4. Dal Makhani
5. Ghana Peshawari
6. Maash ki Dal Khasgi

D. Indian Rice and Bread Items

I. Rice Dishes

1. Shahi Dehradun
2. Yakhni Pulao
3. Plain Pulao
4. Vegetable Biryani

II. Bread

1. Naan
2. Stuffed Paratha
3. Layered Paratha (Lachcha paratha)

E. Indian Sweet Dessert Items

1. Phirnee
2. Rice Kheer
3. Vermicelli kheer
4. Sahi tukri
5. Jafrani halwa
6. Malpua
7. Sheermal
8. Pitha

PREPARATION OF INDIAN STARTERS AND SOUPS

1. Achari Salad

Cauliflower	50 gms.
Carrot	50 gms.
Green peas	50 gms.
Green chillies	2-3 nos.
Snow peas	50 gms.
Mustard oil	
Mustard seeds	
Methi seeds	
Methi powder Pickle masala	20-25 gms.
Dhania powder	
Red chilli powder	
Mustard seed powder	

Pre-Preparation: Clean, wash, dry and cut the vegetables in small cubes. Dust with turmeric powder.

Method

- Heat mustard oil in a pan or kadahi.
- Add mustard seeds for tempering. When tempered, add vegetables. Now add home made pickle masala.
- Finally on top green chilli may be added.

2. Cuchumber

Ingredients	Approx. Quantity
Tomatoes	500 gms.
Cucumber	500 gms.
Green chillies	10 nos.
Lime	2 nos.
Capsicum	300 gms.
Onion	500 gms.
Salt	To taste.

Method

- Cut vegetables into cubes.
- Prepare fresh lemon dressing.
- Toss the cut raw vegetables with dressing before service.

3. Chat Papri (For 6-8 portions)

Ingredients	Approx. Quantity
Flour	150 gms.
Semolina (sooji)	15-20 gms.
Salt	To taste.
Oil	To fry
Boiled chana	100 gms.
Chopped boiled potatoes	2 large one
Tamarind sweet chutney	100-150 ml.
Curd	500 gms.
Green chillies, green coriander, Red chilli powder and chaat masala	To taste

Pre-Preparation: Boil chana. Chop potatoes. Make tamarind chutney. Soak 1 cup tamarind overnight in little water. Mash and strain twice next day. Add I - cup sugar and cook for few minutes. Cool and add I-cup sugar black cardamom, red chilli powder, green chillies and green coriander to taste.

Method

- Sieve flour and suji, and salt and 1 tablespoon oil and rub with the help of palm.

- Make hard dough with little warm water. Divide into small balls and roll out into thin roundles of 1-1½ inch diameter approximately or divide into big size balls and roll out into thin sheet or round and use cutter of 1"-1½".

- Prick with the fork lightly and deep fry till light brown in colour. Papri's should not puff-up.

- Arrange chana, potatoes and papri in plates and top it with beaten up curd, tamarind chutney and masala to taste.

4. Achari Winglets

Ingredients	Approx. Quantity
Chicken winglets	10 nos.
Chicken minced	125 gms.
Garam masala	5 gms.
Coriander leaves	One bunch
Ginger paste	10 gms.
Garlic paste	5 gms.
Red chilli powder	5 gms.
Salt	To taste
Readymade achari masala	30-50 gms.
Refined oil for fry.	
For batter	
Cornflour	50 gms.
Water	100 ml.

Pre-Preparation: Scrape the flesh from the bone of winglets, taking care to leave a little towards the end. Mix chicken mince, garam masala, chopped coriander leaves, ginger-garlic paste, red chilli powder and salt. Make a batter of cornflour and water. Keep aside.

Method

- Stuff the mixture into chicken winglet flesh. Dip in batter and fry in hot oil till golden brown.

Serving

- Coat with mixed pickle mixture and serve hot on a bed of onions rings, before serving.

5. Winter Vegetable Soup

Ingredients	Approx. Quantity
Spring Onions chopped	2 Nos. (100 gms)
Spinach	1 cups
Shelled Peas	1 cups
Milk	1 cups
Butter	2 tablespoons
Tomatoes	2 Nos. (100 gms.)
Grated Nutmeg	1/4 teaspoon
Chopped Cabbage or	
Salad leaves	4 tablespoons
Chopped Mint leaves	1 tablespoon
Vermicilli (Boiled)	1 teaspoon
Salt & Pepper	To taste
Fresh cream	2 tablespoons

Method

- Melt butter in pan and fry green of spring onion, mint, spinach tomatoes and cabbage for 5-6 minutes. Add 4 cups of water and peas and pressure cook for 5 minutes.

- Blend in Mixie and strain the above mixture. Add salt and pepper, milk, grated nutmeg and cream. Mix well and heat for few minutes.

- Garnish with vermicilli, few boiled green peas and boiled chopped carrots and serve hot.

6. Mushroom Soup

Ingredients	Approx. Quantity
Fresh mushrooms	200 gms.
Onions	4 nos.
Fresh cream	100 gms.
Salt and pepper	To taste.
Potato	4 nos.
Milk	4 cups
Butter	4 tablespoons

Pre-Preparation: Chop finely half the onion, 5-6 mushroooms and cook in little butter. Keep aside for garnish.

Method

- Cook remaining onions and mushrooms chopped in butter alongwith peeled and cut potatoes. Add 2 cups water, milk, salt and pepper and pressure cook for 6-8 minutes.

- Blend the above mixture in mixie. Add cooked garnish and boil for few minutes. Before service cream in added.

7. Sweetcorn Soup

Ingredients	Approx. Quantity
Corn (on the cob)	6 nos.
Cornflour	2 tablespoons
Soy sauce	1/2 teaspoon
Sugar	1/2 teaspoon
Salt	1/2 teaspoon
Cream	1/2 cup
Vegetable stock	6 cups.

Method

- Grate the corn from the cob. Add 4 cups stock and cook for 20-30 minutes.
- Dissolve cornflour in 2 cups stock and add to the cooked corn. Now add salt, sugar and reboil for 20-30 minutes. At the final step add cream and soy sauce.

8. Cream of Winter Potato Soup

Ingredients	Approx. Quantity
Potatoes	500 gms.
Onions	1 no.
Fresh cream	1/2 cup
Butter	2 tablespoons
Bay leaf	1 no.
Salt and pepper	To taste
Cooking cheese	50 gms.
Vegetable starch	1½ cups

Method

- Slice peeled potatoes and onion and cook in butter for 5-6 minutes.
- Add bayleaf, I - cups stock and boil for 20-25 minutes till the potatoes are tender.
- Remove bayleaf and strain it. Add salt and pepper to taste. Adjust the consistency by adding stock incase of too much thickness.
- Finally add cream and grated cheese on top.

9. Boula-boula (Green pea soup)

Ingredients	Approx. Quantity
White wine	50 gms.
Onion	1
Garlic	2 cloves
Green pea puree	100 gms
White stock	100 gms.
Salt	According to taste
Pepper	10 gms.
Arrowroot	2 Tsp.
Cream 50 gms	
Parsley	A few.

Method

- Saute onion, garlic, minced beef in white wine.
- Add green pea puree.
- Add white stock and boil it.
- Season with salt and pepper.
- Add diluted arrow root to thicken the soup. Cream and chopped parsley is added before serving.

10. Tomato Coconut Shorba

Ingredients	Approx. Quantity
Tomato	1 kg
Carrot	250 gms.
Onion	2 nos. (large)
Garlic clove	4 nos.
Butter	1 tablespoon
Fresh coconut	5 tablespoons
White sauce	2 cups
Salt and pepper	To taste
Bread croutons	For garnishing
Water	3 cups

Pre-Preparation: Cut tomatoes into large pieces. Grate carrots. Cut onion. Crush garlic. Grate coconut.

Method

- Heat butter in a pan. Add onion and garlic in butter and fry for two minutes.
- Add tomato, carrot, coconut and water and cook at boil.
- Pour the mixture into a liquidizer and strain.

- Boil it with salt for 10-15 minutes.
- Add white sauce and black pepper and mix well before serving bread croutons is added.

PREPARATION OF INDIAN NON-VEG. ITEMS

I. Egg

1. Ande Ka Salan

Ingredients	Approx. Quantity
Vegetable oil	4 tablespoons
Onions	2 nos.
Ginger	1 inch piece.
Garlic cloves	2 nos.
Turmeric	1 teaspoon
Cumin	1 teaspoon
Coriander	2 teaspoons
Cayenne pepper	1 teaspoon
Fennel seeds	1/4 teaspoon
Coriander leaves	1 tablespoon
Tomatoes	450 gms.
Salt	1 teaspoon
Sugar	1/2 teaspoon
Creamed coconut	1/2" slice
Hard boiled duck eggs	6 nos.
Lemon juice	1 tablespoon

Pre-Preparation: Chop onion, ginger, coriander leaves and tomatoes. Crush garlic. Grind cumin seeds, coriander seeds and fennel seeds. Cut eggs in halves length ways.

Method

- Heat the oil in a large saucepan.
- Add the onions, ginger garlic and fry until golden brown.
- Now add turmeric, cumin, coriander, cayenne pepper and fennel seeds. Fry for 8 minutes spices. Add coriander leaves tomatoes, salt and sugar and bring to the boil on slow fire for about 30 minutes.
- Add creamed coconut and after dissolving add the eggs and cook for 20 minutes on slow fire. At last pour lemon juice and serve with boiled rice, paratha etc.

II. Fish

1. Fresh Water Fish Curry

Ingredients	Approx. Quantity
Fish	100 gms.
Lemon	1/2 piece.
Onion	50 gms. (1 small)
Ginger	1/4" piece
Garlic	2 cloves
Tomatoes	50 gms.
Curd	2 teaspoons
Salt	1/2 teaspoon
Red chilli powder	1/4 teaspoon
Turmeric powder	1/4 teaspoon
Garam masala	1/8 teaspoon
Fat	1 T
Black cardamom	1 no
Cloves	2 nos.
Pepper corns	2 nos.
Cinnamon	1" piece
Bay leaf	4 nos.
Potato	
Cauliflower	Optional

Pre-Preparation: Clean, wash and marinate the fish with lemon juice and salt for about one hour and keep aside. Roast cloves, cinnamon and pepper corn. Grind them alongwith ginger and garlic.

Method

- Heat fat in a heavy bottom pan, add bay leaf and black cardamom and fry. Add grated onion and fry till golden brown. Add chilli and turmeric powder and add little water.
- Add masala paste, blanched and chopped tomatoes, beaten curd and salt to the above masala and cook till fat separates out.
- Wash the marinated fish and dry it with a clean cloth. Add to the fried masala. Fry for some more time, then add water to make thick gravy. Bring to a boil, reduce heat and simmer for 3-5 minutes. Before serving chopped coriander leaves and garam masala is added.

Note

- Potato and cauliflower may be added.

2. Red Tomato Fish

Ingredients	Approx. Quantity
Tomatoes	400 gms.
Onion	50 gms.
Garlic	7 cloves
Sugar	2 teaspoons
Vinegar for Cornflour	2 teaspoons
Tomato	2 teaspoons
Butter gravy	2 teaspoons
Red chilli powder	1/2 teaspoon
Salt	1 teaspoon
Fish (Pomfret)	200 gms.
Salt	1 teaspoon
Lemon juice	1 teaspoon
Ginger For	10 gms.
Green chilli	
Fish	2 nos.
Button onion	120 gms.
Fat	2 tablespoon
Potato	
For garnish	120 gms.
Coriander leaves	A few

Pre-Preparation: Make tomato gravy. Cook sliced onion, tomato and garlic with salt till done and then blend and sieve and get a thick puree. After then heat butter and cook tomato puree with red chilli powder and dissolved cornflour. After a few minutes add sugar and vinegar and simmer till sauce become thick. Clean and wash fish, remove head and cut into three parts. Rub salt and lemon juice and leave for half and hour.

Method

- Heat fat and fry button onions and keep aside.
- Fry fish lightly and cook it by simmering with salt and chilli powder till two-third done.
- Slow the fire till fish is tender and sauce penetrates the fish. At last add fried potato pieces and coriander leaves before serving.

3. Goan Styled Fish Curry

Ingredients	Approx. Quantity
Fish (Pomfret prepared)	500 gms.
Onion	50 gms.
Red chillies	8-10 gms.
Turmeric powder	1/2 teaspoon
Cumin seeds	1/2 teaspoon
Coriander seeds	20 gms.
Coconut	120 gms.
Tomatoes	50 gms.
Green chillies	5 gms.
Curry leaves	1 sprig
Tamarind	15 gms.
Salt	10 gms.
Oil	15 ml.

Pre-Preparation: Chop onions. Roast and grind red chillies, cumin seeds and coriander seeds. Grind coconut to a fine paste and mix with spices. Clean and cut fish into slices, wash well and marinate with salt and turmeric. Soak tamarind in a little water and extract pulp.

Method

- Heat oil. Fry onions, add coconut paste and slit green chillies. Fry for 2-3 minutes and then add chopped tomatoes and sufficient water.
- Now add fish to simmering gravy and at the final step add tamarind extract, curry leaves, salt and simmer till fish is cooked.

4. Fish Kundan Kalia

Ingredients	Approx. Quantity
Boneless fish pieces	500 gms.
Onions	250 gms.
Ginger	20 gms.
Garlic	25 gms.
Salt	To taste
Desi ghee	150 gms.
Malai/cream	150 gms.
Dahi	100 gms.
Sone-ka-vark	2 nos.

Ingredients	Approx. Quantity
Coriander powder	5 gms.
Turmeric powder	5 gms.
Red chilli powder	5 gms.
Jafran	1/2 gms.
Garam Masala	
Mace	1 gm.

Pre-Preparation: Clean and wash fish pieces. Keep aside. Slice onions finely and fry in ghee till golden brown. Remove and crush to a fine paste. Grind the garlic to a paste. Grind the masala finely.

Method

- Heat the ghee in a patile and add fish, onions, ginger paste, garlic juice and fry for 10 minutes. Alter them add coriander powder, turmeric powder, chilli powder and salt and fry for five minutes.
- Add beaten curd (1 tablespoon) and fry till the ghee separates.
- Add a cup of water and the ground garam masala and cook covered till the fish is tender and when done remove the pieces of fish from the gravy and keep aside.
- Strain the gravy and add mashed and strained malai to the gravy.
- Add crushed saffron and the yellow colour (if needed). Cook the fish on a slow fire for 5 minutes with gravy.
- At last place the fish pieces in a shallow dish and cover with gold leaf. Mix the rest of the gold leaves in the gravy with a fork so that the gravy looks like emulsified gold 'Kundan Kalia'. Serve with chapati or naan.

5. Chingree (Prawn) Malai Curry

Ingredients	Approx. Quantity
Chingree	500 gms.
Cumin seeds	5 gms.
Ginger	A small piece
Red chilli powder	1/2 teaspoon
Turmeric powder	1/2 teaspoon
Cardamom	1/4 teaspoon
Cloves	5-6 nos.

Ingredients	Approx. Quantity
Cinnamon	2 sticks
Panchporan	1 teaspoon
Coconut milk	1/2 portion.
Sugar	2 teaspoon
Salt	To taste.
Oil	As required.
Water	As required
Cinnamon	2 gms.
Large cardamom	2 gms.
Pepper corns	10-12 nos.
Small cardamom	2 gms.

Pre-Preparation: Shell Chingree, remove intestines and wash well. Season and lightly fry chingree. Keep aside.

Method

- Heat oil. Add panchphoran, bay leaf, ginger, cumin seeds, turmeric powder, red chilli powder and fry till oil comes out.
- Add coconut milk, sugar and salt with required water and let it oil.
- After boiling add fried prawns and cook till gravy is thickened. Serve hot with rice.

6. Kerala Style Fried Fish

Ingredients	Approx. Quantity
Fish fillets	450 gms.
Lemon juice	1 tablespoon
Chilli powder	1 teaspoon
Turmeric powder	1 teaspoon
Black pepper	1/8 teaspoon
Garlic	1 clove
Salt	1 teaspoon

Pre-Preparation: Crush garlic and black pepper. Rub fish with lemon juice. Dry fully with paper towels. Combine chilli powder, turmeric, black pepper, garlic and salt. Rub into fish and mariante for 1 hour.

Method

- Heat oil in skillet and fry fish until brown.

7. Machchi Ka Khalia

Ingredients	Approx. Quantity
Fillets of fish (Murrel, Bhetki, Sole, Pomfret)	90 gms. each (about 12 pieces)

The Marination

Ginger paste	15 gms.
Garlic paste	7 gms.
Lemon juice	30 ml.
Coconut oil (other oil also can be used)	3 tablespoons
Red chilli powder	1.5 gms.
Turmeric powder	1.5 gms.
Salt	To taste

The Khalia paste

Roasted peanuts	75 gms.
Coconut	75 gms.
Sesame seeds	45 gms.
Onions	250 gms.
Coriander powder	12 gms.
Cumin powder	3 gms.
Pathar ka phool powder	1.5 gms.
Bay leaf powder	1.5 gms.

The Gravy

Cooking oil	45 ml.
Cumin seeds	1 gm.
Mustard seeds	2 gms.
(Methi) Fenugreek seeds	1 gm. (Kalongi)
Black onion seeds	0.75 gm.
Curry leaves	24 nos.
Ginger paste	30 gms.
Garlic paste	15 gms.
Turmeric powder	3 gms.
Red chilli powder	3 gms.
Tamarind pulp	45 gms.
Coriander	1.65 gm.
Green chillies	4 nos.
Salt	To taste.
Fish stock	1 litre.

Pre-Preparation: Clean, trim, wash and pat dry the fish. Mix all the ingredients of marination and rub over the fish cubes. Keep aside for 15 minutes.

Make the Khalia paste: Remove the brown skin and grate coconut. Heat a tawa or non-stick frying pan, broil coconut and sesame seeds, separately over very low heat until each emits unique aroma. Peel, wash and roughly chop onions. Put these ingredients in a blender, add peanuts and 180 ml (3/4 cup) water and make a smooth paste. Now mix coriander, cumin, pathar ka phool and bay leaf powders and keep aside.

Make the gravy : Clean, wash and pat dry curry leaves. Clean, wash and coarsley chop coriander leaves. Wash green chilli, slit, deseed and discard the stems.

Make the garnish: Clean and wash coriander leaves.

Method

- Heat oil in a pan, add cumin, mustard, fenugreek and kalonji seeds. Stir over medium heat until they begin to pop. Add half curry leaves, stir, add the ginger and garlic pastes. Stir fry for a minute; add turmeric and red chillies (both dissolved in 30 ml water). Stir until the liquid has evaporated.
- Now add the khalia paste. Stir fry until speeks of fat begin to appear on the surface. Add tamarind pulp; stir for 2-3 minutes.
- Then add fish stock, bring to a boil, reduce to low heat and simmer until reduced by half.
- Add fish, chopped coriander, green chillies and the remaining curry leaves. Bring to a boil. Reduce to low heat and simmer by just gently shaking the pan and not stirring, until the gravy is of medium thin sauce consistency. Remove from fire and adjust the seasoning.

III. Mutten

1. Mutton Curry (Hotel Style)

Ingredients	Approx. Quantity
Coriander powder	20 gins.
Pepper corns	1 teaspoon
Turmeric powder	1 teaspoon
Red onions	50 gms.

Ingredients	Approx. Quantity
Garlic	4 flakes
Ginger	2.5 cm. piece
Green chillies	8 nos.
Oil	30 ml.
Salt	To taste.

Tempering

Ingredients	Approx. Quantity
Cinnamon	1 piece
Cloves	2 nos.
Pepper corns	3 nos.
Red onion	1 no.
Curry leaves	1 spring
Oil or ghee	1 tablespoon

Pre-Preparation: Cut mutton into 1 pieces with the bones and clean it. Make a paste with coriander powder, pepper corns, turmeric and 1 or 2 red onion and garlic. Slit green chillies, slice ginger and rest of the onions.

Method

● Heat oil. Add mustard seeds; when seeds crackle add sliced onions and curry leaves. When onions brown, add mutton and ground spices. Fry a little and then add ginger, green chillies, salt and enough water to cook mutton.

● Heat oil. Add crushed cinnamon, cloves, pepper corns, sliced onions, curry powder and after a few minutes pour this seasoning over curry and mix well.

2. Meat Do Pyaz

Ingredients	Approx. Quantity
Mutton (neck portion)	500 gms.
Fat	50 gms.
Onions (sliced)	115 gms.
Salt	10 gms.
Water	As required

Grind together

Turmeric	a pinch
Red chillies	5 gms.

Ingredients	Approx. Quantity
Coriander	10 gms.
Ginger	a small piece
Oil	100 gms.
Eggs	2 nos.
Breadcrumbs	30 gms.
Salt	to taste.

Pre-Preparation: Clean and cut meat into even size portions.

Method

● Heat fat and fry sliced onions till golden brown. Keep aside.
● Add ground spices and fry well.
● Add meat and continue frying.
● Add fried onion, salt and water.
● Cook till meat is tender and gravy if thickened.

3. Mutton Kasa (Dry Bhuna meat)

Ingredients	Approx. Quantity
Mutton	500 gms.
Vinegar	30 ml.
Onions	225 gms.
Potatoes	115 gms.
Tomatoes	115 gms.
Carrots	115 gms.
Garlic	1 flake
Red chillies (without seeds)	5 gms.
Ginger	a small piece
Oil	100 gms.
Eggs	2 mos.
Breadcrumbs	30 gms.
Salt	to taste

Pre-Preparation: Grind chillies, ginger and garlic to a fine paste. Clean and cut meat, potatoes and carrots into even sized cubes. Chop onions.

Method

● Boil meat with vinegar, half the oil and salt. When half done add ground spices and cook till tender.

- Fry potatoes and carrots in oil.
- Thread onions, potatoes, meat, carrots and tomatoes on a fine sticks and, dip in beaten eggs. Sprinkle with breadcrumbs and fry.

Serving

- Serve hot.

4. Meat Masala

Ingredients	Approx. Quantity
Mutton	100 gms.
Onion	50 gms.
Ginger	1/2" piece
Garlic	2-3 cloves
Tomato	30 gms.
Fat	20 gms.
Red chilli powder	1/4 teaspoon
Turmeric powder	1/8 teaspoon
Salt	1/2 teaspoon
Garam masala	1/4 teaspoon
Cumin seeds	1/4 teaspoon
Coriander seeds	1/4 teaspoon
Clove and pepper corns	2 each
Green cardamom	2 nos.
Coriander leaves	a few

Pre-Preparation: Coriander seeds, cumin seeds, black pepper corns and cloves are to be roasted on a hot skillet, grind ginger, garlic and the above roasted ingredients to a fine paste by using a little water. Grate or grind the onion.

Method

- Heat the fat in a pan, add crushed cardamom and onion paste and fry till golden brown. Now add red chilli powder, salt, haldi and the masala paste, fry on a slow fire, till fat separates out.
- Add chopped tomatoes and fry a little. Add the cleaned and washed mutton and fry for 10-15 minutes till the mutton is browned and fat separates out.
- Add sufficient water and pressure cook for 15 minutes till the pressure drops itself. Chopped coriander leaves and garam masala is added before serving.

Serving

- Serve sprinkled with finely chopped coriander leaves and garam masala.

5. Luckhnawi Meat Korma

Ingredients	Approx. Quantity
Mutton	550 gms.
Dry coconut	30 gms.
Onions	125 gms.
Ginger	5 gms.
Garlic	a few flakes
Red chilies	5 gms.
Curds	115 gms
Coriander powder	15 gms.
Poppy seeds	10 gms.
Green chilies	2 gms.
Cinnanamon	2 gms.
Cloves	2 gms.
Pepper corns	2 gms.

Pre-Preparation: Wash clean and cut (with bones) meat and marinate with curds for half an hour. Grind together half the onion, green chillies, coriander leaves, ginger, garlic, poppy seeds, coconut, red chillies and coriander. Slice remaining onion.

Method

- Heat fat, fry onion slightly, add ground spices and fry for a few minutes.
- Add meat, curd, salt and more water if required and cook till meat is tender.
- When meat is done add roasted and powdered garam masala and remove from fire.

6. Nilgiri Korma

Ingredients	Approx. Quantity
Mutton	500 gms.
Green chillies	5 gms.
Coriander leaves	A bunch
Ginger	A little
Garlic	1 flake
Poppy seeds	20 gms.
Curds	225 ml.

Ingredients	Approx. Quantity
Coconut	35 gm.
Red chillies	5 gms.
Garam masala	A little
Onion	50 gms.
Fat	25 gms.
Salt	To taste.

Pre-Preparation: Wash and cut meat and marinate with curds for half and hour. Grind together poppy seeds, dry coconut, garlic, coriander powder, red chillies (seeds removed), green chillies and half onions.

Method

- Heat fat, fry remaining sliced onions. After a few minutes, add ground spices and meat. Fry for about 15 minutes.
- Add remaining curds and tepid water and cook till meat is tender.
- Add roasted and powdered cinnamon, cloves, pepper corns and cardamoms and cook for 5 to 10 minutes.

Serving

- Serve hot.

7. Achari Ghost

Ingredients	Approx. Quantity
Mutton	600 gms, from chopped portion.
Garam masala	10 gms.
Coriander leaves	15 gms.
Ginger and garlic paste	15 gms. each
Red chilli powder	10 gms.
Salt	to taste
Oil	to fry
Mixed pickle mixture	60 gms.
Vinegar	for marinate

Pre-Preparation: Marinate meat for 2-3 hours. Chop coriander leaves. Mix all the masalas with meat. Keep aside.

Method

- Fry the meat till golden brown.
- Cook using very little water.
- At the final step mix pickle mixture, garam masala and salt. Coriander leaves are added before serving.

8. Dal Meat

Ingredients	Approx. Quantity
Mutton	500 gms. (spine portion)
Masoor dal	125 gms.
Coriander powder	1 tablespoon
Cumin seeds	1 tablespoon
Garam masala	1 tablespoon
Turmeric powder	2 tablespoon
Onion (large)	2 nos.
Garlic	4 flakes
Ginger	2" piece
Salt	to taste
Chilli powder	to taste

Pre-Preparation: Grind ginger and garlic. Slice onion.

Method

- Meat is cooked till half done.
- Cook the dal in meat shorba till soften then pass through a fine sieve.
- Heat 4 tablespoons ghee and fry the onions till soft. Add all the spices with the exception of garam masala and fry.
- Add mutton and fry to a golden brown colour.
- Put meat in the dal, mix well and continue cooking till the mutton is tender. Coriander leaves and garam masala is added before serving.

Serving

- Serve sprinkled with garam masala and coriander leaves.

9. Murg Mussallam

Ingredients	Approx Quantity
Whole chicken	1 no.
Onions	125 gms.
Raw papaya	25 gms.
Garlic paste	1 teaspoon
Ginger paste	1 teaspoon
Salt	to taste
Green cardamom	5 nos.
Black pepper	3 gms.
Cloves	5 nos.
Cinnamon	2 gms.

Ingredients	Approx. Quantity
Poppy seeds	15 gms.
Desiccated coconut	25 gms.
Chironji	15 gms.
Coriander seed	15 gms.
Cumin seed	15 gms.
Saffron colour (edible)	a pinch
Silver leaf	2 nos.
Chilli powder	5 nos.
Curd	1/2 gms.
Ghee	200 gms.
Almonds	25 gms.
Eggs	4 nos.

Pre-Preparation: Clean and wash the chicken well, especially inside portion should be washed well. Prick the chicken with a fork and marinate with raw papaya paste and salt. Keep aside for two hours. Slice onions and fry and grind half of the onion to a pate and keep aside. Make ginger-garlic paste. Roast lightly green cardamom, black pepper, cloves, cinnamon, poppy seeds, coconut, chironjee, coriander seeds and cumin seeds and grind to a paste. Boil eggs (hard) chop and keep aside. Blanch and peel the almonds and cut into fine silvers and keep aside. Dissolve the saffron colour in the kewra water and apply on the chicken. Blend beaten curds and all spices well. Rub this mixture over chicken and marinate for 25 minutes. Mix half of the fried onions in the chopped boiled eggs and stuff inside the body of the chicken. Truss the chicken with a thread.

Method

- Put the degchi on the fire and pour the ghee which was used for frying the onions and the chicken along with the marinate and simmer for 30 minutes or till the chicken is done and the ghee appears on the sides. This can be cooked on a tray in an over at 350° F for about 25-30 minutes. Baste in between with fat or ghee if required.
- After well done, place the Murg on a platter and remove the thread. Place the silver leaf on the chicken and garnish with almond silvers.

10. Sunday Meat Curry

Ingredients	Approx. Quantity
Meat	200 gms.
Onion	200-250 gms.
Garam masala	5 gms.
Haldi powder	5 gms.
Red Chilli powder	5 gms.
Bay leaf	2 nos.
Salt	to taste
Cooking oil	50 gms.

Pre-Preparation: Cut and wash meat. Slice onions.

Method

- Boil meat with salt and turmeric powder. Keep aside.
- Fry onion, Keep aside.
- Heat oil. Add bay leaf and gar am masala and fry for a few minutes. Now add meat, red chilli powder and fry with constant stirring.
- Add water (if required).
- Add fried onion at last and serve.

IV. Chicken

1. Butter Chicken

Ingredients	Approx. Quantity
Chicken	250 gms.
Onion	100 gms.
Ginger	10 gms.
Tomato puree	200 ml.
Salt	1/2 teaspoon
Haldi	1/4 teaspoon
Red chilli powder	1/4 teaspoon
Garam masala powder	1/4 teaspoon
Poppy seeds	1/4 teaspoon
Cumin seeds	1/4 teaspoon
Coriander seeds	1/4 teaspoon
Cloves and pepper corns	1-2 each
Cinnamon	1/2 piece
Green cardamom	2 nos.
Bay leaf	1-2 nos.
Fat	1 tablespoon
Coriander leaves	a few
Ajanta cream	1/2 cup

Pre-Preparation: Clean and wash the chicken. Marinate with tomato puree. Grind ginger, garlic, poppy seeds, cumin seeds, coriander seeds, cloves, peppercorns and cinnamon together to a fine paste. Grate onions. Beat the cream finely.

Method

- Fry the chicken in ghee and keep aside.
- Heat fat in a thick bottomed pan, add cardamom, bay leaf and onion paste and fry to a golden brown colour. Then add turmeric powder, chilli powder, salt, masala paste and fry till the fat comes out.
- Add chicken pieces and fry for 5-10 minutes. Add a little water and cook till done.
- Pour ajanta cream over the chicken and garnish with coriander leaves and garam masala before serving.

2. Dahi Chicken

Ingredients	Approx. Quantity
Garlic	3-4 cloves
Chicken	250 gms.
Dahi (curd)	150 gms.
Onion	100 gms.
Ginger	10 gms.
Garlic	4 cloves
Tomatoes	100 gms.
Salt	1/2 teaspoon
Haldi	1/4 teaspoon
Red chilli powder	1/4 teaspoon
Garam masala	1/4 teaspoon
Cumin seeds	1/4 teaspoon
Sugar	1 teaspoon
Cloves and pepper corns	1/2 each
Cinnamon	1/2" piece
Green cardamom	2 nos.
Bay leaf	1 no.
Fat	1 tablespoon
Coriander leaves	a few

Pre-Preparation: Clean and wash the chicken and cut into pieces. Marinate with beaten curd for 2-3 hours. Grind ginger, garlic, cumin seeds, cloves, pepper corns

and cinnamon together to a fine paste. Grind the onion. Keep aside.

Method

- Heat fat in a thick bottom pan. Add cardamom, bay leaf and onion paste. Fry the onion to a golden brown colour. Add turmeric powder, chilli powder, salt, sugar, masala paste, blanched and chopped tomatoes.
- The above masalas, will be fried till fat separates out.
- Add chicken pieces and fry for 5-10 minutes. Add sufficient water to make gravy and cook till done and a thick gravy is left. Coriander leaves and garam masala is added before serving.

Serving

- Serve, hot garnished with coriander leaves and garam masala.

3. Methi Chicken

Ingredients	Approx. Quantity
Chicken	1000 gms.
Curd	225 gms.
Salt	10 gms.
Ghee	100 gms.
Black cardamom	5 nos.
Cloves	5 nos.
Cinnamon	5 gms.
Bay leaves	2 nos.
Mace	1 gm.
Onions	300 gms.
Ginger	50 gms.
Green chillies	6 nos.
Turmeric	2 gms.
Coriander powder	5 gms.
Chilli powder	5 gms.
Tomatoes	250 gms.
Kasoori methi	5 gms.
Green coriander	30 gms.
Green cardamom	5 gms.

Pre-Preparation: Clean chicken and cut into 8" pieces. Marinate chicken in curd, ginger and lime juice. Mince onion. Heat oil and add onion, ginger, garlic paste, turmeric, red chilli powder, cinnamon, clove, bayleaf, black cardamom, chopped tomatoes and green chilli. Make smooth gravy. Add chicken, where almost done. Add chopped kasoori methi, green coriander and green cardamom.

4. Peshawari Bharawan Murg (Mince stuffed Chicken)

Ingredients	Approx. Quantity
Chicken	1 Kg
Lemon juice	1 tablespoon
Ghee	As required
Mint leaves	1 tablespoon
Salt	To taste
Ginger	4 cm piece
Garlic ground to	10 cloves
Coriander leaves a paste.	1 cup
Green chillies	4 nos.
Salt	To taste
For Stuffing	
Minced meat (Keema)	400 cms.
Khoya	100 gms.
Onion	1 no.
Ginger garlic paste	1 teaspoon
Green chillies	2 nos.
Cardamom	10 nos.
Cinnamon	2 cms. piece
Ghee	As required
Salt	To taste

Pre-Preparation: Clean chicken. Add lime juice and the ground paste. Rub lime juice to the chicken inside and outside and marinate for one hour in the ground masala paste. Tie up the legs of the chicken well to retain shape and steam in a pressure cooker. Chop mint leaves, green chillies. Slice onion.

Method

- **Make stuffing:** For making stuffing heat 4 tablespoons ghee and fry the sliced onion till meat is tender and dry. Stuff the chicken with half the keema mixture and tie up again with a thread.
- Heat 5 tablespoons ghee in a large pan. Add two pieces of crushed cinnamon and the remaining keema. Place the chicken on it. Clover the pan with a tight

fitting lid and cook on a low fire. A few drops of water may be added. As soon as the keema at the bottom starts to brown, place live coals in the lid. When chicken become brown on top, remove from fire. Garnish it with coriander and mint leaves.

- At the final step arrange chicken on a bed of keema with green salad.

5. Handi Chicken

Ingredients	Approx. Quantity
Chicken	250 gms.
Onion	100 gms.
Ginger	10 gms.
Garlic	3-4 cloves
Tomatoes	100 gms.
Capsicum	100 gms.
Salt	1/2 teaspoon
Haldi powder	1/4 teaspoon
Red chilli powder	1/4 teaspoon
Garam Masala	1/4 teaspoon
Poppy seeds	1/4 teaspoon
Cumin seeds	1/4 teaspoon
Coriander seeds	1/4 teaspoon
Cloves and pepper corns	1-2 each
Ginnamon	1/2" stick
Green cardamom	2 nos.
Bay leaf	1-2 nos.
Fat	1 tablespoon
Coriander leaves	a few

Pre-Preparation: Clean and wash the chicken and cut into pieces. Grind ginger, garlic, poppy seeds, cumin seeds, coriander seeds, cloves, pepper corns and cinnamon together to a fine paste. Grate onion. Chop capsicum.

Method

- Heat fat in a *'Mitti Ki Handi'*. Add bay leaves, cardamom and onion paste. Fry to a golden brown colour. Add turmeric powder, chilli powder, salt, masala paste, blanched and chopped capsicum and tomatoes. Fry till the fat separates out.
- Add Chicken pieces and fry for 5-10 minutes. Add sufficient water to make

gravy and cover with a lid and put live coals on the lid. Cook over slow heat till done and a thick gravy is left. Coriander leaves and garam masala is added before serving.

6. Murg-sagwala (Chicken with spinach)

Ingredients	Approx. Quantity
Chicken	1/2 Kg
Spinach	1/2 Kg
Ghee	As required
Cardamoms	2 nos.
Cloves	3 nos.
Black pepper corns	6 nos.
Bay leaf	1 no.
Curd	1/2 cup
Soda bi. carb	pinch
Salt	to taste
Cumin seeds	
Coriander seeds	
Ginger	ground to a paste
Onions	
Garlic	
Kashmiri red chilli	

Pre-Preparation: Chop spinach and onions. Grind pepper corns. Beat curd. Cut chicken into cubes.

Method

- Boil spinach with soda bi. carb in just enough water and strain it. Keep aside.
- Heat 4 tablespoons ghee and add ground masala paste and saute till browned well. Then add chicken, cardamom, cloved, ground peppercorns and bay leaf. Fry till the chicken is brown in colour.
- Add spinach. Cook till the meat is tender and the gravy is thick.
- Lower the heat and cook till the spinach and the meat are well blended. Add beaten curds and simmer till the gravy is aromatic.

Serving

- Serve hot with parathas.

PREPARATION OF INDIAN VEGETARIAN ITEMS

I. Paneer Ki Subji (Main Paneer food items)
1. Pea-paneer

Ingredients	Approx. Quantity
Fresh peas	450 gms.
Paneer	115 gms.
Coriander powder	5 gms.
Chilli powder	1/2 tsp.
Turmeric	a pinch
Garam masala	1/8 tsp.
Onion	55 gms.
Fat	30 gms.
Garlic	3 flakes
Ginger	a small piece
Tomatoes	225 gms.
Salt	to taste
Blanched almonds or Cashewnuts	30 gms.
Curds	30 gms.
Coriander leaves	a few sprig.

Pre-Preparation: Grind together onion, coriander powder, chilli powder, turmeric, ginger and garlic to a fine paste. Grind almond or cashewnuts separately.

Method

- Heat fat. Fry paneer cubes till light brown and keep aside.
- Now fry spices for a few minutes and then add peas and fry.
- Add tomato pulp, salt and a little water.
- Cook till peas are tender. Add fried paneer. Cook on a low heat.
- Add the ground nuts and beaten curds and mix well. Bring to boil. Coriander leaves are added before serving.

2. Paneer Sagwala

Ingredients	Approx. Quantity
Spinach or Serson sag or Methi leaves (green)	150 gms.
Water	1 T
Paneer	50 gms.

Ingredients	Approx. Quantity
Salt	1/2 t
Cumin seeds	1/4 t
Onion	25 gms.
Ginger	5 gms. (1/2" piece)
Tomatoes	50 gms.
Garlic	2 flakes
Fat	1/2 t

Pre-Preparation: Clean, wash and chop spinach. Cook spinach, adding salt and lt water in an open pan. Grind to a paste or blend in a blender.

Method

- Heat fat in a pan, fry cumin seeds. Add finely chopped onion, ginger and garlic and fry lightly. Now add the chopped tomatoes. Cook till masalas are done.
- Add ground spinach and long thin pieces of paneer and cook on a low heat for a few minutes.

3. Sahi Paneer

Ingredients	Approx. Quantity
Paneer	250 gms.
Cashewnuts	50 gms.
Tomatoes	500 gms.
Cream	50 gms.
Salt	1 teaspoon
Green chillies	2-3 nos.
Thick curd	1 cup.
Flour	2 tablespoons
Black pepper powder	a pinch
Red chilli powder	1 tablespoon
Green coriander	few sprig
Masala (To grind)	
Ginger	10 gms.
Salt	1/2 teaspoon
Green chilli	1 no.
Red chilli powder	1/2 teaspoon
Onions	2 nos. (100 gms.)
Turmeric powder	1/4 teaspoon
Clove and green cardamon	2 nos. each
Coriander powder	1 teaspoon

Pre-Preparation: Cut paneer and capsicum into 1" pieces. Chop tomatoes and coriander leaves. Crush garlic and ginger.

Method

- Heat fry. Fry paneer pieces till golden brown. Keep aside.
- Add ginger, garlic, red chilli powder, coriander powder,, green chilli and tomatoes and fry.
- Now add paneer, fry for a few minutes and then add sufficient water to make gravy.
- Add lime juice, green masala and kasoori methi at the final step.

4. Kadahi Paneer

Ingredients	Approx. Quantity
Paneer	200 gms.
Capsicum	100 gms.
Salt	10 gms.
Ghee	100 gms.
Garlic	30 gms.
Red chilli	6 nos.
Coriander powder	10 gms.
Tomatoes	500 gms.
Onion	100 gms.
Green chilli	4 nos.
Ginger	50 gms.
Green Coriander	25 gms.
Garam masala	5 gms.
Kasoori methi	3 gms.
Lime juice	30 ml.

Pre-Preparation: Cut paneer into 2½ cm x 3- slices. Mix chopped cashewnuts, green coriander, green chillies and salt. Stuff this mixture in between 2 slices of paneer and press keep aside. Prepare a batter of flour, salt and pepper powder.

Method

- Deep fry the paneer slices coated with batter.
- Prepare tomato paste. Grind and combine all spice mentioned for masala alongwith onions and fry in oil.
- Add tomato paste and fry for sometime. Now mix curd, degi mirch, salt and cook. Add little water and boil for few minutes.
- Arrange fried paneer pieces in a serving dish and pour gravy on top decorate with cream and green coriander.

Serving

- Serve hot.

5. Paneer Durbar

Ingredients	Approx. Quantity
Paneer	50 gms.
Cornflour	2 teaspoons
Salt	1/4 teaspoon
Red chilli powder	1/8 teaspoon
Garam masala	a pinch
Fat	for frying
Tomato gravy (Makhani gravy)	As required
Cream	2-10 gms.
Khoya	10 gms.
Current	15-20 nos.

Pre-Preparation: Grate and knead the paneer. Add cornflour, salt, khoya, currant, red chilli powder and mix well. Beat cream. Make even size balls. Make gravy.

Method

- Heat fat in a deep frying pan and fry koftas till golden brown.
- Add koftas (balls) in gravy and cook on slow fire to 4-5 minutes.
- Pour beaten cream over it.
- Sprinkle garam masala and coriander leaves before serving.

II. OTHER VEGETABLE ITEMS

1. Cashew Potato Curry

Ingredients	Approx. Quantity
Potato	3 kg.
Cashewnut	500 gms.
Onion	200 gms.
Ginger	10 gms.
Garlic	30 gms.
Charmagas	100 gms.
Poppy seeds	60 gms.
Refined oil	250 ml.
Green chillies	50 ml.
Coriander leaves	as required.

Pre-Preparation: Boil potato peel and cut into quarters. Prepare past of charmagas and poppy. Slice onion and prepare ginger-garlic paste.

Method

- Heat oil, fry cashewnut and keep aside.
- Add sliced onions and fry to a golden brown colour. Add ginger garlic paste milk of charmagas and poppy seeds.
- Add potatoes and mix it well. Check seasoning and add fried coconut.
- Arrange chopped green chillies and coriander leaves on top.

2. Dum Aloo

Ingredients	Approx. Quantity
Potatoes	100 gms.
Salt	1 teaspoon
Fat	for frying
Coriander seeds	1/4 teaspoon
Poppy seeds	1/4 teaspoon
Desiccated coconut	5 gms.
Cumin seeds	1/4 teaspoon
Clove	1 no.
Pepper corns	2 nos.
Black cardamom	1 (small)
Grated nutmeg	a pinch
Fat	1 tablespoon
Salt	1/4 teaspoon
Red chilli powder	1/4 teaspoon
Turmeric powder	1/4 teaspoon
Onion	30 gms.
Garlic	2 flakes
Coriander leaves	a sprig.
Green chilli	1 no.
Garam masala	1/4 teaspoon.

Pre-Preparation: Peel and prick potatoes with a fork and soak in a little water in 1 teaspoon of salt for about half an hour. Dry it. Roast coriander seeds, poppy seeds, coconut, cumin seeds,- clove, pepper corns, black cardamom and nutmeg and grind to a paste. Grate or grind onions and garlic to a paste.

Method

- Heat fat. Deep fry the potatoes on medium heat till golden brown.

- Heat fat and fry onion, garlic paste till brown, add salt, red chilli powder, turmeric powder and ground masala paste and cook on slow fire.
- Add a little beaten curd to the above mixture at a time.
- Add fried potatoes and cook for another five minutes. Then add remaining curd and about 50 ml. water. Keep it in slow oven (250°F) for about 30 minutes, or on slow fire for 10 minutes. Arrange coriander leaves on top and dust garam masala powder before serving.

3. Vegetable Tak-a-tin

Ingredients	Approx. Quantity
Beans	100 gms.
Carrots	100 gms.
Colocatia	100 gms.
Cauliflower	100 gms.
Lotus stem	100 gms.
Potato	100 gms.
Tomato paste	200 gms.
Onions	50 gms.
Coriander leaves	10 gms.
Green chillies	2 gms.
Salt	to paste
Cooking oil	80 ml.
Red chilli powder	2 gms.
Turmeric powder	2 gms.
Coriander powder	3 gms.
Garam masala	2 gms.
Chaat masala	2 gms.
Ginger	10 gms.

Pre-Preparation: Clean the small brinjal in running water. Peel and cut colocatia in halves. Clean lotus stem. Cut diagonally in 1" shape. Cut potatoes into cubes and keep in cold water. Cut cottage cheese in cubes and keep. Chop green coriander, green chilli, tomato and onions.

Method

- Fry small brinjal, lotus stem, colocatia and potato. Boil green peas and dust salt and chaat masala over vegetables.

- Take a pan. Add oil to it. Add tomato dices and onion to it and cook for sometime, then add red chilli powder, dhania powder, turmeric powder, garam masala and make a thick gravy. Now add the vegetables into gravy and simmer.
- Green coriander and finely sliced ginger and arranged over the vegetable at the final step.

4. Hare Chane Ki Sabji

Ingredients	Approx. Quantity
Hara chana	100 gms.
Onion	50 gms.
Ginger	5 gms.
Garlic	2 cloves
Tomato	50 gms.
Green chilli	1 no.
Fat	1 tablespoon
Salt	1/2 teaspoon
Red chilli powder	1/4 teaspoon
Garam masala	1/4 teaspoon
Turmeric powder	1/4 teaspoon
Coriander leaves	few
Cooking oil	6-8 gms.

Pre-Preparation: Grind onion, ginger, garlic and green chilli to a fine paste. Blanch tomato. Clean and wash channa.

Method

- Heat fat in a pan and fry onion, ginger and garlic paste to golden brown colour till the fat separates.
- Add salt, red chilli powder, haldi and fry for two minutes.
- Add tomato and continue frying till fat separates.
- Add hara chana and fry a little.
- Add sufficient water, cover and let simmer till chana is tender. Chopped coriander leaves and fried garam masala may be added at the time of serving.

5. Sauted Winter Vegetables
(a) Cauliflower, Potato, Beans, Carrots, Green Peas, Capsicum, Mushroom

Ingredients	Approx. Quantity
Cauliflower	400 gms.
Potato	200 gms.
Beans	All peeled, 100 gms.
Carrot	cleaned & 100 gms.
Green peas	cut in cubes. 50 gms.
Capsicum	50 gms.
Mushrooms	50 gms.
Panchphoran	2 gms.
Cumin powder	2 gms.
Red chilli powder	5 gms.
Turmeric powder	5 gms.
Garlic ginger	5 gms. each
Salt	to taste
Sugar	to taste
Cooking oil	60 gms.
Kaju	
Coriander leaves	To garnish

Pre-Preparation: Make ginger garlic paste.

Method

- Heat oil in kadahi. Add panchphoram for tempering.
- When tempered, add vegetable cubes and saute for sometime with added turmeric powder.
- Now add ginger, garlic paste, red chilli powder, cumin powder, cumin powder and fry till the masala is done. Add a very little water and cook on slow fire till vegetable are done and fully dried. Add salt and sugar to taste accordingly at the last step, (cover may be used for better result).
- Broken fried kaju and coriander leaves may be added for decoration, hot ghee and fried garam masala powder may also be added over the vegetables at the time of serving.

(b) Cabbage + Potato + Capsicum + Green Peas

Ingredients	Approx. Quantity
Cabbage	400 gms.
Potato All	peeled 200 gms.
Capsicum and	cleaned 50 gms.
Green peas and cut	in cubes. 50 gms.
Baby corns	As required
Garlic	5 gms.
Cumin	5 gms.
Turmeric powder	5 gms.
Red chilli powder	5 gms.
Tomatoes	2 nos.
Green chilli	1 no.
Salt	to taste
Sugar	to taste
Green mango powder	5 gms.
Garam masala	5 gms.
Coriander leaves	20-25 gms.
Oil	50 gms.

Pre-Preparation: Chop garlic, tomatoes, green chilli and coriander leaves.

Method

- Heat oil in a kadahi, add panchphoran for tempering.
- When tempered, add vegetable pieces and saute for sometime with added turmeric powder.
- Now add ginger garlic paste, red chilli powder, cumin powder and fry till the masala is done. Add a very little water and cook on slow fire for 10-15 minutes. Add salt and sugar to taste accordingly at the last step. Cover may be used for better result.
- Dust with mango powder and garam masala powder and pour hot ghee over the vegetable at the time of serving.

(c) Aloo + Gobi + Beans

Ingredients	Approx. Quantity
Aloo	All peeled and 200 gms.
Gobi (cauliflower)	cleaned and. 200 gms.
Beans	cut in cubes 100 gms.
Cumin seeds	5 gms.

Ingredients	Approx. Quantity
Onion	100 gms.
Red chilli powder	5 gms.
Turmeric powder	5 gms.
Garlic and ginger	5 gms. each
Salt	to taste
Sugar	to taste
Kaju	
Coriander leaves	to garnish
Cooking oil	30 gms.

Pre-Preparation: Make ginger garlic paste. Slice onions.

Method

- Heat oil in kadahi. Add cumin seeds for tempering.
- When tempered add onions and fry a little. Then add vegetables cubes and saute for some time with added turmeric powder.
- Now add ginger-garlic paste, red chilli powder, and fry till the masala is done. Add a very little water and cook on slow fire till the vegetable is done and fully dried. Add salt and sugar to taste accordingly at the last step. Cover may be used for better result.
- Broken kaju and coriander leaves may be added for decoration. Hot ghee and fried garam masala powder may also be added over the vegetable at the time of serving.

(d) Patna Kadoo

Ingredients	Approx. Quantity
Kadoo	500 gms.
Tomatoes	100 gms.
Onion	100 gms.
Cumin seeds	5 gms.
Red chilli powder	2 gms.
Turmeric powder	2 gms.
Ginger	5 gms.
Salt	to taste
Sugar	to taste
Black pepper	5-6 nos.
Coriander leaves	to garnish
Ghee	
Cooking oil	30 gms.

Pre-Preparation: Peel, wash and cut kadoo into cubes. Peel and crush ginger. Chop tomatoes and onions.

Method

- Heat oil in kadahi. Add cumin seeds for tempering.
- When tempered add onions and fry a little. Then add kadoo and saute 2-3 minutes with added turmeric powder.
- Now add ginger, red chilli powder, tomatoes and stir well. Add half cup of the water and cook on slow fire till vegetable is done and fully dried. Add salt and sugar to taste accordingly at the last step. Cover may be used for better result.
- Hot ghee, fried garam masala and coriander leaves may be added over the vegetable at the time of serving.

6. Brinjal with Chilli Garlic Gravy

Ingredients	Approx. Quantity
Baigan (brinjal)	(4" to 5") 500 gms.
Oil	40-50 gms.
Turmeric powder	1 teaspoon
Salt	to taste
Chilli garlic gravy	as required

Pre-Preparation: Wash and cut brinjals to halved, keeping the stem intact. Sprinkle salt and turmeric powder and keep for sometime.

Method

- Heat refined oil in a suitable container and deep fry the brinjals. Keep aside.
- Keep the brinjals flat over a flat serving dish, (edible portion up).
- Now, hot chilli garlic gravy. Pour over the brinjal and keep for about 5-10 minutes before serving.

7. Vegetable Augratin

Ingredients	Approx. Quantity
Mixed vegetable (carrots, Cauliflower, potatoes, peas, french beans, etc.)	500 gms.
Onion	100 gms.

Ingredients	Approx. Quantity
Salt	to taste
White sauce	4 tablespoons
Butter	2 teaspoons
Green chillies	to taste
Green coriander	to taste
Black pepper powder	to taste

Pre-preparation: Wash and cut vegetables. Make white sauce. Boil the vegetables.

Method

- Place the vegetables, in a flat dish greased with 2 teaspoons butter. Sprinkle salt, black pepper powder and arrange onion rings on top. Add white sauce over it.
- Cover with a polythene sheet.
- Keep in oven for 15-18 minutes at 350°F. Then give top heat for 10 minutes to give brown colour on top.
- Remove the dish from oven, decorate with green chillies and green coriander and serve hot.

8. Shyaamagadda Pulusu

Ingredients	Approx. Quantity
Arbi	16 nos.
Lemon juice	10 ml.
Cooking oil	75 ml.
Garlic	6 flakes
Rai/Mustard seeds	2 gm.
Cumin seeds	1 gm.
Husked Urad dal	5 gms.
Dried red chilli	4 nos.
Curry leaves	16 nos.
Onions	200 gms.
Fresh tomato puree	180 ml.
Tamarind pulp	60 gms.
Dhania/coriander powder	12 gms.
Red chilli powder	4-5 gms.
Turmeric powder	3 gms.
Salt	to taste
Gur/Jaggery	15 gms.

Pre-preparation: Wash thoroughly the Arbi. Put in a pan. Cover with enough water and boil until cooked. Add lemon juice and bring to a boil again, drain, cool, peel quarter lengthwise and keep aside in a panful of water. Wipe and clean the red chilli with moist cloth. Clean, wash and pat dry the leaves. Peel, wash and finely chop the onions. Grate the jaggery and keep aside in 45 ml. of water.

Method

- Heat oil in a pan, add garlic. Fry till mustard seeds, cumin seeds, urad dal and red chilli get a light brown colour.
- Add curry leaves and onions and saute until golden brown.
- Then add tomato puree, tamarind pulp, red chillies and turmeric, and stir fry until the fat leaves the sides. Add 3 cups of water and salt and when it starts to boil slow the heat.
- Now add arbi and jaggery and bring to a boil, stirring occasionally, until the gravy gets a thin sauce consistency.
- Remove from fire and adjust the seasoning.

III. PREPARATION OF DAL (MAIN DAL ITEMS)

1. Dal Maharani

Ingredients	Approx. Quantity
Whole lentil with seeds	1.25 Kg.
Onion	250 gms.
Ginger	30 gms.
Garlic	60 gms.
Red chilli powder	30 gms.
Tomato puree	300 ml.
Double cream	250 ml.
Salt	as required
Butter	200 gms.
Coriander leaves	30 gms.
Green chillies	20 gms.
Garam masala	10 gms.

Pre-preparation: Clean and wash dal. Slice onion. Prepare ginger garlic paste.

Method

- Add dal and boil.

- Cook rajma separately in pressure cooker and add to dal. Season it.
- Add cream to dal before finishing.
- Decorate with finely chopped coriander leaves at last.
- Simmer for at least 4 hours.
- Add cream gradually to dal and decorate with chillies and coriander leaves before serving.

2. Dal Panchmahal

Ingredients	Approx. Quantity
Lentil (with skin)	300 gms.
Moong dal	300 gms.
Kali dal	300 gms.
Toor dal	300 gms.
Rajma	300 gms.
Onion	250 gms.
Ginger	30 gms.
Garlic	30 gms.
Red Chilli powder	30 gms.
Double cream	250 gms.
Butter	250 gms.
Coriander leaves	30 gms.
Green chillies	20 gms.
Garam masala	10 gms.
Salt	as required.

Pre-preparation: Clean and wash dal. Slice onion and make a ginger garlic paste.

Method

- The dal is boiled with salt and ginger garlic paste were added.
- Fry onions to a golden brown colour, and add it to the dal.
- Add garam masala, butter, red chilli powder and tomato puree.

3. Moti Mahal Dal

Ingredients	Approx. Quantity
Black gram (urad dal) whole	200 gms.
Refined oil	1 tablespoon
Ginger paste	1 teaspoon
Cream	50 gms.
Onions	2 nos. (100 gms.)

Asafoetida	a pinch (hing)
Rajma (kidney beans)	1 tablespoon
Salt	to taste
Butter	2 tablespoons
Full cream milk	2 cups
Tomatoes	2 nos. (100 gms.)

Pre-preparation : Pick, wash and soak urad and rajma. Chop ginger, onion and garlic. Blanch and chop tomato.

Method

- Add water, soaked rajma and urad, chopped ginger, garlic and salt in a pressure cooker for half an hour.
- Mash the cooked dal. Leave it on slow fire for another half an hour. Stir frequently.
- Heat fat fry chopped onions till golden brown. Add chopped tomato. Fry for a few minutes. Add spices and curd and let it cook for few minutes.
- Heat fat, fry chopped onions till golden again. It should become red in colour at brown. Add chopped tomato. Fry for a few the time of serving.
- Add the boiled dal to the masala and cook on slow fire till well mixed.

Serving

- Serve hot with cream.

4. Dal Makhani

Ingredients	Approx. Quantity
Urad whole	30 gms.
Rajma	10 gms. (soaked)
Water	1 - cup
Ginger	1/2" piece (5 g)
Garlic	2-3 cloves
Onion	1/2 (small)
Tomato	1 (small)
Curd	25 gms.
Salt	1/2 t
Red chilli powder	1/4 t
Garam masala	1/4 t
Fat	1 T
Cream	1 t (optional)

Pre-preparation: Wash dal and rajma 2-3 times and soak in 8-10 cups water for 15-20 minutes with salt and oil.Method

Method

- Cook for half an hour with hing at high flame and again half an hour at slow flame.
- Now open the cooker and add milk in case of over cooking. Cook for 30 minutes

5. Ghana Peshawari

Ingredients	Approx. Quantity
Kabuli chana	500 gms.
Onion	150 gms.
Corn	50 gms.
Ginger	5 gms.
Onions	40 gms.
Coriander	50 gms.
Cloves	4 nos.
Pepper corns	5 nos.
Cinnamon	2 nos. 1" piece
Cumin seeds	1 teaspoon
Mustard seeds	1 teaspoon
Oil	30 ml.
Water	200 ml.

Pre-preparation: Soak chana overnight and then marinate for half an hour. Make a paste of onion. Chop ginger and green chillies, grind coarsely. Separately broil coriander seeds till brown and finely powder. Broil the finely powder cardamom, cloves, pepper corns, cinnamon, cumin seeds and mustard seeds.

Method

- Pour oil in a thick bottom pan, add marinated chana and fry for 10 minutes.
- Pour enough water to cover the chana and cook it over slow fire till done.
- When cooked, add 1 teaspoon of garam masala. Adjust seasoning.

Serving

- Serve hot with steamed rice.

6. Maash Ki Dal Khasgi

Ingredients	Approx. Quantity
Washed urad dal 500 gms.	
Curd 250 gms.	
Milk 500 ml.	
Green chillies	5 nos.
Ginger	10 gms.
Chilli powder	5 gms.
Cardamon	4 nos.
Coriander powder	10 gms.
Cream	125 gms.
Saffron	1/4 gm.
Green chillies	2-3 nos.
Mint leaves	1/4 bunch
Pure ghee	2 tablespoons
Salt	to taste.
Garam Masala	
Small cardamom	5 nos.
Clove	5 nos.
Cinnamon	1 gm.
Black pepper corns	5 gms.

Pre-preparation: Pick, wash and soak the dal for 15 minutes. Slice onions, Grind garam masala to a paste. Finely chop the ginger, green chillies and mint leaves.

Method

- Heat the ghee and fry the sliced onions till crisp and golden.
- Add the dal, chilli and coriander powder and saute for 5 minutes. Now add milk, cream, salt, garam masala and about 2 cups of water, or sufficient to cook the dal. It should be cooked in a covered patili or deep vessel, on a slow fire till done.
- Remove from the fire. Sieve the curd and pour evenly on the cooked dal.
- Cook dal again on a slow flame and tilt it gently from side to side till all curd is absorbed by the dal.
- Make a tempering using ghee, mint leaves and green chillies and pour over cooked dal. At last pour dissolved saffron and garnish with fried onions.

PREPARATION OF INDIAN RICE AND BREAD ITEMS

I. Rice Dishes
1. Shahi Dehradun

Ingredients	Approx. Quantity
Dehradun rice	1 kg
Salt	as required
Water	as required
Black cardamom	4-5 nos.
Cinnamon	2 sticks
Green bay leaf	4-5 nos.
Ghee	3 tablespoons

Pre-preparation: Clean and wash rice.

Method

• Boil water along with a pinch of salt.
• Add rice and cook till done.
• Strain off the excess water.
• Heat ghee, add bay leaf, cardamom, cinnamon and pour over the rice.

2. Yakhni Pulao

Ingredients	Approx. Quantity
Mutton chops	500 gms.
Mutton (Yakhni cuts)	(nalli, 750 gms.
Basmati rice puth, neck 1 kg and seens)	
Cloves	12-15 nos.
Ginger	30 gms.
Cinnamon	2 gms.
Green cardamom	5 nos.
Onions	250 gms.
Ghee	250 gms.
Brown cardamom	5 gms.
Garlic	30 gms.
Whole wheat flour	500 gms.
Kewra water	1/2 tablespoon
Pepper corns	to taste
Salt	to taste
Fresh curd	150 gms.

Pre-preparation: Slice onions. Make ginger garlic paste.

Method

• Heat the ghee in a pressure cooker and fry onions. Keep aside.

• Heat 2/3rd ghee and add half the cinnamon, brown cardamoms, yakhani meats, cloves, ginger-garlic paste and salt and cook covered for sometime in meat juices. Continue to turn over till the meat pieces are light brown in colour. Now add sufficient water to cover the meat and above 1½ inch. Cook for about 45 minutes.
• Strain yakhni through muslin cloth. Strain meat puree in yakhni through a sieve.
• Heat remaining ghee in pressure cooker and add half of the rest cinnamon and seasoning. Saute it for 5 minutes cover and cook till done.
• *Mix* 1 litre yakhni with beaten curd and red chilli powder. Strain through muslin cloth and remove excess fat. Par boil rice to 3/4 done stage with salt and rest of whole masala and 2 tablespoons of fat removed from yakhni. Strain and arrange layers of rice and chops in a degchi, add yakhni seal with atta dough and dum for 20-30 minutes. Remove and open just before service.

3. Plain Pulao

Ingredients	Approx. Quantity
Rice	75 gms.
Water	Double the amount
Onion	50 gms.
Cumin seeds	1/4 t
Black cardamom	1 no.
Clove	1 no.
Cinnamon	1 small stick
Bay leaf	1 no.
Salt	3/4 - 1 t
Fat	1 T

Pre-Preparation: Clean, wash and soak the rice in water for half an hour.

Method

• Heat fat in a heavy bottomed pan, add whole spices and thinly sliced onion. Fry till the onion is light brown in colour.
• Add drained rice to the onions and fry for 2-3 minutes more. Then add water and salt and cook on slow till boiling.

- Now reduce the heat and cook covered till the rice is done and the water dries up.

Serving

- Serve, hot with curry or raita.

4. Vegetable Biryani

Ingredients	Approx. Quantity
Rice	100 Gms.
Potato	50 gms.
of rice by volume.	
Peas	50 gms.
Beans	50 gms.
Carrots	50 gms.
Cauliflower	50 gms.
Onion	100 gms.
Tomato	50 gms.
Curd	1 T
Zeera	1/2 t
Black cardamom	1
Bay leaves	1-2
Pepper corns	3-4
Cloves	2
Cinnamon	1/2" piece
Ginger	1/2" piece
Garlic	3-4 cloves
Salt	1- t
Haldi	1/4 t
Red chilli powder	1/2 t
Saffron	1 packet
Milk	1 T
Fat	4T

Pre-Preparation: Clean, wash and soak the rice. Roast dry spices on a tawa and grind alongwith ginger and garlic.

Method

- Take 2 T fat in a heavy bottomed pan and fry onions till golden brown. Add ground spice paste and fry a little more. Add salt, haldi, red chilli powder, blanched and chopped tomatoes and beaten curd and fry for some more time.
- Add cut vegetables to fried masala, cover and cook over slow fire till vegetables are tender and fat separates out.
- Prepare rice as for boiled rice.

- Take a heavy bottomed pan. Add 1 T of fat and spread 1/3rd of boiled rice. Then layer half the vegetable and again spread 1/3rd rice. Layer with the rest of the vegetable and finally spread the last layer of rice and at last pour melted fat over it.
- Dissolve saffron in milk and sprinkle on top. Cover with a lid. Keep over a hot tawa for 15-20 minutes. Alternately, keep in moderately hot oven for half an hour.
- Serve the biryani with fried onion rings.

II. BREAD (Main bread and naan items)

1. Naan

Ingredients	Approx. Quantity
Flour	3 cups
Fresh curd	3-4 cups
Butter	4 teaspoons
Sugar	2 teaspoons
Refined oil	2 teaspoons
Salt	1 teaspoons
Milk	1/2 cup
Baking powder	1/2 teaspoon
Fat	1 teaspoon
For Topping:	
Poppy seeds	1 teaspoon
Kalonji	1 teaspoon
Melted butter or fat	2 teaspoons

Pre-Preparation: Sieve flour, add salt, sugar and butter, rub and make small depression in the centre of the flour. Put baking powder and fill with curd. With the help of milk and little warm water make dough. Apply little fat on both hands and knead the dough once again. Keep aside covered with damp cloth for 3 hours. Divide into balls.

Method

- Roll out the balls into triangles (exact shape is 'tear-drop') and bake in gas tandoor or heat griddle plate (with handle). Apply little water on triangles and put it on griddle plate (tawa). Apply little ghee and sprinkle items for topping and press lightly. After few minutes, turn griddle plate upside down and when naan is gloden brown, remove and puff on flame. Butter is applied before serving.

2. Stuffed Paratha

Ingredients	Approx. Quantity
Atta (Flour)	300 gms.
Dried and powdered green and green mint leaves	1 teaspoon each
Green chilli chopped	1 teaspoon
Coriander powder	1 teaspoon
Anardana	2 teaspoons
Refined oil	To fry
Salt	To taste

Pre-Preparation: Sieve atta with little salt and knead well to make medium soft dough, keep aside for 2 hours. Take dried powder of green coriander and green mint leaves, add salt, chopped green coriander and green mint leaves, add salt, chopped green chillies, coriander powder, anardana and mix. Divide the dough into equal size balls. Roll each ball one by one into small discs then apply oil and sprinkle dry atta and stuff with above masala. Make ball again and roll out like chapati.

Method

• Cook on griddle plate (tawa) and apply oil on both sides till light brown in colour.

Serving

• Serve hot.

3. Layered Paratha

Ingredients	Approx. Quantity
Flour	250 gms.
Oil	1 tablespoon

Pre-Preparation: Sieve 250 gms flour, add 1 tablespoon oil and make dough with luke warm water. Keep aside for 4 hours.

Method

• Divide the dough into equal size balls, bigger than roti's ball. Then cut into two halves:

• Stretch each half from corner and roll it to make ball. Again roll out like roti and

shallow fry on heavy hot griddle plate. It is served with halwa.

PREPARATION OF INDIAN SWEET DESSERT ITEMS

1. Phirnee (for 1 portion)

Ingredients	Approx. Quantity
Milk	250 gms.
Rice	10 gms.
Sugar	1½ T
Almonds	2
Kewra essence	1 drop

Pre-Preparation: Soak the rice for 1-2 hours and grind with little cold milk in the liquidizer. Add rest of the milk.

Method

• Cook the milk and powdered rice mixture with constant stirring till it is of creamy consistency.

• Add sugar and after giving one boil remove from fire. Add a drop of essence.

• Place the mixture in fridge and after setting top decorate with shredded almonds.

2. Rice Kheer

Ingredients	Approx. Quantity
Rice	10 gms.
Water	1/2 cup
Milk	250 ml.
Sugar	1 T
Green cardamom	1
Almond	1
Raisins	4-5

Pre-Preparation: Pick, wash and soak the rice in half cup of water for half an hour.

Method

• Boil the rice in the same water till it is tender.

• Add milk and simmer on slow fire for 15-20 minutes with frequent stirring. Mash the rice while stirring.

• When it is of creamy consistency, add sugar and stir till it is dissolved. It is

cooked until a creamy consistency is attained.
- At last, add crushed green cardamom seeds and top decorate with almonds and raisins.

3. Vermicelli Kheer

Ingredients	Approx. Quantity
Milk	200 gms.
Vermicelli	10 gms.
Sugar	1½ T
Ghee	1/2 t
Almond	1
Raisins	4-5

Pre-Preparation: Heat ghee in a karahi and fry the vermicelli lightly.

Method

- Boil milk and simmer for 10 minutes. Add vermicelli to the milk and cook for sometime on slow fire till kheer thickens to an even consistency.
- Add sugar and cook for a few minutes stirring constantly.
- Remove from fire.
- At the last step garnish with shredded almond and raisins.

4. Sahi Tukri

Ingredients	Approx. Quantity
Condensed milk	1/2 tin
Almond, Pistachio	to taste
Small cardamom	6-7 nos.
Silver leaves	4-5 nos.
Bread slices	12 nos.
Fat	to fry
Kewra	1 teaspoon

Pre-Preparation: Cut bread pieces into desired shapes. Heat condensed milk in a pan.

Method

- Heat fat in a pan or Karahi and deep fry bread pieces till crisp and light brown in colour.

- Dip bread pieces in condensed milk and then arrange in a serving dish. Pour remaining milk on top.
- Now sprinkle kewra and apply varq. Decorate with nuts. Cardamom powder may be added at last.
- Keep in freeze for 1 hour before service.

5. Jafrani Halwa

Ingredients	Approx. Quantity
Suji	250 gms.
Ghee	200 gms.
Sugar	200 gms.
Water	1 litre
Blanched almonds	12-13 nos.
Raisins	15-18 nos.
Cashewnut	15-16 nos.
Green cardamom	5 nos.
Jafran (Dissolved in water)	a few

Pre-Preparation: Add water and sugar in a sauce pan and bring to boil to make syrup of sugar and water. Keep aside.

Method

- Heat ghee in a karahi and fry suji, till light brown in colour. (Slow fire is used for better result)
- Cook, stirring continuously, till the mixture emits good flavour.
- Add syrup to fried suji being cooked on slow fire. Add jafran dissolve in water.
- Keep cooking with constant stirring till all the syrup is absorbed and halwa starts leaving the sides of karahi.
- At last step dust powdered cardamom and arrange chopped almonds, cashewnut and raisin on top.

6. Malpua

Ingredients	Approx. Quantity
Maida (refined flour)	80-100 gms.
Powdered milk	30-35 gms.
Aniseed	10 gms.
Baking powder	1/4 teaspoon
Saffron	1/2 teaspoon
Almonds	10 nos.

Ingredients	Approx. Quantity
Cardamoms	8 nos.
Sugar	1 - cups
Milk	1/2 cup
Ghee	for frying
Salt	a pinch

Pre-Preparation: Grind saffron. Chop almonds.

Method

- Mix powdered milk, flour baking powder aniseeds, milk, a pinch of salt and 8 tablespoons sugar and make a smooth paste.
- Make a syrup with 1 cup of sugar and 2 cups of water. Add ground cardamom and saffron to it. Keep aside.
- Heat ghee in a pan and make small pureas of the batter and fry till golden brown. Dip in the sugar syrup.
- Decorate almonds before serving.

7. Sheermal

Ingredients	Approx. Quantity
Flour	1 kg
Milk	1 litre
Green cardamom powder	1/2 teaspoon
Fat or ghee	700 gms.
Saffron	1 teaspoon
Sugar	1 teaspoon
Kewra essence	1/2 teaspoon

Pre-Preparation: Soak saffron in warm milk. Prepare a dough with flour and milk and cardamom powder. Now add melted fat with sugar and leave it to get incorporated into it.

Method

- Mix fat in dough with the help of fingers till the fat is incorporated into the dough and it gets a string consistency.

- Cover the dough with a damp cloth and keep in a cool place for half an hour.
- Divide the dough into 12 balls of equal size and then roll out rotis of six inch diameter. Prick it and bake in an iron tandoor or in an oven at 220°C for 5-7 minutes.
- Baste with saffron and kewra flavoured milk.
- Wrap in a damp napkin and serve with Kormas, Nehari etc.

8. Pitha
(A dish made with rice flour and stuffing like khoya, potato, chana dal, jaggery, green peas, etc.)

Ingredients	Approx. Quantity
Rice flour	500 gms.
Milk	2 kg.
For Stuffing	
Khoya	100 gms.
Sugar	400 gms.
Raisins	25 gms.
Cardamom	2-3 nos.

Pre-Preparation: Make a dough with rice and tepid water. Keep aside. Boil milk with a little cardamom powder till it gets thickens. Keep aside. Mash khoya. Add half of the sugar (powdered) raisins and remaining cardamom powder to khoya and mix well. Keep aside.

Method

- Make walnut size balls with flour.
- Make a well in the centre of the ball and fill with 1 teaspoon of khoya mixture and then again shape into a ball.
- Dip the balls into boiling milk and cook for some time.
- When done remove, from fire and let it cool before serving.

THAI COURSE : ITEMS AND PREPARATIONS

A. Appetiser

Fruit salad
Fresh fruit
Fruit punch

B. Soups

1. Tom Kha Kai
   (Chicken coconut soup)

2. Tom Yam Kung
   (Hot and sour shrimp soup)

C. Beef/Chicken/Vegetable/Rice

1. Kaeng Khiao Wan Nuea
2. Yam Nuea (beef)
3. Satay (Chicken)
4. Phat Thai
5. Thot Man Pla
   (Curried fish cakes)

6. Khao Phat
   (Fried Rice)

7. Mi Krop
   (Crispy noodles)

8. Kai Yan
   (Barbecued chicken)

9. Khao Niao and Som Tom
   (Sticky rice and green papaya salad)

D. Desserts

1. Sangkhaya Fakthong
   (Custard pumpkin)

2. Bua Loi Phuak
   (Taro balls in coconut cream)

3. Kluai Buat Chi
   (Banana cooked in coconut milk)

INTRODUCTION

Thai food is internationally famous. Whether chilli-hot or comparatively bland, harmony is the guiding principle behind each dish. Thai cuisine is essentially a marriage of centuries-old Eastern and Western influences harmoniously combined into something uniquely Thai. **Characteristics of Thai food depend on who cooks it, for whom it is cooked, for what occasion, and where it is cooked.** Dishes can be refined and adjusted to suit all palates. Originally, Thai cooking reflected the characteristics of a water-borne lifestyle Aquatic animals, plants and herbs were major ingredients. Large chunks of meat were eschewed. Subsequent influences introduced the use of sizeable chunks to Thai cooking. With their Buddhist background, Thais shunned the use of large animals in big chunks. But cuts of meat were shredded and laced with herbs arid spices. Traditional Thai cooking methods were stewing and baking or grilling. Chinese influence; saw the introduction of frying, stir-frying and deep-frying. Culinary influences from the 17th century onwards included Portuguese, Dutch, French add Japanese. Chillies were introduced to Thai cooking during the late 1600s by Portuguese missionaries who had acquired a taste for them while serving in South America. Thais were very adapt of 'Siameseising' foreign cooking methods; and substituting ingredients. The ghee used in Indian cooking was replaced by coconut oil, and coconut milk substituted for other dairy products. Overpowering pure spices were toned down and enhanced by fresh herbs such as lemon grass and galanga. Eventually fewer and less spices were used in Thai curries, While the use of fresh herbs increased', it is generally acknowledged that Thai curries burn intensely, but briefly, whereas other curries, with strong spices, burn for longer periods, Instead of serving dishes in courses, a Thai meal is served all at once, permitting diners to enjoy complementary combinations of different tastes. A proper Thai meal should consist of a soup, a curry dish with condiments, a dip with accompanying fish and vegetables A spiced salad may replace the curry dish. The soup can also be spicy, but the curry should be replaced by a non - spiced item. There must be harmony of tastes and textures within individual dishes and the entire meal.

Eating and Ordering Thai Food

Thai food is eaten with a fork and spoon. Even single-dish meal; such as fried rice with pork, or steamed rice tapped with roasted duck, are served in bite - sized slices or chunks obviating need for a knife. The spoon is used to convey food to the mouth. Ideally, eating; Thai food is a communal affair involving two or more people, principally because the greater the number of Diners the greater the number of dishes ordered. Generally speaking, two diners order three dishes in addition to their own individual plates of steamed rice, three diners four dishes; and so on. Diners choose whatever they require from shared dishes and generally add it to their own rice. Soups are enjoyed concurrently with other dishes, not independently. Spicy dishes are 'balanced' by bland dishes to avoid discomfort. Ideal Thai meal is a harmonious blend of the spicy, the subtle, the sweet and

sour, and is meant to be equally satisfying to eye, nose and palate. A typical meal might include a clear soup (perhaps bitter melons stuffed with minced pork) a steamed dish (mussels in curry sauce), a fried dish (fish with ginger), a hot salad (beef slices on a bed of lettuce, onions, chillies, mint and lemon juice) and a variety of sauces into which food is dipped. This would be followed by sweet desserts and / or fresh fruits such as mangoes, durian, jackfruit, papaya, grapes or melon.

THAI COURSES
Titbits

These can be hors d'Oeuvres, accompaniments, side dishes, snacks. They include spring rolls, satay, puffed rice cakes with herbed topping they represent the playful and creative nature of the Thais.

Salads

Harmony of tastes and herbal flavours are essential. Major tastes are sour, sweet and salty. Spiciness comes in different degrees according to meat textures and occasions.

General Fare

A sweet and sour dish, a fluffy omelette, a stir fried dish help make a meal more complete.

Dips

Dips entail some complexity. They can be the major dish of a meal with accompaniments of vegetables and some meats. When dips are made thinly, they can be used as salad dressings. A particularly popular and simple dip is made from chilli, garlic, dried shrimps, lime juice, fish sauce, sugar and shrimp paste.

Soups

A good meal for an average person may consist simply of a soup and rice. Traditional Thai soups are unique because they embody more flavours and textures than can be found in other types of food.

Curries

Most non-Thai curries consist of powdered or ground dried spices, whereas the major ingredients of Thai are fresh herbs. A simple Thai curry paste consists of dried chillies, shallots and shrimp paste. More complex curries include garlic, galanga coriander roots, lemon grass, kaffir, lime peel and peppercorns.

Single Dishes

Complete meals in themselves, they include rice and noodle dishes such as Khao Phat and Phat Thai.

Desserts

No good meal is complete without a Thai dessert. Uniformly sweet, they are particularly welcome after a strongly spiced and herbed meal.

Titbits

A simple kind of titbit is fun to make. You need shallots, ginger, lemon or lime, lemon grass, roasted peanuts and red phrik khi nu chillies; Peeled shallots and ginger should be cut into small fingertip sizes. Diced lime and sliced lemon grass should be cut to the same size. Roasted peanuts should be left in halves. Chillies should be thinly sliced, combinations of such ingredients should be wrapped in fresh lettuce leaves and laced with a sweet - salty sauce made from fish sauce, sugar dried shrimps and lime juice.

DIPS

Mixing crushed fresh chillies with fish sauce and a dash of lime juice makes a general accompanying sauce for any Thai dish. Adding some crushed garlic and a tiny amount of roasted or raw shrimp paste transforms it into an all purpose dip (nam phrik). Some pulverised dried shrimp and julienned egg-plant with sugar makes this dip more complete. Serve it with steamed rice, an omlette and some vegetables.

Salad

Salad dressings have similar base ingredients. Add fish sauce, lime juice and sugar to enhance saltiness, sourness and sweetness. Crushed chillies, garlic and shallots add spiciness and herbal fragrance.

Lemon grass and galanga can be added for additional flavour. Employ this mix with any boiled, grilled or fried meat,

Lettuce leaves, sliced cucumber, cut spring onions and coriander leaves help top off the salad dressing.

Soup Stocks

Soups generally need good stock. Add to boiling water crushed peppercorns, salt, garlic, shallots, coriander roots, and the meats or cuts of one's choice. After "Prolonged boiling and simmering, you have the basic stock of common Thai soups, Additional galanga lemon grass, kaffir lime leaves, crushed fresh chillies, fish sauce and lime juice create the basic stock for Tom Yam.

Curries

To make a quick curry, fry curry or chilli paste in heated oil or thick coconut milk. Stir and fry until the paste is well cooked and add meats of one's choice. Season with fish sauce or sugar to taste. Add sliced eggplant with garnish of basil and kaffir lime leaves. Make your own curry paste by blending fresh (preferably dried) chillies, garlic, shallots, galanga, lemon grass, coriander roots, ground pepper, kaffir lime peels and shrimp paste.

Single Dish Meals

Heat cooking oil, fry in mixture of crushed chillies, minced garlic, ground pepper and chopped chicken meat. When nearly cooked, add vegetables such as cut beans or eggplants. Season with fish sauce and garnish with kaffir lime leaves, basil or balsam leaves. Cooked rice or fresh noodles added to the frying would make this a substantial meal.

TOM KHA KAI
Chicken Coconut Soup

Ingredients	Approx. Quantity
coconut milk	2 Cups (500 ml)
young galangal (kha on)	6 thin slices
lemon grass	2 stalks
(ta, khrai]	lower portion cut into 1 in (2.5 cm) lengths and crushed
kaffir lime leaves	5 fresh (bai ma krut) torn in half
boned chicken breast	250 g sliced
fish sauce (nam pla)	3 table spoons
sugar	2 table spoons
lime juice	1/2 cup (125 ml)
black chilli paste (nam phrik pao)	1 tablespoon
cilantro/coriander leaves (bai phak chi) torn	1/4 cup
Green Thai chilli peppers (phrik khi nu) crushed	5

Method

- Combine half the coconut milk with the galangal lemon grass and lime leaves in a large saucepan and heat to boiling Add the chicken, fish sauce, and sugar Simmer for about 4 minutes or until the chicken is cooked and then add the remaining coconut milk. Heat just to boiling. Place the lime juice and chilli paste in a serving bowl and pour the soup over them, garnish with cilantro leaves and crushed chill peppers.

TOM YAM KUNG
Hot and Sour Shrimp Soup

Ingredients	Approx. Quantity
water	3 cups
light chicken stock	(24fl or 750 ml)
shrimps prawn, shelled and deveined	8 oz (250 g)
garlic cloves minced	2
kaffir lime leaves (bai ma krut)	5
fresh or dried galangal (kha)	3 thin slices
fish sauce (nam pla)	1/4 cup

lemon grass citronella (ta khrai) 2 stalks
lower 1/3 portion only cut
into 1 in (2 - 3 cm) lengths
green onions   2
hot green Thai chilli peppers
(phrik khi nu)   sliced 5
optional 1/2 cup sliced straw mushrooms
lime juice   1/4 cup (2 fl oz / 60 ml)
roasted chilli paste (nam
phrik pao)   1 teaspoon
chopped cilantro coriander
leaves (bai flak chi)   1 tablespoon

Method

- Bring the stock to a boil over medium heat. Add the garlic, lime leaves galangal fish sauce, lemon grass and shallots, then the mushrooms and chilli papers, if using simmer for 2 minutes.
- Add the shrimp and reheat to boiling. Cook until the shrimps are pink, opaque, and firm but no longer than 1 minute. When the shrimps are cooked, place the lime Juice and chilli paste in a serving bowl. Pour the soup into the bowl, stir and garnish with cilantro leaves

KAENG KHIAO WAN NUEA
Green Curry with Beef/Chicken

Ingredients

2 stalks lemon grass/citronella, bottom part only. Cut into 1/2 in (1 cm) pieces
1 tablespoon sliced galangal (kha) or fresh ginger
1 teaspoon cumin
1/2 cup fresh cilantro/coriander root (rak phak chi)
8 garlic cloves
10 green Thai chilli peppers (phrik khi nu)
10 jalapeno peppers (phrik chi fa)
1 teaspoon shrimp paste (kapi)
1 tablespoon chopped shallot
1/4 teaspoon minced kaffir lime skin (phio ma - krut)
2 cups (500 ml) coconut milk
450 g beef, cut into 1/2 in x 2 in (1 cm x 2.5. cm) pieces

Ingredients

1/4 cup (60 ml) fish sauce (nam pla)
3 tablespoon sugar
1 cup Thai eggplant (ma kheua phuang) or
1 cup tinned bamboo shoots
1/2 cup (125 ml) coconut cream.
6 fresh kaffir lime leaves (bai ma - krut)
1/4 sweet basil leaves (bai harapha) red jaiapeno pepper (phrik chi pha daeng for garnish

Method

- Place all the green curry paste ingredients in an electric blender and process until smooth, or pound in a mortar. Pour the coconut milk and green curry paste into a large saucepan and heat to boiling. Add the beef, fish sauce, and sugar. Cool at a slow boil for 5 minutes. Add the eggplant and simmer for 2 minutes.
- Add the coconut cream and stir to combine Add the kaffir lime leaves and basil leaves. Remove the contents to a serving bowl and garnish with the red pepper.

Yam Nuea

Ingredients

450 g prime beef tenderloin,
2 garlic cloves fresh coriander leaves,
1/4 cup sugar
2 teaspoons light soya sauce
2 teaspoon fresh lime juice,
salt to taste,
freshly ground black pepper
2 spring onions, thinly sliced
6 fresh red chillies thinly sliced
2 tablespoons vegetable oil,
lettuce leaves.

Method

- Cook the beef until medium rare, or as preferred and cut into small thin slices. Pound together the garlic. 2 chopped coriander leaves, sugar, soya, sauce, lime juice, salt and ground black pepper until smooth. Heat the oil in a saucepan and stir-fry the spice paste for 3-4 minutes. Add the beef and cook for a further minute. Remove the beef and allow to cool. Serving on a plate. Then, sprinkle the chillies on top and garnish the remaining coriander leaves.

Satay

Ingredients

750 gm chicken breast
1/4 teaspoon roasted coriander seeds powder
1/4 teaspoon roasted cumin seeds powder
1/4 teaspoon pepper
1/4 teaspoon turmeric (roots) power
1/2 teaspoon curry powder
3 slices galangal
1/2 tablespoon finely chopped lemon grass
1 tablespoon salt
3 garlic cloves
1 cup coconut milk
2 table spoon vegetable oil
2 tablespoons sugar.
Small wooden skewers.

Method

- Slice the chicken breast finely, width approximately 1½ inches. Pound together, or blend in a blender, the coriander seeds, cumin seeds, pepper turmeric curry powder, galangal lemon grass, salt and garlic. Pour the blended ingredients into the coconut milk. Add sugar and vegetable oil and blend again so that all ingredients are well mixed. Add the chicken slices and marinate for 2 hours. Thread the chicken slices onto the skewers Pour the marinating sauce into a pot and heat until boiling. Place the chicken slices over a charcoal grill (barbecue) and apply the sauce to the chicken while turning over. When cooked through serve with Satay sauce and cucumber sauce.

Phat Thai

Ingredients

3 cups narrow rice noodle
1/3 cup sliced chicken meat, small stripe
4 shrimps
2 eggs
1/3 cup soya bean curd, cut into small sliver
1 tablespoon pickled white radish chopped
1/2 cup cooking oil
1 tablespoon garlic, chopped
1 tablespoon shallot or onion chopped
1 tablespoon ground dry red chilli or paprika
4 tablespoon sugar
4 tablespoon fish sauce
4 tablespoon vinegar 1/3 cup bean sprouts
1/3 cup spring onion, chopped to
1½ in lengths 1 lime for garnishing
1/4 cup carrot, for garnishing sliced thinly
1/4 cup cabbage for garnishing sliced thinly
2 tablespoons ground roasted peanut.

Method

- Fry the chopped garlic and onion until turned yellow. Add chicken and fry until cooked. Pour in the shrimp, pickled white radish, soya bean curd. Break the eggs into the pan and scramble. Add sugar, fish sauce, vinegar, ground dry red chilli and stir well. Pour in the noodles, stir-fry until mixed well, add spring onion, 3/4 or half a cup of bean sprouts (the remainder, clipped both ends, used for garnishing) and stir-fry until cooked. Spoon onto platter. Garnish with ground roasted peanut, bean ˙sprouts carrot, cabbage and sliced lime.

Stir-Fried Mixed Vegetables

Ingredients

1½ cup cabbage cut bite size
6 broccoli, cut bite size
10 snow pea ends clipped
10 pealed carrot sliced across
2 asparagus, cut to 1 in lengths

Ingredients

3 mushroom, halved
1/2 cup green and red bell chilli sliced lengthways
4 baby corn, medium size
1/4 cup ear mushroom thinly sliced
1/2 cup bean sprouts clipped both ends
2 teaspoon chopped garlic
4 tablespoon cooking oil
1 tablespoon dark soya sauce
2 tablespoon light soya sauce
1 pinch ground pepper.

Method

- Fry the garlic for a little while in the oil and add the cabbage, broccoli, snow peas, carrot, asparagus mushrooms, chillies, baby corn, and ear mushrooms and saute. Add dark soya sauce light soya sauce and bean sprouts and stir - fry until mixed well. Spoon up onto platter and sprinkle with ground pepper.

THOT MAN PLA
Curried Fish Cakes

Ingredients

1/2 kg boneless fish steak minced
1/4 kg winged beans or Fresh beans, finely chopped
1 egg, beaten
1/4 CUP chopped shallots
1/4 cup chopped garlic
1/4 cup chopped lemon grass
1/2 tablespoon chopped coriander root
1/2 tablespoon chopped galanga root
1/2 teaspoon pepper corns
1/2 teaspoon grated kaffir - lime rind
1 tablespoon shrimp paste
5-10 dried chillies, seeded, soaked and shredded
1/2 tablespoon salt, 1 cup vegetable oil.

Method

- Pound or grind together the shallots, garlic, lemon, grass coriander root, galanga root, krachai root, pepper corns, grated kaffir lime rind, shredded dried chillies, salt and shrimp paste to a fine paste. Put the minced fish in an electric blender, arid blend in the curry mixture. Add the beaten egg. Pour the curried fish mixture into a large bowl. Mix in the chopped beans. Make flat round fish cakes. Use about I spoonful of the fish mixture at a time. Heat the oil in a frying pan and deep - fry the fish cakes until golden brown. Serve with the cucumber dressing.

KHAO PHAT
Fried Rice

Ingredients

3 tablespoon peanut or corn oil
200 g boneless skinned chicken breast cut lengthways into 1/2 in/1 cm thick slices
1 tablespoon chopped garlic 1 medium sized onion sliced, 2 eggs
4 cups/13 lb/750 g cooked rice
1 tomato, cut into 8 wedges
1 spring onion (scallion) chopped
2 teaspoons white soya sauce
1 teaspoon fish sauce
1 teaspoon sugar
1 teaspoon ground white pepper.

Method

- Heat the oil in a wok or pan, add the chicken and garlic, and nix well over the heat for 1 minute. Add the onion and cook for 1 minute, break in the eggs, mix very well and then stir in the rice and the rest of the ingredients. Stir well. Cook for 8 minutes and serve immediately with cucumber slice and whole spring onions.

MI KROP
Crispy Noodles

Ingredients

4 cups (1 qt / 1) oil
200 g rice vermicelli
Sauce
1/2 cup (125 g) sugar
1/2 cup (125 ml) vinegar
1 teaspoon salt

Ingredients

1 teaspoon tomato paste
1 tablespoons garlic pickle (krathiam dong)
Garnish
2 eggs beaten (optional)
1/4 cup chopped green onions
1/4 cup chopped red bell pepper
1/8 cup chopped chives
125 g fried tofu diced
1 tablespoon chopped cilantro/coriander leaves (bai phak chi)

Method

In a wok or deep - fryer heat the oil to 375° F (190°C) and fry the rice vermicelli untill puffed. Remove and set aside. Combine the sauce ingredients in a large skillet and cook over medium heat for 4 minutes until of a syrupy consistency. If desired, fry the beaten eggs in a small pan. When cooked remove and slice into thin strips. Set aside. Add the noodles to the sauce and mix quickly so that they are evenly coated. Place on a serving dish, sprinkle with the garnish, and lay the eggs strips on top. Serve immediately.

KAI YANG WITH
Barbecued Chicken with

Ingredients

1 whole chicken, about 1.5 kg cut in half
1 teaspoon salt 4 garlic cloves, chopped
1 teaspoon white pepper
1 tablespoon minced cliantro/coriander leaves and root
3 tablespoon cognac, whisky or rice wine
2 tablespoons coconut milk
1 tablespoon fish sauce (num pla)
1 teaspoon chopped fresh ginger
2 tablespoon soya sauce.

Method

- Rub the entire chicken with the combined marinade ingredients and allow to marinate for 15 minutes. Bake at 350° F (180°C) for 45 minutes and then broil/grill 10 minutes or until done. Cut into smaller pieces before serving.

KHAO NIAO AND SOM TAM
Sticky Rice

Ingredients

1 kg sticky (glutinous) rice,
Water

Method

- Place 4 cups sticky (glutinous) rice, in a saucepan and add water to cover. Rub the rice between your hands several times and drain of the milky water; add clean water and repeat until the water is clear. Soak overnight in water to cover or, to save time, it can be soaked in hot water for 3 hours before steaming. Drain the rice and place in a cloth lined basket or in a steaming basket. Place the basket over a pot of boiling water, cover and steam for approximately 30 minutes.

Papaya Salad

Ingredients

1 medium dark green papaya
4 garlic cloves
6 green Thai chillies (phrik khi nu)
2 tomatoes cut into wedges
1-2 cup green beans chopped into 1/2 in (2-5 cm) pieces
2 tablespoons anchovy sauce
1/2 teaspoon salt
1/4 cup (60 ml) lime juice or turmarind juice.

Method

- Peel the papaya and rinse under running water. Remove the seeds and shred the flesh with a grater. Set aside. Place the garlic cloves and chillies in a mortar and mash with a pestle until crushed into chunks. Add the papaya and the re-maining ingredients and gently combine oil with the pestle and a spoon. Serve cold.

PO PIA THOT
Spring Rolls

Ingredients

2 tablespoon oil
1 teaspoon minced garlic
250 g minced pork
2 cups grated carrots
2 cups chopped celery
1/4 cup (60 ml) fish sauce (nam pla)
1 tablespoon Maggi seasoning
2 tablespoon sugar
1/8 teaspoon white pepper
1 cup bean sprouts
20 spring roll wrappers
2 egg yolks, beaten
3 cups (750 ml) oil for deep frying

Method

- Heat a large skillet, add the oil, garlic, and pork and saute until the pork is cooked. Add the carrots, celery, sauces, sugar and pepper. Cook for 1 minute on high heat to reduce the sauce, drain whatever liquid is left from the pan. Allow the filling to cool and then add the bean sprouts. Place a wrapper as a diamond with a corner towards you and place two table spoon in the lower portion. Fold the corner up, rolling once. Bring the sides in and brush the upper portion of the wrapper with egg yolk. Roll the wrapper up, sealing the entire spring roll. Repeat with the rest of the wrappers. Heat the oil to 350°F (180°C) and deep-fry the spring rolls until golden brown. Serve with a sweet and sour sauce.

THAI DESSERTS

SANGKHAYA FAKTHONG
Custard in Pumpkin

Ingredients

small pumpkin
5 chicken eggs
1/3 cup palm sugar
pinch of salt
1 cup coconut cream

Method

- Cut a slice off the top of the pumpkin, remove the seeds and most of the soft pulp, in a mixing bowl, lightly whisk the eggs, add the sugar, salt and coconut cream and stir until well blended. Pour the mixture into the pumpkin and cook in a steamer (for approximately 20 minutes) until the custard is set. Make 4 servings.

BUA LOI PHUAK
Taro Balls in Coconut Cream

Ingredients

1 cup cooked taro, mashed
2 cups glutinous - rice flour
1 cup corn flour
4 cups coconut milk
1 cup palm sugar
1/8 teaspoon salt
6-8 tablespoon water

Method

- Put the glutinous - rice flour and the corn flour in a bowl. Add a little water at a time and knead to a soft dough. Add the mashed taro and knead well. Roll into tiny balls and set aside. Dissolve the palm sugar and salt in the coconut milk over a low heat, stirring constantly. Bring to the boil and add the taro balls. When they are cooked, remove from the heat. Serve hot. Make 4-6 servings.

KLUAI BUAT CHI
Banana Cooked in Coconut Milk

Ingredients

2-3 small, slightly green bananas
4 cups (900 ml) thin coconut milk
1 cup (175 g) sugar
1/4 teaspoon salt.

Method

- Slice the bananas lengthways, then in half. Pour the coconut milk into a pan, add the sugar and salt. Bring to the boil, add the bananas, bring back to the boil for 8 minutes and then remove from the heat. Serve hot or cold.
  4 Sevings

APPENDICES

STANDARD WEIGHTS AND MEASURES

1. Commonly used weight conversion

Pounds (lbs)	Ounces (Oz)	Grams (g)	Kg	G (rounded off)
—	1	28.350	—	25 or 30
—	2	56.699	—	55 or 60
—	3	85.094	—	85
—	4	113.398	—	115
—	5	141.748	—	140-145
1	16	454	—	455
2	32	907	—	910
3	48	1361	1	360
4	64	1814	1	815
5	80	2268	2	270

2. Kilograms to Pounds

Kg	lb	Rounded	off
1	2.210	2 lb	3 Oz
2	4.409	4 lb	7 Oz
3	6.614	6 lb	10 Oz
4	8.818	8 lb	13 Oz
5	11.023	11 lb	

3. Commonly used Volume conversions

Pints	Litres	Litres	Pints
1	0.568	1	1.759
2	1.136	2	3.520
3	1.705	3	5.279
4	2.273	4	7.039
5	2.841	5	8.799

4. Conversion factors useful when Planning layouts

Inches × 2.54 = Centimetres (cm) × 0.0254 = Metres (m)
Square inches × 6.451 = Cm:
Feet × 30.48 = Cm
× 0.304 = m
Sq. ft × 0.092 = m²
Yd. 1 × 0,914 = m
Sq. Yds. × 0.836 = m²
Miles × 1609.3 = m
Miles × 1.069 = km

5. Oven Temperatures used in Cooking

Description	Gas Mark	°F	°C
Very Hot	9	475	246
Moderately Hot	8	450	232
	7	425	218
	6	400	204
Moderate	5	375	191
Very Moderate	4	350	176
	3	225	163
Slow	2	300	149
Very slow	1	275	135
	1/2	250	.121
Cool	1/4	225	107
	—	200	93

Appendix II

A typical 5-star Kitchen Organisation Chart

Chef de Cuisine
(Head chef)

Sous Chef
(Assistant Head Chef)

Chef Potager
(Soup Cook)

Chef Entremettier
(Vegetable Cook)

Chef Rotisseur
(Roast Cook)

Grillardin
(Grill Cook)

Chef Poissonnier
(Fish Cook)

Night Cook
Breakfast Cook
Staff Cook

Chef Saucier
(Sauce Cook)

Commis
(Assistant)

Apprentis
(Apprentice)

Chef Tournant
(Relief Cook)

Chef Grade Manger
(Larger Cook)

Chef Froitier
(Cold Buffet Cook)

Boucher
(Butcher)

Hors d'Oeuvrier
(Hor d'Oeure Cook)

Chef Patissier
(Pastry Cook)

Tourier
(Pastry Cook)

Confiseur
(confectioner)

Glacier
(ICE Cream Cook)

The complete kitchen brigade includes the following ancillary personnel:

Kitchen Clerk and Aboyeur
Kitchen Porters
Plongeur
Plongeur (Pot washer)
Stillroom Assistant
Storeman

GLOSSARY OF CULINARY TERMS

Aperitif : An alcoholic drink taken before a meal to stimulate the appetite.

Appetizer : A small portion of fruit, juice, or savoury titbits, served as the first course of a meal.

Aspic : A clear, savoury jelly made from meat or vegetable stock and used to garnish or mould fish, meat and poultry.

Au gratin : A dish covered with sauce, breadcrumbs or cheese and then baked or grilled and served in the same dish.

Bain-Marie : A device for keeping foods hot without actually boiling by standing the dish containing the food in a large pan filled with water which is kept just below boiling point

Bake blind : Pastry, especially flan cases and individual tartlets, baked before the filling is put in. The pastry case is lined with foil or grease proof paper cut to shape, weighed down with dried beans, and baked in the centre of a pre-heated oven at 400°F for fifteen minutes. The beans and foil are then removed and it is baked further for five to ten minutes or until the pastry is dry and lightly browned.

Bake : To cook food in an oven or a similar appliance by dry heat.

Barbecue : To roast slowly on a spit, over coal or under a heat unit, usually basting with a highly seasoned sauce.

Baste : To moisten meat or other foods while cooking to add flavour and to prevent drying of the surface. The liquid is usually melted fat or meat drippings.

Batter : A mixture of flour, liquid, and other ingredients which is soft enough to be beaten or 'battered'. Used for pancakes, cakes, fritters, dropscones, or coating foods for frying.

Bavarian : A moulded cold dessert made with gelatine, eggs, cream and flavourings.

Beat : To make a mixture smooth by introducing air with a brisk, regular motion.

Bechamel : A rich white sauce.

Bind : To add eggs, cream, melted fat, flour or roux panada to a dry mixture to hold it together.

Birishta : Thinly sliced onion fried slowly till crisp and golden brown. It is then ground and added to a dish. Used in mughlai cooking.

Bisque : A thick, rich cream soup usually made with shellfish or pureed vegetables.

Blanch : Dipping foods into boiling water either to whiten, remove strong flavour, soften, cleanse, or loosen the skin to facilitate peeling.

Blend : To mix thoroughly two or more ingredients.

Boil : To cook in liquid in which bubbles rise constantly to the surface and break.

Bouillon	:	A clear, seasoned soup usually made from beef or chicken. Also obtained by dissolving a bouillon cube in boiling water.
Bouquet garni	:	Several herbs, usually including cloves, cardamom, parsley and bayleaf tied in cheesecloth or muslin cloth. Added to stews, sauces and soups for flavouring and removed before serving.
Braise	:	To cook food slowly in a small amount of liquid in a covered pan. Food may or may not be browned first in a small amount of fat
Broil	:	To cook by direct heat.
Brown	:	To give a dish, usually already cooked, an appetizing golden brown colour by placing under a grill or in a hot oven for a few minutes.
Broth	:	An unclarified thin soup.
Brush	:	To apply a coating of milk, egg, sugar and water mixes etc. to pastry, cakes and other baked products to give it a glaze or even for browning.
Canape	:	Plain or toasted bread or crackers topped with a savoury mixture, served as an appetizer.
Caramelize	:	To heat sugar over low heat until it melts and develops a characteristic flavour and golden brown colour.
Casserole	:	A covered utensil in which food may be baked and served.
Coating	:	Covering one food with a thin layer of another in liquid form. Usually applied to food dipped in beaten egg or in a batter.
Compote	:	Fruit stewed in syrup.
Consistency	:	Thickness or texture of a mixture.
Consomme	:	Thin clarified soup.
Cream, to	:	To beat or soften fat until light and fluffy.
Creamed	:	A term applied to foods that are either cooked in or served with a white sauce.
Croquette	:	A mixture of chopped or minced food, made into various shapes, coated with egg and crumbs and deep fried.
Crouton	:	Small, diced and fancy shapes of toasted or fried bread used for garnishing soups and savoury dishes
Cut and fold	:	To mix flour very gently into an aerated mixture.
Cut in	:	To distribute solid fat in dry ingredients by chopping with knives or pastry blender until finely divided.
Dariole	:	A small flowerpot shaped mould used for steamed or baked puddings, setting jellies etc.
Dash	:	Less than one-eighth teaspoon of an ingredient, usually a spice.
Deep fry	:	To cook in hot fat, deep enough to cover the food.
Devilled	:	Any highly seasoned dish. Various mixtures of dry condiments are used but they usually include some hot and piquant ingredient like mustard.

Dice : To cut into small, even cubes.

Disjoint : To cut meat or chicken into smaller pieces at the bone joints.

Dot : To put small pieces of butter, cheese, cream etc. over die surface of a dish.

Dough : A mixture of flour, liquid, and other ingredients thick enough to be shaped by hand or rolled out on a board. Used for chapattis, mathris, samosas, bread, biscuits, pastry, scones.

Dredge : To cover or coat with dry ingredients such as flour, sugar, breadcrumbs, grated coconut, poppy seeds.

Dress, to : Clean, pare, trim, decorate. Drippings : Fat and juices drawn from meat or poultry as it cooks.

Dust : To sprinkle lightly with flour or sugar.

Emulsion : A suspension of a light liquid, like oil, in a heavier liquid, like egg; such as, mayonnaise, French dressing.

Entree : This is the third course served in an old-fashioned formal meal of many courses. It is a savoury dish, usually of meat served in a sauce but may also be a fish dish or a cold dish.

Escalopes : Thin slices of meat dipped in egg and breadcrumbs and then fried.

Farce : Any kind of stuffing.

Fillet : A piece of meat, fish or poultry without the bones.

Flake : To break into small pieces with a fork, being careful not to mash the pieces.

Flan : A pastry case made in a flat tin filled with a sweet or savoury mixture either before or after cooking the pastry.

Flute : To make an edge with a scalloped effect; used for pie crusts.

Fold in : To combine delicate ingredients like whipped cream, beaten egg whites with other foods using a gentle circular motion.

Fondant : Sugar cooked to soft-boiled stage (112°C, 234°F) and then beaten to a 'fudge-like' smoothness. It can be used as an icing or sweet.

Forcemeat : Same as farce.

Frappe : Sweetened fruit juice, half frozen.

Fricassee : A stew generally made with meat or poultry and thickened with white sauce.

Fritter : A small quantity of a batter mixture, often containing meat, vegetables or fruit, fried until crisp.

Frosting : Sugar icing used to cover cakes. Fry : To cook in hot fat.

Garnish : To decorate.

Gateau : Cake, ice cream or anything made in the shape of a cake and lavishly decorated.

Giblets : The trimmings of certain parts of poultry, such as heart, liver, kidney, gizzard, feet and neck.

Gild	:	To brush with beaten egg.
Glace	:	To coat with a thin sugar syrup cooked to the cracked stage.
Glaze	:	To brush the tops of pies, buns and other baked products with egg and water, sugar and water or some preparation which gives the surface a glossy appearance.
Grate	:	To shave into small shreds on a grater. Grill : To cook by direct heat. Same as broil.
Grind	:	To reduce to particles by crushing.
Hors-d'oeuvres	:	Small savoury titbits usually served as appetizers.
Infuse	:	To soak flavouring materials such as tea leaves, herbs, bayleaf in hot liquid in order that the liquid may absorb the flavouring.
Julienne	:	Food cut into thin long sticks.
Knead	:	To work a dough lightly by bringing the outside of the dough into the centre, using the knuckles of the hand.
Knock back	:	To knead yeast dough once again after it has risen.
Leavening	:	Substances like baking powder or yeast which create bubbles of gas in batters and doughs causing them to rise.
Liaison	:	Binding and thickening ingredients added to soups and sauces, such as butter and cream liaison, egg yolks or egg whites, flour, cornflour or arrowroot, roux.
Macaroons	:	Biscuits made from egg whites, sugar and ground almonds, though other nuts are also used.
Macedonies	:	A mixture of raw or cooked fruits and vegetables cut into pieces of similar size.
Macedonies	:	A mixture of vinegar, oil, spices, curd, lime In which meat is steeped before cooking in order to improve the flavour and to make it more tender.
Marinate	:	To soak in a marinade.
Mask	:	To coat a dish with sauce or to line a mould with jelly.
Meringue	:	A mixture of stiffly beaten egg whites and sugar baked until the mixture is dry and firm.
Mince	:	To cut or chop into very small pieces.
Mono-sodium glutamate	:	A white crystalline salt that enhances the natural flavour of foods. Also called Ajinomoto or Chinese Salt.
Mousse	:	A cold dessert with whipped cream or beaten egg whites.
Panada	:	Mixture of flour, butter and liquid used as a foundation for mixtures like souffle and for binding ingredients together.
Panbroil	:	To cook food uncovered on an ungreased or lightly greased hot surface, pouring off fat as it accumulates.

Parboil : To boil until partially cooked usually before completing cooking by another method.

Parfeit : Ice cream served in a tall glass and decorated with a variety of nuts and fruits.

Pare : To peel thinly.

Pasta : The name of the national staple starchy food in Italy, such as noodles, spaghetti, macaroni, vermicelli

Pit : To remove seeds and stones from fruits and vegetables.

Poach : To cook in simmering liquid.

Potage : A nourishing broth or soup.

Prove, to : To keep aside yeast dough in a warm place to let it rise and double in bulk

Puree : To press food through a fine sieve or blend in a blender so it becomes a smooth, thick paste.

Raising Agents : Same as leavening.

Raspings : Dried, sieved, browned breadcrumbs used for coating.

Rechauffe : Any dish made with re-heated food.

Reconstitute : To restore concentrated foods such as dry milk or frozen orange juice to their normal state by adding liquid.

Reduce : Allowing a mixture to boil rapidly in an open pan thus reducing the volume by evaporation of water and therefore concentrating the flavour.

Render : A highly-seasoned food used as an accompaniment, like pickles and chutneys. To free fat from animal tissues by heating at low temperatures.

Rissoles : Mixture similar to that of croquettes enclosed in pastry and fried.

Roast : To cook uncovered in hot air. Roux : A thickening made of flour and fat and used for soups or sauces.

Rub-in : A method used for mixing fat in Sour (as is done for making short-crust pastry) using the tips of the fingers and thumb till the mixture looks like breadcrumbs.

Saute : To lightly fry and toss in a small amount of hot fat.

Scald : To heat to just under the boiling point or to dip certain foods in boiling water.

Scalloped : A method of preparing cooked fish, egg, or vegetables by mixing with a sauce, usually white or Bechamel, and re-heating in the oven with buttered crumbs as topping.

Score : To make light cuts in a surface such as a piece of pork before roasting. Making a pattern of squares or diamonds on pastry crust

Sear : To brown the surface of meat by a short application of intense heat

Season : To improve the aroma and flavour of food by adding seasonings like salt, pepper, mustard, : garlic.

Sherbet	:	Frozen mixture of fruit juice, egg whites, sugar, milk or water.
Sift	:	To put dry ingredients through a sieve or strainer.
Simmer	:	To cook in liquid just before the boiling point.
Singe	:	To pass through a flame and burn the surface for removing hair, as in poultry.
Sippet	:	Fingers or triangles of toasted or fried bread which are used for garnishing savoury dishes.
Souffle	:	A very light preparation made of a sauce foundation, egg yolks, flavouring ingredients and beaten egg whites.
Steam	:	To cook in steam with or without pressure. Steep : To allow food to stand in hot liquid to extract colour and flavour.
Stew	:	To cook by simmering in a little liquid.
Stock	:	A soup or broth made by boiling meat, bones, vegetables or fish in water with or without spices. The liquid forms a foundation for a number of soups and sauces.
Temper	:	To heat fat and fry various spices before adding to a dish.
Toast	:	To brown by dry heat. Toss
	:	To turn food in a pan or dish by holding the container and by using a quick, jerky movement.
Truss	:	To tie up or skewer meat, poultry and fish for roasting.
Whip	:	To beat rapidly to incorporate air and increase volume.
Whisk	:	To beat cream or eggs till a stiff froth is obtained.
Zest	:	The rind of a lemon or orange, grated or pared thinly without any pith.

DAILY ALLOWANCES OF NUTRIENTS FOR INDIANS
(Recommended by the Nutritions Expert Group)

Group	Particulars	1 Net calories	2 Proteins (gm.)	3 Calcium (gm.)	4 Iron (mg.)	5 Vitamin A Retinol (ug.)	5 Vitamin A B-carotene (ug.)	6 Thiamine (mg.)	7 Riboflavin (mg.)	8 Nicotinic acid (mg.)	Ascorbic acid (mg.)	9 Folic acid (ug.)	10 Vitamin B,12 (ug.)	11 Vitamin D (I.U)
Man	Sedentary work	2400	55	0.4-0.5	20	750	3000	1.2	1.3	16	50	100	1	200
	Moderate work	2800						1.4	1.5	19				
	Heavy work	3900						2.0	2.2	26				
Woman	Sedentary work	1900	45	0.4-0.5	30	750	3000	1.0	1.0	13	50	100	1	
	Moderate work	2200						1.1	1.2	15				
	Heavy work	3000						1.5	1.7	20				
	Pregnancy (second half of pregenancy)	+300	+10	1.0	40	750	3000	+0.2	+0.2	+2.50	150-300	1.5		
	Lactation (up to 1 year)	+700	+20	1.0	30	1150	4600	+0.4	+0.4	+5.80	150			
Infants	0-6 months	120/kg	2.3-1.8/kg		1.0 mg.	400	—							
	7-12	100/kg	1.8-1.5/kg		0.5-0.6	300	1200							
Children	1-year	1200	17	0.4-0.5	15-20	250	1000	0.6	0.7	8	25	0.2		
	2 yrs. / 3 yrs.		18			300	1200	0.8	0.8	10	30-50	50.100	0.5-1.0	
	4-6 yrs.	1500	22			40	160	0.9	1.0	12				
	7-9 yrs.	1800	33			60	240	1.0	1.2	14				
	10-12 yrs.	2100	41			750	3000	1.3	1.4	17				
Adolescents	13-15 yrs. Boys	2500	55	0.6-0.7	25	750	3000	1.1	1.2	14				
	13-15 yrs. Girls	2200	50		35									
	16-18 yrs. Boys	3000	60	0.5-0.6	25			1.5	1.7	21				
	16-18 yrs. Girls	2200	50		35			1.1	1.2	14				

Sufficient nutrients have been provided to compensate for loss in cooking which varies depending on the method used.

NUTRITIVE VALUE PER 100 GRAMS OF SOME COOKED FOODS

Sl. No.	Preparation	Calories	Protein (g.)	Carbohy-drate(g.)	Fate (g.)	Calcium (mg.)	Iron (mg.)	Phosph-orus(mg.)
	Recipes common to the whole country							
	A. 1. Sweets—Wheat							
1.	Barbi	409	5.3	57.1	17.9	65	2.4	152
2.	Biscuits							
	(i) Sweet biscuits	349	6.8	58.1	10.1	21	3.9	177
	(ii) Butter biscuits	482	4.4	70.1	20.4	9	0.4	37
	(iii) Milk biscuits	399	6.4	62.2	13.8	44	3.6	174
3.	Bun	281	5.0	45.9	8.7	91	2.1	139
4.	Cake							
	(i) Plain cake	492	5.1	49.5	30.5	15	0.7	58
	(ii) Semolina cake	371	8.3	51.9	14.5	43	3.9	198
5.	Gulab jamun	387	6.8	37.8	24.2	260	2.4	186
6.	Halwa							
	(i) Atta halwa	263	2.6	34.1	13.0	12	1.4	72
	(ii) Khesari	136	1.7	23.7	3.8	10	1.1	53
7.	Jaebi	494	4.4	42.0	34.3	31	1.4	89
8.	Paadurshah	485	5.6	63.5	22.7	11	0.7	57
9.	Sponge cake	286	7.6	53.8	4.5	25	1.0	97
10.	Surma Ladoo	464	3.2	60.8	23.1	30	1.5	100
11.	Toffee							
	(i) Chocolate	464	5.1	65.2	20.3	11	2.5	129
	(ii) Coconut	429	4.2	70.2	11.5	5	0.6	46
	A. 2. Sweets-Rice							
12.	Kheer	141	4.1	21.1	4.5	80	1.0	98
13.	Kheer (without milk)	168	2.9	34.4	2.0	26	2.9	74
14.	Sweet rice	267	2.5	44.6	8.8	15	0.8	65
	B. I. Savouries-Wheat							
15.	Bread	275	8.1	50.0	4.7	26!	4.8	217
16.	Meat puffs	603	13.9	36.9	44.1	95	1.7	140
17.	Potato kachori	166	2.0	15.2	10.710	0.2	23	
	B.2. Savouries-Rice							
18.	Cauliflower palao	149	2.6	21.4	6.0	43	1.3	65
19.	Chewra	420	4.2	40.2	27.0	23	3.9	134

Sl. No.	Preparation	Calories	Protein (g.)	Carbohy-drate(g.)	Fate (g.)	Calcium (mg.)	Iron (mg.)	Phosph-orus(mg.)
20.	Ghee rice	223	2.8	21.6	13.8	27	0.8	71
21.	Godham pakora	163	3.0	18.6	8.5	35	1.6	81
22.	Ompodi	444	11.4	50.5	21.8	148	6.4	174
23.	Paapari	444	5.3	59.7	20.4	44	2.1	122
24.	Plain khicher	168	4.7	21.0	7.3	32	0.8	60
25.	Red gram khicheri	171	4.1	24.8	6.0	27	1.9	66
26.	Rice gruel	121	2.3	27.7	0.2	11	0.7	49
27.	Vadi palao	230	6.2	37.2	6.2	40	2.4	108
28.	Vatel	500	3.4	64.2	25.5	24	1.8	77
29.	Vegetable biryani	148	2.3	22.0	5.7	26	0.8	52

Recipes in common use in the Eastern region

A. 1. Sweets-Wheat

30.	Choshi peetha (Savian kheer)	180	0.5	29.7	4.6	124	0.5	104
31.	Fried biscuits	509	5.8	48.6	32.0	15	2.1	105
32.	Gujia	501	8.2	57.9	26.5	141	2.8	182
33.	Pathi shapte	290	6.0	38.2	12.7	107	1.5	151
34.	Peetha	307	4.6	48.4	10.5	19	1.4	81

A. 2. Sweets-Rice

| 35. | Maalpura | 278 | 2.3 | 37.4 | 13.1 | 22 | 0.7 | 78 |
| 36. | Khicheri | 298 | 3.9 | 39.8 | 14.4 | 24 | 1.0 | 73 |

B. 1. Savouries- Wheat

37.	Mathi	521	0.4	40.5	37.219	1	2.2	114
38.	Khicheri (with mutton)	190	6.5	14.3	11.8	60	1.6	75
39.	Khicheri (with vegetable)	127	3.9	16.7	5.0	29	0.7	50
40.	Pish pash	166	4.4	16.3	9.2	55	1.0	58
41.	Rice chapati	212	3.4	42.9	3.0	6	1.1	76

Recipes in common use in the Western Region

A. 1. Sweets-Wheat

42.	Bombay paka	484	3.3	640	23.9	33	0.3	42
43.	Cheeroti	240	4.4	26.6	12.7	81	1.6	119
44.	Gulpoli	374	6.9	47.1	16.5	55	5.1	117

Sl. No.	Preparation	Calories	Protein (g.)	Carbohy-drate(g.)	Fate (g.)	Calcium (mg.)	Iron (mg.)	Phosph-orus(mg.)
45.	Karanji	508	5.7	51.8	30.8	14	1.5	99
46.	Ladoo powder	563	8.2	51.2	36.3	143	4.1	230
47.	Magmal puri	507	6.0	71.4	21.9	29	3.5	138
48.	Milk cake	331	4.6	45.5	14.6	71	2.0	100
49.	Mutkuli	348	5.4	54.8	11.9	18	3.2	144
50.	Mutkuli iadoo	534	5.9	53.2	33.1	43	3..1	168
51.	Nankhatai	584	5.6	62.9	34.5	12	0.5	61
52.	Paaktali cheeroti	506	5.1	51.6	31.2	34	0.5	56
53.	Puran poll	462	6.6	51.9	25.5	52	4.3	87
54.	Satu-kaa-peeth	429	9.3	68.6	13.1	60	5.4	198
55.	Shakarpara	691	3.7	37.9	58.3	12	2.2	100
56.	Shakarpara-chi-wadi	400	4.9	52.3	19.0	13	1.7	88
57.	Suji biscuits	373	4.5 j	40.9	21.3	39	1.4	88
58.	Surat khaari	519	7.3	47.7	33.2	71	2.1	103
59	Sweet thaalipeeth	339	4.5	50.2	14.1	40	5.5	115

A. 2. Sweets- Rice

Sl. No.	Preparation	Calories	Protein (g.)	Carbohy-drate(g.)	Fate (g.)	Calcium (mg.)	Iron (mg.)	Phosph-orus(mg.)
60.	Adraswada	415	3.4	76.1	10.7	52	5.3	75
61.	Anarasa	499	3.7	63.4	25.2	26	3.4	65
62.	Banana vadai	359	2.9	67.8	8.2	33	4.1	64
63.	Kadhiele	152	1.6	36.1	0.1	25	2.5	36
64.	Modak	209	2.8	35.3	6.1	5	0.6	74
65.	Rice halwa	339	2.7	42.6	17.4	5	0.6	79
66.	Rice ladoo	502	3.6	64.3	25.3	5	0.5	55
67.	Shakarpara-chi-wadi	489	4.5	70.5	21.0	11	2.1	111
68.	Zibrutenchi kheer	174	1.4	27.0	6.8	17	2.5	50

B. 1. Savouries-Wheat

Sl. No.	Preparation	Calories	Protein (g.)	Carbohy-drate(g.)	Fate (g.)	Calcium (mg.)	Iron (mg.)	Phosph-orus(mg.)
69.	Buttermilk	218	5.3	28.8	8.8	40	3.2	162
70.	Ghawan	279	5.8	35.0	12.8	19	3.4	156
71.	Savain uppuma	196	6.0	28.3	6.3	39	1.0	68
72.	Thaalipeeth	392	8.3	49.3	18. 0	39	5.1	222
73.	Tikhet-mithachi karanjee	333	5.7	33.1	19.7	77	0.8	89
74.	Uppuma	233	4.9	30.0	10.2	49	2.7	133
75.	Wheat flour chakali	798	6.1	36.6	69.7	20	3.6	163

Sl. No.	Preparation	Calories	Protein (g.)	Carbohy-drate(g.)	Fate (g.)	Calcium (mg.)	Iron (mg.)	Phosph-orus(mg.)
			B. 2.	Savouries-Rice				
76.	Chewre	394	14.9	55.1	12.3	82	6.8	224
77.	Dhokra	122	4.2	21.0	2.1	85	1.0	93
78.	Dosai	360	6.3	37.2	20.6	33	2.9	134
79.	Gharvada	264	3.5	25.3	16.2	61	0.6	78
80.	Kanki	92	1.9	20.1	0.3	15	0.7	42
81.	Kaya vada	384	4.8	59.1	14.5	18	1.5	102
82.	Kharri bhaat	124	1.7	19.0	4.6	50	0.9	46
83.	Khicheri (with curd)	117	3.8	21.8	1.4	25	0.9	54
84.	Paankie	193	4.8	33.7	2.1	90	1.3	129
85.	Poha	118	2.9	21.2	2.2	31	2.0	70

Recipes in common use in the Northern region

Sl. No.	Preparation	Calories	Protein (g.)	Carbohy-drate(g.)	Fate (g.)	Calcium (mg.)	Iron (mg.)	Phosph-orus(mg.)
			A 1.	Sweets-Wheat				
86.	Balushai	469	5.4	62.6	22.0	35	1.1	67
87.	Churi	454	6.9	56.1	22.5	23	4.1	186
88.	Goja	499	5.9	86.7	13.9	11	0.6	50
89.	Halwa paratha	382	5.9	48.3	18.3	19	3.5	157
90.	Jaggery roti	445	5.5	54.0	23.0	36	5.7	153
91.	Jalebi	412	4.9	72.0	11.6	10	0.5	41
92.	Kungania	196	2.4	34.6	5.4	8	1.4	65
93.	Leepie	248	3.1	36.6	9.8	26	3.9	96
94.	Maalpua	325	4.4	44.8	14.3	14	2.6	118
95.	Nashasta	627	10.9	90.9	24.7	46	6.0	279
96.	Panjiri	528	5.5	56.6	30.7	30	2.9	145
97.	Pathura	296	4.1	40.5	13.1	27	4.3	115
98.	Pura	447	6.1	61.6	19.6	20	3.6	163
99.	Pinni	492	8.9	51.2	27.9	232	4.4	255
100.	Seera	181	4.0	19.7	9.4	91	1.2	114
101.	Shakarpara (sweet)	403	5.4	80.7	6.8	49	59	62
102.	Sohan halwa	399	3.0	62.9	.15.2	15	1.5	78
103.	Sweet Dalia	217	7.7	30.5	7.1	240	1.6	213
104.	Sweet mathi	495	5.5	54.0	28.6	36	5.7	153

Sl. No.	Preparation	Calories	Protein (g.)	Carbohy-drate(g.)	Fate (g.)	Calcium (mg.)	Iron (mg.)	Phosph-orus(mg.)
105.	Sweet roti	454	6.9	56.1	22.5	23	4.1	186
106.	Sweet samosa	415	11.0	51.2	21.5	251	2.5	201

A. 2. Sweet-Rice

Sl. No.	Preparation	Calories	Protein (g.)	Carbohy-drate(g.)	Fate (g.)	Calcium (mg.)	Iron (mg.)	Phosph-orus(mg.)
107.	Rice carrot kheer	226	5.9	36.0	6.9	173	1.1	156
108.	Rice with jaggery	244	2.0	50.7	3.7	27	3.9	60
109.	Rice phirni	166	4.9	22.7	6.4	120	1.0	127
110.	Shri palao	379	5.6	46.4	12.2	154	1.3	150

B.   1.   Savouries-Wheat

Sl. No.	Preparation	Calories	Protein (g.)	Carbohy-drate(g.)	Fate (g.)	Calcium (mg.)	Iron (mg.)	Phosph-orus(mg.)
111.	Chaat	474	4-1	53.8	26.4	70	5.5	65
112.	Dalia	78	2.5	8.9	3.6	12	1.1	41
113.	Ghee roti	463	8.1	48.8	26.2	26	4.8	217
114.	Kachori	500	7.4	37.7	35.5	35	1.7	82
115.	Khamiri roti	220	7.5	45.1	1.1	24	4.4	200
116.	Maida papper	580	7.2	46.3	40.9	26	0.9	66
117.	Matheri	495	6.8	46.2	31.4	13	0.7	57
118.	Milk puri	529	10.0	55.1	29.9	73	5.3	269
119.	Potato puri	247	4.9	33.4	9.6	15	1.8	88
120.	Radish paratha	246	5.4	32.6	10.7	40	3.1	147
121.	Samosa	256	3.8	31.2	12.8	23	0.7	44
122.	Tomato loli	303	6.7	38.9	13.4	30	3.7	176

B. 2.   Savouries-Rice

Sl. No.	Preparation	Calories	Protein (g.)	Carbohy-drate(g.)	Fate (g.)	Calcium (mg.)	Iron (mg.)	Phosph-orus(mg.)
123.	Biryani	244	7.0	15.8	17.0	71	1.5	92
124.	Kheecha	467	5.7	65.4	20.4	26	2.1	126

Recipes in common use in the Southern region

A. 1. Sweets-Wheat

Sl. No.	Preparation	Calories	Protein (g.)	Carbohy-drate(g.)	Fate (g.)	Calcium (mg.)	Iron (mg.)	Phosph-orus(mg.)
125.	Ashgourd halwa	398	2.9	50.7	20.7	11	0.6	62
126.	Badam puri	341	2.8	42.9	17.2	6	0.3	23
127.	Banana bajji	355	3.0	40.2	20.4	10	0.4	46
128.	Banana vadai	373	5.0	64.7	10.6	13	0.6	57
129.	Barbi	503	2.6	68.6	24.3	10	0.3	33
130.	Bengal gram payasam	87	1.5	20.4	0.3	35	2.2	29
131.	Coconut tablets	457	3.0	67.1	19.7	9	1.5	109

Sl. No.	Preparation	Calories	Protein (g.)	Carbohy-drate(g.)	Fate (g.)	Calcium (mg.)	Iron (mg.)	Phosph-orus(mg.)
132.	Coconut vadai	400	4.0	55.7	17.9	33	4.9	128
133.	Egg-maida-dosai	238	4.0	30.6	11.1	12	0.7	85
134.	Gulaabipoo	403	4.9	49.3	20.7	16	2.9	130
135.	Kalkal	348	8.3	57.1	19.7	21	0.9	85
136.	Khazoor	365	5.0	49.8	16.3	11	0.5	50
137.	Paadarpeni	227	4.5	25.9	11.7	94	1.5	127
138.	Papaya halwa	345	2.3	61.3	10.3	8	1.2	54
139.	Rawa appam	318	5.1	48.1	11.7	13	1.4	84
140.	Rawa putu	56	4.5	38.1	9.5	14	2.4	149
141.	Surul puri	424	9.8	55.4	18.0	31	4.4	190
142.	Sweet appam	656	6.3	85.2	32.2	62	9.3	196
143.	Sweet iddli	213	4.9	35.6	5.6	88	2.1	138
144.	Sweet poli (Holige)	451	8.5	64.0	17.9	49	2.6	121
145.	Sweet vadai	405	5.7	55.3	17.9	31	3.2	154
146.	Watte appam	168	2.7	34.5	2.3	10	1.4	80
147.	Wheat halwa	285	2.3	41.4	12.3	12	1.2	60

A. 2.   Sweets-Rice

Sl. No.	Preparation	Calories	Protein (g.)	Carbohy-drate(g.)	Fate (g.)	Calcium (mg.)	Iron (mg.)	Phosph-orus(mg.)
148.	Adapradaman	207	2.4	32.8	7.3	29	2.4	61
149.	Adirasam	482	3.8	83.1	14.4	44	6.0	85
150.	Appam (sweet)	251	2.4	35.6	11.0	—	0.5	54
151.	Awalosepodi	248	2.7	42.0	7.9	28	2.7	88
152.	Chanderkantai	608	12.7	102.7	16.4	67	4.1	179
153.	Cheedai	413	4.5	73.8	10.6	65	5.7	101
154.	Idiappam	264	3.1	42.7	10.9	6	0.7	90
155.	Jack-fruit adai	294	4.2	46.1	12.8	13	0.6	66
156.	Kolaputu	190	2.4	37.7	3.1	4	0.2	49
157.	Konmpal	280	3,3	42.3	10.7	7	0.8	98
158.	Neyyappam	515	4.4	74.7	21.6	10	0.8	112
159.	Paalputu	183	2.9	34.0	3.6	34	0.4	65
160.	Pachora	211	2.3	31.9	8.1	5	0.5	73
161.	Pal (milk) kolkattai	117	3.3	18.3	3.8	68	1.1	76
162.	Rice cake	290	6.2	54.9	4.8	20	1.0	105
163.	Somasi (Sweet)	448	5.6	45.5	26.4	12	1.5	113

Sl. No.	Preparation	Calories	Protein (g.)	Carbohy-drate(g.)	Fate (g.)	Calcium (mg.)	Iron (mg.)	Phosph-orus(mg.)
164.	Sweet kolkattai	194	2.5	33.5	5.4	15	1.9	70
165.	Tambittoo (Mavilakku mavu)	368	4.6	54.9	14.5	35	4.5	151
166.	Watapu	397	4.0	57.6	17.2	11	1.4	139
167.	Yela adai	232	2.9	47.5	6.0	31	3.1	77
	B. 1. Savouries-Wheat							
168.	Bhaath	172	3.7	17.3	9.6	13	1.6	84
169.	Godam dosai	263	3.7	28.1	15.1	25	1.0	56
170.	Godam pongal	356	6.4	24.7	25.8	28	3.0	215
171.	Godam tenkuzhal	576	7.1	40.6	43.0	64	3.6	194
172.	Karapuri	493	11.5	69.8	18.6	42	6.8	310
173.	Kaaram somasi	275	5.5	27.5	15.8	47	1.2	80
174.	Kaaram khazoor	536	12.9	59.6	29.4	62	6.1	271
175.	Kodbara	450	7.4	43.0	27.6	22	1.3	99
176.	Maida dosai	239	4.7	30.9	10.7	15	0.6	47
177.	Masala dosai	205	4.8	26.6	8.7	58	1.6	87
178.	Masala iddli	299	5.8	26.8	18.8	84	2.8	160
179.	(i) Muruku	465	9.9	61.6	19.7	32	5.2	255
	(ii) Muruku	529	6.8	61.2	28.4	23	3.0	155
180.	Poli (hot)	196	5.0	23.3	9.1	33	2.7	107
181.	Rawa adai	326	6.1	31.7	19.5	18	3.3	193
182.	Rawa dosai	203	5.3	25.6	8.7	68	2.5	155
183.	Rawa vadai	578	6.4	41.6	42.8	18	3.0	176
184.	Rawa pakora	491	8.7	43.9	31.2	97	4.4	239
185.	Savain iddli	91	3.2	15.8	1.7	32	2.1	93
186.	Shakarpara	583	6.2	38.2	44.7	22	3.6	165
187.	Semolina roti	399	7.8	44.1	21.3	31	4.4	224
188.	Siri vadai	338	6.8	35.4	18.7	92	3.3	191
	B. 2. Savouries-Rice							
189.	Adai	571	13.4	65.8	28.2	110	5.5	226
190.	Aappam	226	3.5	39.3	6.1	19	0.5	52
191.	Black gram kolkattai	108	3.2	21.5	0.9	23	1.0	53
192	Broken.rice roti	251	7.3	26.0	13.0	66	3.0	113

Sl. No.	Preparation	Calories	Protein (g.)	Carbohy-drate(g.)	Fate (g.)	Calcium (mg.)	Iron (mg.)	Phosph-orus(mg.)
193.	Coconut dosai	312	2.9	23.4	23.1	5	1.0	96
194.	Conjeevaram iddli	132	5.9	23.2	1.7	86	2.1	113
195.	Kodombuttu	105	2.1	23.3	0.1	3	0.3	33
196.	Kodballa	590	6.9	61.0	34.8	2V	2.1	147
197.	Kunku	387	10.3	35.8	22.4	78	4.5	173
198.	Lime rice	152	3.2	23.5	4.4	20	1.0	91
199.	Muruku	521	10.2	68.6	22.9	86	4.5	186
200.	Noy-pongal	191	2.8	27.9	7.1	28	1.7	52
201.	Onion dosai	314	5.0	34.5	17.1	72	1.9	93
202.	Rice flour roti	409	5.4	43.6	23.4	29	1.5	—
203.	Rice kolkattai	271	4.5	38.4	10.8	17	1.1	91
204.	Sesame rice	168	2.8	27.1	5.0	33	0.6	50
205.	Sour rice paka	175	2.0	19.9	9.5	27	1.3	41
206.	Tattal	461	5.9	45.8	28.4	32	2.4	128
207.	Thenguzhal	366	9.1	42.8	17.4	80	3.5	139
208.	Uthappam	330	6.4	37.8	17.1	46	2.1	112
209.	Yellu-podi anna	145	2.0	21.0	5.6	22	1.2	37

INDEX OF DISHES